BATTLE
FOR THE ASHES

Other books by David Frith

Runs in the Family (with John Edrich)
"My Dear Victorious Stod": a biography of A.E. Stoddart
The Archie Jackson Story
The Fast Men
Cricket Gallery (ed.)
Great Moments in Cricket (as "Andrew Thomas", with
Norman Harris)
*England versus Australia: a Pictorial History of the Test matches
since 1877*
The Ashes '77 (with Greg Chappell)
The Golden Age of Cricket
The Illustrated History of Test Cricket (ed. with Martin Tyler)
The Ashes '79
Thommo (with Jeff Thomson)
Rothmans Presents 100 Years England v Australia (co-ed)
The Slow Men
Cricket's Golden Summer: Paintings in a Garden (with Gerry Wright)
England v Australia Test Match Records 1877–1985 (ed.)
Pageant of Cricket
Guildford Jubilee 1938–1988
By His Own Hand
Stoddy's Mission: the First Great Test Series 1894–95
Test Match Year 1996–97 (ed.)
Caught England, Bowled Australia (autobiography)
The Trailblazers: the First English Cricket Tour of Australia 1861–62
Silence of the Heart: Cricket's Suicides
Bodyline Autopsy
The Ross Gregory Story

BATTLE FOR THE ASHES

DAVID FRITH

FOREWORD BY ASHLEY GILES

*TEST MATCH PHOTOGRAPHS BY
PATRICK EAGAR*

EBURY
PRESS

First published in Australia by ABC Books 2005

First published in Great Britain by Ebury Press 2005

1 3 5 7 9 10 8 6 4 2

Ebury Press, an imprint of Ebury Publishing.
Random House,
20 Vauxhall Bridge Road, London SW1V 2SA

Random House Australia (Pty) Limited
20 Alfred Street, Milsons Point, Sydney, New South Wales 2061, Australia

Random House New Zealand Limited
18 Poland Road, Glenfield, Auckland 10, New Zealand

Random House South Africa (Pty) Limited
Isle of Houghton, Corner of Boundary Road & Carse O'Gowrie,
Houghton 2198, South Africa

The Random House Group Limited Reg. No. 954009

www.randomhouse.co.uk

Typeset and designed in Australia by Midland Typesetters

Printed and bound in Great Britain by Mackays of Chatham plc, Chatham, Kent

Project management in Australia by Richard Smart Publishing

A CIP catalogue record for this book is available from the British Library

Cover design by Two Associates
Cover images © Getty Images
Back flap image of David Frith by Mark Ray
Test match images by Patrick Eagar
Other photographs from the David Frith Collection

ISBN 0 091910846

This offering is dedicated to the author's two
longest-standing cricket pals and supporters:
Murray Hedgcock, conversationalist and gatherer of facts,
and Richard Smart, who first backed me by publishing
my work thirty crowded years ago.

Acknowledgements

My warmest thanks are extended to Ashley Giles for contributing the Foreword. He had quite a series and is the only England player to emerge from his home village of Ripley, Surrey apart from George Griffith, who played for All England in the days before Test cricket was known as such. Poor Griffith, who toured with the first-ever English team to Australia in 1861-62, hanged himself eight years later. In contrast, everything in "Gilo's" life looks rosy, which pleases everybody who knows this fine fellow who some years ago wisely ignored my advice to remain a fast bowler.

Elsewhere, my gratitude is due to my beloved and tolerant Debbie, who never expected me to get involved with yet another book (somehow this was the happiest of them all); and to Murray Hedgcock for keeping an eagle eye on the media coverage while I fixed my own gaze on either the Test matches or the keyboard; to Richard Smart for suggesting this book after sensing something in the wind early this year; and to Stuart Neal at ABC Books in Sydney and Andrew Goodfellow and Alex Hazle at Ebury Press in London for doing the rest.

Contents

Foreword

The dust hasn't settled yet and I'm not sure I ever want it to. It's been a rollercoaster ride of emotion. I've felt proud and happy, depressed and sad. At times I thought I was going to cry. When Glenn McGrath dismissed Michael Vaughan and Ian Bell with consecutive balls that Monday morning at The Oval, I just couldn't watch any more. Matthew Hoggard and I went into the dining-room behind the players' dressing-rooms and played cards, something I'd never ever done during a game. Before long we'd also lost Marcus Trescothick to Shane Warne, and I was forced back into the dressing-room to prepare to bat. Just before lunch Freddie Flintoff also fell to Warne and I think we all now feared the worst.

I felt physically sick. Everything we'd worked so hard for over these five matches, and the years of preparation before then, seemed as though it would all be for nothing after all.

Kevin Pietersen and Paul Collingwood began after lunch with still more than 70 overs left in the match, Warne bowling as well as we have ever seen him. Our lead was a slender 133. Colly's selection in the team here was crucial. If we had gone in with five bowlers, Geraint Jones would now have been batting and I'd have been next up. Paul at No.7 strengthened both our batting and chances of saving the match.

I was in the coach's office by now. With the door open I could see the cricket from my chair. For ages I sat there on my own as KP opened an assault on Brett Lee: 16 off one 96 mph over. It was a truly amazing passage of play, exhilarating for spectators but nail-biting when you are next man in. I still felt sick.

Kev and Colly forged an incredibly important partnership, batting for over an hour together after lunch, but at 2.18 pm Ricky Ponting took a sharp catch off Colly's glove from Warne. I'm next in. How am I going to stop myself shaking?

At 2.42 pm Geraint gets bowled by one that stays down a little bit from Shaun Tait. As I put my gloves and helmet on my game head kicks in. It's a strange sensation. The horrible feelings of nausea and uncontrollable nerves leave my body. Things are so often worse for a spectator. But as a player your focus on the job in hand takes over.

There are still about 55 overs left and our lead is only 205. It's a tall order, but who knows? I remember thinking that I must just stay with Kevin and see where we can get to. We must count these overs down, take time out of the game.

We are still together at tea, with a lead of 227 and a maximum of 49 overs remaining. KP has got his first hundred in Test cricket – a decent time to pull out your finest performance. In the dressing-room there is a little excitement, some anticipation, but still plenty of nerves. We are far from safe. I take myself back into the coach's office and away from everybody. I feel as focussed as I ever have, and I don't want that to soften.

Since I was a child all I've ever wanted to do is play cricket for England and to be part of the team that won the Ashes. This was not a time to relax. Every day in this series has seemed like a week. Just over two weeks before Hoggy and I had been there at the end at Trent Bridge. Then I thought I might possibly have hit the winning runs for the Ashes. Now, at tea-time on the final afternoon of this amazing series, it seemed I still had a lot of work to do to make sure this would be the case.

After the interval Kev and I decided we would just try to eat away at the overs. We would tackle them in blocks of five, just 30 balls at a time. I remember Brett Lee bowling very quickly – 92, 94, 96 mph. Warne was tricky. But we had a feeling he was getting tired and was trying to really force the issue. We had a chat after every ball: "Keep going! Keep going!" A tap of the gloves. Another ball down.

I feel a special bond with all my team-mates. We have been through a lot together: hours in the gym and practising in the nets, watching videotapes of the opposition, preparing plans, sleepless nights, days in the field together, wicketless sessions. It's Band of Brothers stuff. That's what makes this England side so good. We love each other's company. It's easier to dig deep and find that extra 2% when it's for your mates.

Kevin Pietersen will always have a special place in my heart now. You couldn't play a more important innings for your country, your team, your mates. It was such a pleasure to bat with him. He kept me going through some really tough overs. At times I just stood in awe at the shots this guy was playing.

At drinks a maximum of 35 overs remained and we had a lead of 283. Surely the Aussies couldn't get that many in the time remaining? No relaxing though. You never know with this opposition.

Around 5 o'clock Kev's innings comes to an end. But we are safe by now. We have won the Ashes back. Shortly afterwards I manage to complete my fourth Test half-century – the most amazing feeling. My team-mates were overjoyed for me.

I had mixed feelings now. I didn't want to get out, but I also wanted to get up to the dressing-room to hug my team-mates. I was desperately trying to stay focussed. But I also kept smiling to myself. We'd actually won the Ashes! Soon after 6 o'clock it was official.

I've come a long way since my cricket days began on Ripley village green. Fortunately I ignored the author's advice when we played together for Guildford. When, at the age of 15, I was considering giving up seam bowling for spin because of recurrent back problems, David told me to "stick with the quick stuff; you'll go a long way".

Well, I ignored him, and here we are: Ashes winners. But in David Frith's defence, he doesn't get it all wrong. After all, he did say many months ago, in the face of doubters everywhere, that England would regain the Ashes this year.

ASHLEY GILES

1

Odds and Omens

The precise moment when the forthcoming 2005 Ashes battle seized my mind remains clearly defined. During an on-air discussion in ABC Radio's studio at the Sydney Cricket Ground early in January, thoughts turned to Australia's upcoming defence of the little urn over in England, and naturally enough Jim Maxwell asked for a prediction. Whether it came from the brain or the heart I cannot say, but I found myself blurting out this sentiment: "I fully expect England to regain the Ashes in September." Jim blinked, and blinked again, and I thought I detected a flush to his cheeks.

Worse was to follow. That same week, at a Surry Hills gathering of a group of seriously serious cricket folk who call themselves the Company of Cricket Scribes, convened by cricket academic Stephen Gibbs, the question that was now seemingly on everybody's lips popped up again. All eyes swung across to me, presumably because I was the only Anglo-Australian in the room. I repeated the assertion. Apparently to some it seemed absurd. One member cleared his throat – rather ostentatiously, I thought – while John Benaud reached into his trouser pocket and murmured: "Here's fifty bucks to say they won't." Fortunately, since he was still seated, his hand seemed to become trapped. The atmosphere in Abdul's Restaurant thereafter seemed a little distracted.

As the months rolled by the resounding opinion surfacing was that England would probably give Australia a better fight than in the preceding eight – yes, *eight* – Ashes series (they could hardly do much worse) but that there could really be only one winner. Australia's sole survivor from pre-war Test cricket, the much-respected 92-year-old Bill Brown, who was also a member of Don Bradman's unbeaten 1948 side in England, went as far as to predict that Ricky Ponting's team would go through England undefeated. Against this, some other Test veterans had been polite enough to suggest that England might somehow steal one of the five Test matches. Even Geoff Boycott was not all that upbeat: "I think England will win a Test. My concern is Australia will probably win two."

Now I like to think of myself as a fair-minded chap, one who carries around the burden or maybe the privilege of allegiance to two countries. As I made clear in 2002 in laying out the intro-duction to my book on the 1932–33 "Bodyline" series, I care deeply about these two nations, England and Australia, and the bonds between them, and about the cricket relationship in particular (though sometimes I despair). Offsetting a longish list of drawbacks (I've been shot at by both sides, and often), one of the benefits this hybrid condition affords is that it allows me to stand back neutrally to weigh the foibles of both countries with even-handed amusement.

From this position, I can easily rise above Cyclopean partisan-ship, looking instead, with sleep-ruining anxiety, at the health of the world's oldest Test relationship. It's fundamental to my nature that I feel for the underdog. Ashes cricket had been ailing for some time. Even hardened Australian sportsmen and -women, a little bored by Steve Waugh's team's ongoing superiority, were praying for a stronger challenge, something to stimulate the tastebuds. Not than any – in my sphere, at any rate – seemed ready to go that extra inch by hoping for an England series victory. It is widely agreed, nonetheless, that the culture and heritage of Ashes Test cricket are in need of fortification.

I can recall the inbuilt inferiority complex endured by English cricket-lovers of another time. In the late 1940s and early 1950s, across the length and breadth of the worn-out, battle-scarred country where cricket had first blossomed so many centuries earlier, nobody really expected Bradman's much-admired Australia to be beaten, even with Len Hutton, Denis Compton and Alec Bedser wearing the crown and three lions. The pessimism was just as widespread after Lindsay Hassett succeeded Bradman. Four-one was the lopsided outcome of the 1950–51 series, though the margins were breathtakingly close in Australia's first two Test victories.

The feeling come the English spring of 1953 was therefore much as it was to be in the spring of 2005: after Australia's retention since 1934 – 19 years – surely it was time for the Ashes to change hands? Sid Barnes, Australia's pig-headed, high-scoring batsman, wrote in early 1953 words which might equally well have applied to the situation in 2005: ". . . and then to find in 1953 a complete change of front, a real fighting spirit and unbounded confidence, not falsely assumed but built on strong, sound fact, I felt that our lads were going to meet some determined opposition this time, that they were really going to be embroiled in a fight and that England on the cricket field would be the England of old pre-war vintage."

England then, in addition to the lion-hearted Bedser, had the fiery black-haired Fred Trueman to return the fire of the ageing Ray Lindwall and Keith Miller, and they also had spinners Tony Lock, Johnny Wardle and Jim Laker to bemuse Australia's batsmen, several of whom were still a bit damp behind the ears.

It worked. Four draws were followed by a memorable England victory at The Oval. Hassett and his men were gracious in defeat, and in the depths of their hearts they might even – the older players anyway – have felt a gladness for England.

That is hardly the case now, 52 years later. In these abrasive times, when winning is all-important, money is a craze, and demonstrative national pride has reached ferocious levels in sport, no Australian cricketer wanted to be part of what would unhappily be perceived as the *disgrace* of relinquishing the Ashes in 2005. Nor was there any cause to feel sympathy for the England of today, for in contrast to the exhausted nation in the wake of the Second World War, 60 years on it is money-mad, unsentimental and bullish – well, much of the younger generation at least.

My unsupported conjecture about the outcome of the Test series found its way into print in June, so I had something either to fall back on or to cover up when the outcome was finally known. Brian Viner of *The Independent* picked up on the January forecast during our casual conversation at Lord's in June. By then, events had persuaded more people to come round to a more positive line of thinking. Some must even have placed hard-earned money on it. Now that might have been getting a little too carried away.

***

The springtime toast, then, was to the regaining of the health of Ashes Test cricket. And that could mean only one thing: England had to win in 2005.

Reflect on the poor fare served up by successive England teams:

1989. Against widespread prediction, it was all Australia, from David Gower's insertion of Allan Border's resurgent team at Headingley (they made 601 for seven and won by 210 runs), Steve Waugh's torrent of runs there and at Lord's (after a delay of 27 Tests before his first century), followed by Dean Jones's 157 at Edgbaston, to the David Boon sweep shot at Old Trafford which secured the Ashes 19 months after Mike Gatting's team had held onto them at Melbourne. Manchester saw Australia's 100th victory in Tests against England, who were now a ragged outfit for whom it seemed that anybody stringing a few scores together or taking a few wickets was instantly called to the colours. Astonishingly, 29 players were used that summer. Painfully for him, Ian Botham simply could not recapture his match-winning ways of former years, and the sudden mid-series recruitment of several England players for a rebel tour of

South Africa was just as disturbing. Terry Alderman's 42 wickets in the six-Test 1981 series had been in vain, but his 41 wickets now in the six Tests of 1989 were a key factor in Aussie victory.

England 0, Australia 4 (2 drawn).

1990–91. Australia took the initiative immediately, running off with the Brisbane Test by 10 wickets after 30 wickets had crashed for 460 runs. West Australian beanpole Bruce Reid's 13 wickets at Melbourne put them two up, and the Ashes were safe with a hard-fought draw at Sydney. And Australia seemed to be getting better, for here came another successful debutant in Mark Waugh (138 at Adelaide). It was not that England had no talented players: there was bulldog Graham Gooch and young Michael Atherton, and the rugged Allan Lamb and polite, self-effacing, richly talented Robin Smith. But somehow they didn't always seem to be scrumming down as a team.

Australia 3, England 0 (2 drawn).

1993. That ball from Shane Warne at Old Trafford: seated in the Press-box right behind the bowler's arm, I found it hard to believe what we had just seen. The television replays (since watched dozens and perhaps hundreds of times) showed it to be true. Given warning of it, Mike Gatting might have been able to counter it, but there can be no certainty. That evening I had the pleasure of informing Warne that he was the first bowler from either side in the long history of Australia v England Test cricket to hit the stumps with his maiden delivery. He seemed pleased at the knowledge, a pleasure grown manifold in the years since, with the hundreds of scalps in his bag finally coupling with his unchallenged reputation as the finest wrist spinner of all time. A third crushing victory in the fourth Test at Headingley secured the prize again, Border making 200 not out and grinding England's nose in it with an unbroken stand of 332 with Steve Waugh. Here Boon made his third successive century.

Lord's, for the want of a single, would have seen centuries by the first *four* Australians in the order, Mark Waugh being bowled through his legs by Tufnell when 99 after hundreds by Michael Slater, Mark Taylor and David Boon. It was here that England really did touch rock bottom, for they not only went down by an innings but the visitors lost only four wickets in raising 632 runs and played *a man short* after Craig McDermott's twisted gut compelled his repatriation. Australia's team spirit was so robust that a cardboard cut-out of the ailing Queenslander was installed in his place. Depressed English cynics were beginning to believe that 11 cardboard figures of Australian cricketers might have been sufficient to overthrow England.

With Gooch stepping down and Atherton now in command, the sixth and final Test, at The Oval, brought England their first victory in 19 Australian battles in just on seven years. It was something which became known as the phenomenon of the "dead rubber syndrome". Did Australia relax, albeit subconsciously, once the major task had been accomplished? If they were a long time shrugging off this odd habit, at least it went with the appetising habit of winning series after series.

England 1, Australia 4 (1 drawn).

1994–95. With Border, cricket's Marciano, now nudged into retirement laden with honours and records, Australia raced off with substantial victories at the Gabba and the MCG (where Warne secured a hat-trick, the first in Ashes Tests since Hugh Trumble's on the same ground 91 years before). Sydney staged a tense draw, with centuries by Taylor and Slater on the final day. Almost as if by custom, England then earned themselves a follow-up win at Adelaide, where veteran Gatting made 117. Even so, yet more Australian talent came on stage when Greg Blewett made a century on debut. He was to become the first batsman ever to make hundreds in his first three Ashes Tests, and in a less affluent era would surely have played many more than his ultimate 46 Tests. Australia sent England home with another thrashing at Perth.

It was time for "the Poms" to lick fresh wounds and think hard, really hard. There was talent in the ranks. Consider Graham Thorpe: century on debut in '93, runs in almost every Ashes Test since then except when injured, and now 123 in the Perth debacle. Why was Australia's talent supply-line so prolific? How did they keep doing it? Was it the climate, the pitches, the structure, the training and preparation? My belief was that, granted the regeneration of heaps of natural talent, a near-fanatical national pride had a lot to do with it – that and the prototype cricket academy, which England would soon be adopting (enlisting the unlikely aid of that successful Australian regimental sergeant-major Rod Marsh while they were at it). There also dawned the slow realisation that you cannot expect to shape a Test team as solid as Australia's if you keep messing about with the personnel. In the early 1990s I counted around 60 current players in county cricket who had England Test caps in their cricket bags. It was close to incredible. At Nottingham in 1993, England called up *seven* new players into the squad, five of whom played, four of them Test debutants. Thorpe and Nasser Hussain alone paid off long-term (Hussain having played three Tests in the West Indies three years previously). Australia continued to be a dedicated, well-organised, compact unit. England just shuffled mournfully along.

Australia 3, England 1 (1 drawn).

1997 – Might the trend have swung come June 1997? Hussain made a double-century and Thorpe another century at Edgbaston, where England won the opening contest. But the truly significant performance there was Mark Taylor's 129, which ended a very long slump for the square-jawed, bear-like Australia captain. Glenn McGrath sounded his trumpet loudly in the rain-spoilt Lord's Test with 8 for 38, and in the next three Tests Australia toyed with England as if they were a school team. At Headingley they played like a school team, spilling crucial catches. And here Ricky Ponting, on Ashes debut, made the first of what looked like many Test centuries to come, and Jason Gillespie stamped an indelible mark with 7 for 37, the best ever by an Australian at Leeds, beating Charlie Macartney's 7 for 58 with spin in 1909.

When McGrath bowled England out for 180 at The Oval in the final Test of that summer, it looked like yet another walkover. But naughty-boy Phil Tufnell spun out seven Australians in the first innings and four more in the second, when Andy Caddick took five, and a consolation 19-run victory went England's way. Had Australia eased off again, even subconsciously? Somehow, bearing the innate victory-lust in mind, it seems unlikely. But fatigue might have been a factor. Victors often take more out of themselves.

England 2, Australia 3 (1 drawn).

1998–99. For once an Ashes series began with a draw, bringing English pessimists relief at so swift a removal of the spectre of a complete green-and-goldwash. Unlikely top scorer at Brisbane? Wicketkeeper Ian Healy, 134. However, it soon became here-we-go-again time: Australia by seven wickets inside three days at the WACA (Damien Fleming nine wickets) and by 205 runs at Adelaide Oval, where Justin Langer announced himself with an unbeaten 179. An epic match at Melbourne saw England home by 12 runs after the longest day's play in Test history, just over eight hours. Then it was back to reality. Australia won at Sydney largely thanks to leg-spinner Stuart MacGill's 12 wickets and Slater's second-innings century (after being reprieved early by the third umpire on a run-out referral). It was the volatile NSW batsman's third hundred of the series, and apart from his 123 in an innings total of 184 only Mark Waugh (24) reached double figures.

"Tubs" Taylor was presented with the larger-than-life crystal replica of the Ashes urn, and when I altruistically asked him at the Press conference how it felt to have something tangible at last to hold on high, he growled back that he'd happily drop the bloody thing and see it shatter into smithereens. Such is the intensity of Australian resentment that Ivo Bligh's little symbol, the most precious in sport, remains always in the glass case at Lord's. There is no acceptable substitute. Darren Gough at least now had the memory of his hat-trick, the first achieved for England against Australia since 1899, when J.T.Hearne took the most fabulous three-in-three of all, getting Clem Hill, Syd Gregory and Monty Noble. Memories. They continued to be almost all England had to live on.

Australia 3, England 1 (1 drawn).

2001. After a bizarre beginning (Alec Stewart and Caddick belting 103 for England's tenth wicket) the pattern was sustained: nearly 600 by Australia, centuries on Ashes debut for Damien Martyn and Adam Gilchrist, a further three-figure score for Steve Waugh, then collapse by England to an innings defeat when the series – now restored to five matches – kicked off at Edgbaston. England had beaten Australia only once at Lord's in the 20th Century – Hedley Verity's match (15 for 104) in 1934 – and now the new century was launched at Lord's with yet another win for the visitors at the Home of Cricket. Fast men McGrath and Gillespie did most of the damage, and England now understood what a phenomenon was Gilchrist, thrashing away at No.7. Mark Waugh, that most silken of cricketers, wrapped his soft fingers around his record 158th Test catch here, and was at the crease at Trent Bridge in the next Test to see Australia to their third victory in only 11 days of play. The Ashes had quickly been made safe yet again.

With Steve Waugh now out with a leg injury, Gilchrist, after weather interruption and hopeful of an eventual 5-0 series win, declared at Headingley to set England a target of 315 in 90-odd overs. A dazzling 173 not out by left-hander Mark Butcher brought unexpected victory in this 300th Anglo-Australian Test match – only for England a week later to crash to defeat by an innings and 25 runs at The Oval. There the Waugh twins made centuries, as did Langer, restored to the side at the expense of the distressed Slater. Mark Ramprakash, the man with all the talent but questionable temperament, made a superb hundred for England, and Marcus Trescothick made his third half-century of the series. But Warne's 11 wickets here were decisive.

England 1, Australia 4.

2002–03. A figure not dissimilar to the Incredible Hulk threw a great shadow over English hopes from the start of this rubber. Nasser Hussain kindly gave Australia first use of a decent Gabba pitch, and Matt Hayden plundered 197 and 103 from it. Ponting made a trim century, Simon Jones, the Welsh fast bowler, suffered an excruciating knee injury in the outfield, and England were away to another deplorable start. Further huge Australian victories at Adelaide and Perth (Ashes safe again already) were followed by another comfortable win at Melbourne, where Langer ground out an awesome 250 and Hayden made another hundred.

For England there was one distinctly encouraging string of performances. Michael Vaughan's centuries at Adelaide and Melbourne were made with such panache, as was yet another in the final Test, at Sydney – and they were all big ones – that it was clear that England had found a batsman of the highest class. This last Test was won, with another important century coming from Mark Butcher, and England's pace bowlers doing the business at last (Caddick 7 for 94 in the final innings). Yet Sydneysiders will remember the match as much for Steve Waugh's dramatic final Ashes century, his Bradman-equalling 29th overall, reached off the final ball of a day of huge expectation, followed by another spectacular century from Gilchrist. England won all right, and again spared themselves the ignominy of a green-and-goldwash, but McGrath and Warne were missing from the opposition on this occasion.

Against that was the extraordinary roll-call of injuries in the English ranks. Major hopes Darren Gough and Andrew "Freddie" Flintoff were repatriated before they could bowl a ball, Gough having been the only original selection who had ever taken a Test wicket in Australia. On top of that, missing from one or more of the

2002–03 Ashes Tests because of injury were Steve Harmison, John Crawley, Ashley Giles, Andy Caddick, Alec Stewart and Craig White. That was some handicap, made more severe by further mishaps to several replacement players, and the bloodied eye of Alex Tudor, felled by Brett Lee at Perth. There was, too, the little matter of England's best batsman, Graham Thorpe, not even embarking on the tour. His private life was a mess and he withdrew before the start.

Upon these misfortunes has been based much of the hope regarding the 2005 series. Surely England will now be capable of mustering all their best players without hindrance? Nasser Hussain aired the cautious belief that had there not been such an injury scourge throughout the 2002–03 series, England would have taken the fight much further than they managed in the first three Test matches. Pretty obvious perhaps. Upon this, and the supposition that Australia's average age was so high as to indicate a peaking, lay the major hopes that England under Vaughan would do the job in 2005.

Australia 4, England 1.

❉ ❉ ❉

So the tally (leaving aside the drawn 1988 Bicentennial Test, when the Ashes were not at stake) since Mike Gatting's England team won the Ashes series of 1986–87 is Australia 28, England 7, drawn 8. Remarkably, six of those England successes came after the various series had been decided.

The Ashes were now just cold dust after eight lop-sided rubbers. Would the cinders of the bail – or was it a lady's veil? – now reheat and burst into flames? The build-up, the fervid anticipation and expectation, had become quite wearing. It was surely unique in its intensity. With a year still to go before the start of the series England spinner Ashley Giles muttered that the public already seemed incapable of talking about anything else. It was obviously becoming rather wearing, and it would unquestionably be a great relief when the battle of 2005 finally got under way.

One thing could be stated with confidence. Despite the perpetual one-sidedness, the attendances at Ashes Test matches have invariably been huge, with advance bookings always heavy. If only English cricket grounds could match Australia's for size, the numbers admitted to the big matches would climb astronomically. Applications for tickets for the 2005 series suggested that the small English grounds, even or perhaps especially Lord's, could have been filled three, four, five times over. After the early sell-out, tickets began to appear on internet websites for many, many times face value, prompting the authorities to mount an investigation. Any MCC member found guilty of profiteering was to suffer a two-year suspension of membership, yet another symptom of the compassionate society.

❈ ❈ ❈

The programming for the 2005 English season was lousy. All sorts of fare was on offer during the first half of the summer – county one-day and Championship cricket, some frantic Twenty20 cricket (20 overs a side, all over in an hour and a half, satisfying the masses who can't concentrate on anything for more than a few minutes).

There were two forgettable England v Bangladesh Test matches, each settled in a fraction over two days, with Ian Bell's run-glut (65 and 162, both not out: Test average now 297) useful to the cause, though it might have been wise to have blooded Kevin Pietersen at Test level at the same time. Marcus Trescothick gorged himself with 194 at Lord's and then 151 at Chester-le-Street, the most northerly Test ground in the world. Michael Vaughan recovered his stride with 120 at Lord's, where for once Andrew Strauss (69) failed to make a Test century. Against New Zealand on Test debut there in May 2004 he had scored 112 and 83 – run out by Nasser Hussain in his final Test innings: he finished with an unbeaten 103 and retired from Test cricket on the spot. Strauss followed up with

137 against West Indies at Lord's two months later, when Robert Key bashed 221 and Vaughan recorded a pair of centuries.

Floods of runs for England, a further flood of new confidence, and cheeky peeks at Australia's two Test results against Bangladesh in the Australian winter of 2003: an innings and 132 at Darwin and an innings and 98 at Cairns. Stuart MacGill picked up 17 wickets and there were centuries from Darren Lehmann and Steve Waugh (two each) and 100 not out in probably his final Test innings by Martin Love, the classy Queenslander born into the wrong era, like so many other talented current Australian cricketers.

England, then, at the start of this uniquely eventful summer, had polished off Bangladesh faster and more embarrassingly (losing only six wickets in the two matches combined) than their major foe had done a year previously. England had thus taken their record series of consecutive home wins to an impressive 10 Test matches. It added fuel to the bonfire which was signalling the Greatest Ashes Contest in Living Memory or Even of All Time.

The five Ashes Tests of 2005 were to be crammed into a 54-day schedule in the second half of the summer, denying fans the opportunity to savour the series with a proper and enjoyable reflective time between each contest. There was also a feeling that the England & Wales Cricket Board had been none too clever in launching the Test series at Lord's. Surely they were aware that England had won there against Australia only once since 1896? It was surely known that the visitors drew inspiration from the historic ground, in contrast to England's players, who, absurd as it seems, often played as if overawed. The places for raucous English patriotism were Edgbaston and Headingley, where players were lifted by the sort of stadium-rocking vocal support and mass waving of St George flags more usually found in the realms of that less-than-beautiful game football.

Offsetting the belief that the usually warmer weather and harder pitches of July to September might favour Australia, there was the risk that the tightly-packed schedule would weigh against the touring team should anyone become injured. Anybody breaking a finger would miss the following Test or maybe two, so close together were they scheduled. Not that there was a shortage of possible reinforcements among the counties. The English game is teeming with Australians.

A peep at tour schedules in the old days is eye-opening: the Australians would sail away as soon as the Sheffield Shield season ended, sometimes dallying along the way with games in Tasmania or elsewhere. The sea voyage took around five weeks. The cricketers were then allowed to find their land legs, having gentle net sessions and attending rounds of hospitality at high-profile dinners in London. Then a programme of 34 matches began to unfurl, starting with (in the case of the 1956 Australians) a showcase one-dayer at Arundel, followed by three-day matches at Worcester, Leicester, Bradford, Nottingham, The Oval, Cambridge, Manchester, Lord's, Oxford and Hove before the first Test match in early June, by which time the players had already been away from home for nine or 10 weeks.

A further 11 weeks later they began the fifth and final Test, at The Oval, and when that was over they *still* had six matches to play – including one against *Minor Counties* – before the last ball was bowled (by wicketkeeper Gil Langley, as it happened) on September 15. The slightly jaded Australians embarked for the voyage home, where they hoped to be greeted by their wives and families about six months after leaving them, and then resumed their everyday jobs as teachers, sales reps and bank clerks. They were lucky if they were not out of pocket, tour fees being so modest and opportunities for sponsorship and side earnings unspectacular. Keith Miller was envied for his Brylcreem advertising contract, which met with less than the full approval of the Australian Cricket Board.

And yet the cricketers who undertook those lengthy tours loved almost every minute of them, and the survivors positively do not feel envious of the moderns for their numerous compressed programmes (even though their wealth might have come in handy). This is partly because that very compression of tours has squeezed out much of the sense of leisure. The modern highly-paid professional has no knowledge or experience of the protracted tours of days gone by. Instead, he has many – too many, in fact – shortened tours. And the media attention is uncomfortably intense. The newspapers of the first three-quarters of the twentieth century were virtually scandal-free as far as cricketers were concerned.

Nor were the Press conferences as numerous or as orchestrated. Players, especially captains, were quietly cornered by trusted journalists, and confidences were not betrayed. The mandatory Press conferences of today are sometimes amusing for their sheer automatism and blandness. Cricketers are actually coached in public-relations skills, all good preparation, no doubt, for a later career on television. How refreshing and unexpected it was to read England new boy Kevin Pietersen's remark in a magazine in the spring of 2005. He revealed that in a text message from Freddie Flintoff concerning the forthcoming Ashes series, the bluff Lancastrian promised: "We are going to do some damage together!"

Pietersen, nursing a tumultuous soul like most of us bi-nationals, was born in June 1980 in Pietermaritzburg and qualified for England by virtue of the nationality of his mother, Penny, who came from Canterbury, Kent. Like so many white South Africans, he perceived a future in the land of his birth in which his opportunities would be severely restricted. He was probably aware that all the photographs of the pre-1970 South African teams have been removed from the walls at Newlands, Cape Town, and doubtless elsewhere as well, and that Barry Richards has remarked not only that the racial quotas system was not good but that he and his generation were being punished twice for the former government's apartheid policy. First there had been the 1970 expulsion from Test cricket when Richards was approaching his peak (he was for several years, in the opinion of the majority, the finest batsman in the world) and now he and his contemporaries were being airbrushed out of Test history. There will be more and more South Africans (and white Zimbabweans) playing county cricket, just as those of Asian parentage are prolific names in the daily county scorecards. The demographic pattern is shifting, for there is also a sharp diminution in the once-large number of West Indian players.

Pietersen's batting skill and natural aggression first displayed themselves at international level when he returned to South Africa in England colours after a four-year qualification in county cricket with Nottinghamshire. Clive Rice had signed him up, but temperamental clashes with team-mates prompted Pietersen to move to Hampshire, where, in 2005, he was in the odd position of playing under the captaincy of Shane Warne, who would be prosecutor-in-chief should Pietersen make it into the England Test side. Despite a glaring preference for the leg side, on that first major tour the lantern-jawed, extrovert "KP" crashed an unbeaten century at better than a run a ball in the tied one-day match at Bloemfontein, an even more spectacular one (69 balls) at East London, and followed all that with yet another at Centurion. He averaged 151.33 in the series and, equally importantly, demonstrated that the raucous teasing and taunting by the crowds who saw him as a traitor, far from intimidating him, actually inspired him. With that last century he had them on his side, which lifted him further. His beaming self-confidence made him an ideological successor to those other up-and-at-'em South Africa-born Englishmen (how that term irritated them) Tony Greig and Allan Lamb. What many did not know, and what is so very significant, is that all of these players had one or two British parents. Anybody who cares to pontificate on the complex issue of birthplace is welcome to do so – preferably out of this author's earshot.

It is just sad that Pietersen wasted his boyhood hero-worship on the discredited late Hansie Cronje, who notoriously took money from match-fixers. Now Pietersen, with his bizarre punk hair-do and tattoos, and after his shift of counties, was wanted by the majority, it seemed, to be selected for England's Test team against Australia. It says something for England's new strength that despite his showing in South Africa and in county cricket, whereas five years earlier he would have been tossed into the Test side without further ado, in 2005 he faced stiff competition for a middle-order place.

***

Great expectations indeed. What omens have there been? Well, while maybe not too much should be read into Ricky Hatton's beating of the "unbeatable" adopted Australian Kostya Tszyu for the world light-welterweight boxing title on June 5, who won the last Test played between Australia and England to date (Sydney, January 2003)? Answer: Vaughan's England, by the solid margin of 225 runs. Who won the last one-day international between the two countries? Well, in the Champions Trophy semi-final at Edgbaston in September 2004, England got home with some comfort by six wickets. Marcus Trescothick made 81, Vaughan 86, Andrew Strauss, England's discovery of the decade, 52 not out, and Gough, now strictly a one-day international player, took 3 for 48, Vaughan, the talented but reluctant off-spinner, 2 for 42 off his 10 overs. The ball with which Vaughan dismissed Tendulkar in a Trent Bridge Test curved and spun so beautifully that it was a candidate for the Ball of the Decade, delivered as it was nine years after Warne's bobbydazzler to Gatting. Then again, there was Ashley Giles's 100th Test wicket, a ball of similar beauty which completely befuddled Brian Lara at Lord's in July 2004. But we mustn't get carried away. England are not once more in possession of a Laker and Lock, and that's that.

Some years ago, Ted Dexter, when England's chairman of selectors, was mocked mercilessly when he attributed events on the field to astral influences. But who knows? Who really knows?

***

There was nothing in Australia's international season at home in 2004–05 to suggest that the great days were near to ending. Their passage against India in the home series of 2003–04 had not been easy, with one victory apiece and the visitors making the highest total in their history (705 for seven declared: Tendulkar 241 not out, Laxman 178) in the final, drawn Test at Sydney. That was Steve

Waugh's final Test, and as he was carted shoulder-high around his beloved home ground, music blaring, local fans cheering themselves hoarse, there were many who wondered if his departure would mark the dividing line between world domination and a slide back into the general pack.

Within weeks England were mowing down West Indies at Kingston (Steve Harmison 7 for 12 in West Indies' second innings of 47), then Port-of-Spain, then Bridgetown, only for that genius Brian Lara to regain his world Test record from Matt Hayden. His 400 not out in a total of 751 for five declared was at the cost of a real chance of winning the match, an angle smartly seized upon by Australia's new captain Ricky Ponting: "They ran out of time in the game. That's not the way the Australian team plays." Too right.

The manner in which the Australian team plays became of acute interest during 2004. Ponting had joined select company in stroking double-centuries in successive Tests at home against India during the 2003–04 season, and in the minds of many he stood clear as the world's best batsman – a title which tends to rotate from one name to another with greater frequency in this richly-endowed age than in any previously. However, in the calendar year of 2004, the gifted Tasmanian failed to reach three figures in any of his 19 Test innings. It was just one of those things. He missed three Tests through injury and another following the death of his aunt. Ponting reached 92 against Sri Lanka in Colombo in March and was stumped for 98 at Perth against Pakistan in December, besides notching three other half-centuries. He felt the frustration, but the new year, the year of the eagerly awaited Ashes clash, began rather well for him. After a beautiful 207 against Pakistan at Sydney to help seal a 3-0 result, he led his men to a 2-0 victory in New Zealand in March 2005, finishing with 105 and a not-out 82 at Auckland.

The English media were quick to put to him, upon the team's arrival in England on June 5, that his team was well past the flush of youth. Some may have been aware that last year the Australia XI taking part in the Darwin Test against Sri Lanka was the oldest (average 32 years 212 days per man) since Bill Woodfull's team in the angst-ridden Adelaide Test during the 1932–33 "Bodyline" series (33 years 15 days). If the 50-year-old Bert Ironmonger and the 41-year-old Clarrie Grimmett, both spinners, had been replaced by men of, say, Bill O'Reilly's age (27), then the search for an older team than Ponting's would have had to go back even further.

But surely it was not yet panic time for Australia? None of the 2005 squad landing at Heathrow was older than 35, and even if the oldest was Glenn McGrath, the pillar of the pace attack, perched on 499 Test wickets, it was perhaps a little early to start panicking? Still it didn't smother either the speculation or the astonishment at the fact that for almost the first time in Ashes history England had youth on their side.

The Australia captain, brown eyes sparkling, and with that pointed nose and mouse-like lower features giving him the most cheeky facial image in the long history of the Test captaincy, said all the right things upon arrival. His team had benefited from a seven-week break; they had worked hard at the Brisbane training camp; all the one-dayers before the Ashes Test series would help Australia. He also reiterated that "an Ashes tour is always special," adding: "But this one is more so because it is the No.1 in the world versus the No.2. England's recent record speaks for itself. They have beaten virtually everyone else, and you don't get to No.2 in the rankings without achieving a lot."

It would not have thrilled those Australians who relentlessly espouse the supposed new order (Australia's Test matches against India and Sri Lanka being, in their eyes, the new blue riband) when Ponting asserted that "this is the tour every Australian wants to get on because it is the best tour there is".

All around Ponting have been high-scoring team-mates: Damien Martyn, the Leonardo DiCaprio lookalike, who goes quietly about his business in this fruitful second life of his after the frustrations of Part One of his Test career (1992–94); Justin Langer and Matthew Hayden, the aggressive left-hand openers, judged by some to be the most successful of all time, Hobbs and Sutcliffe and Greenidge and Haynes notwithstanding; Simon Katich, the polite left-hander who managed a rebirth by moving from the western to the eastern extremity of Australia; the essentially modern Michael Clarke, who brought not only a little relief to the worryingly high average age of the side but great excitement as he displayed his remarkable talent in his maiden Test innings away and home, big centuries at Bangalore and Brisbane; and, of course, the phenomenal Adam Gilchrist.

It has been calculated that Gilchrist is the fastest run-scorer in Test history, and by popular vote among today's world stars, the most destructive batsman, one to whom many bowlers simply fear to bowl; and he holds most of the catches on offer behind the wicket in those capacious orange gloves of his.

Gilchrist's simple power and flailing bat time and again seem to spell out a kind of ingenuousness that a scheming fielding captain ought surely to be able to counter. Bowl around the wicket? Tuck him up against the cut? Deceive him with a good slower ball? Bounce him? Do him with a wrong'un? All this has been tried by a galaxy of bowlers from all the Test nations. And still he rides high. Take the first five Australian wickets and then you are facing perhaps the biggest problem of the afternoon. He doubles and sometimes trebles the score following his entry to the arena, and he does it at top speed. Dealing with Gilchrist was very high in England coach Duncan Fletcher's dossier of matters arising. He made his Test debut at the Gabba in 1999. The date was November 5. How appropriate: Guy Fawkes Night. The number of "parliaments" Adam Gilchrist has blown up in world cricket is awesome to behold.

A long time ago I played first-grade cricket for Paddington, in Sydney, alongside Stan Gilchrist. Stan was a country-bred leg-spinner who would toil through a hot afternoon, giving his all, before slumping exhausted in a corner of the dressing-room in the evening, usually with something approaching anguish radiating from his flushed countenance. (We usually fielded for ages against the big guns from Wests or District or Bankstown, the Simpsons, the Davidsons, the Burkes, the Philpotts, the Thomases.) If *only* we could have known that one day Stan's often wicketless devotion to the game would be rewarded with the pride he now feels in having produced such a son as Adam, who has played a key role in elevating Australia to probably the highest ranking in the history of cricket.

I came across Stan Gilchrist some decades later, when we were waiting for our passes into the Gabba. It was taking a long time and it was frustrating. Stan, from his steady leg-spin of old and his top-rate coaching skills, knew all about frustration. He was patient. And what did we discuss? We compared notes on the termite problems affecting our respective properties. With the start of play imminent and the pair of us still adrift on the forecourt, I urged him to threaten to pull his boy out of the Test match unless our tickets were found quick smart. Whether the remark was overheard I know not, but our passes materialised a minute later! Adam Gilchrist scored 126, pouched four catches and made a stumping, and Australia won by the little matter of an innings and 156. As so often, they owed him a lot.

***

Whether Australia had reached the absolute peak and were about to slide was about to be revealed in the 2005 Ashes series. This was universally understood. The previous 12–18 months warranted careful study. Australia stood comfortably atop the world rankings, with the fast-rising England in second place. During 2004, England were the only unbeaten Test side in the world. Australia would have achieved that condition as well but for the 13-run defeat at Mumbai (Bombay) early in November. That was when India's spinners exploited a dreadful surface on the third day to roll Australia over for 93.

Players are gagged nowadays, so when Jason Gillespie was asked what he thought of the pitch, he wisely declined to offer an opinion for fear of official punishment. But he mentioned instead that a mate of his had remarked that it was easily the worst *he'd* ever seen. If only Michael Vaughan had had such quick wit and diplomatic skills he might have ducked the ridiculous full-match-fee fine imposed by match referee Clive Lloyd (mastermind of the West

Indies fast-bowling juggernaut of the 1980s now turned adudicator) in Johannesburg in January 2005. Vaughan's "crime" was to say, inoffensively, that he felt the umpires (Steve Bucknor and Aleem Dar), in calling a halt to play in variable light on the second evening when England were batting and Vaughan and his No.10, Harmison, had already put on 82, had not been consistent. The England captain would have been better advised to refer the questioner to the remarks of Bob Willis (if he had only known about them) up in the commentary box: the former England fast bowler had told viewers that Bucknor's decision was "disgraceful" and that the umpire should "sail off into the sunset".

England still went on to win that match against a fairly strong South Africa, and they also took the series (2-1), even though they sometimes played well short of potential. Andrew Strauss, back in the land of his birth, scored 126 and 94 not out at Port Elizabeth on debut against South Africa as England chalked up their eighth win in eight Tests, surpassing their previous best of seven under Percy Chapman (three, all by an innings, against the newly-elevated West Indies in 1928, and the first four in Australia in 1928–29, when Don Bradman and Archie Jackson made their Test debuts).

Strauss, the cool and calm Middlesex left-hand opener, had now made remarkable history by recording a century on debut against three different countries: New Zealand, West Indies and South Africa. Those who had watched his fairly ordinary grade cricket performances in Sydney with the Mosman club a few years earlier were scratching their heads in amazement. Early in the 2005 season Strauss lost a golden chance to make it *four* debut centuries when, on 69, he got a pad in front of one from Mortaza of Bangladesh. That left Australia next in his sights.

***

No sane soul would suggest that Australia's 16-year stranglehold over England was attributable to luck. A check on those 43 Test matches since 1989, however, reveals that Australia won 25 tosses to

England's 18. In more recent focus, Australia led in tosses 16-6 since Perth 1995. Four times Australia put England in and went on to win, seizing the initiative in 2001 by doing it in the first two Tests, where England's sloppy fielding contributed greatly to their defeats.

Once in that time, at Melbourne in that heart-stopping Test in 1998–99, Australia lost after putting England in. Infamously, Australia were timidly put in by Nasser Hussain at Brisbane in the opening encounter of 2002–03, and Hayden's heavy punching from the opening bell led to a stunning Australian victory. "Oh God, Nass, what have you done?" the England captain muttered to himself as the Australians settled down for a fat score. He later wrote that not only his coach but Steve Waugh too would have inserted the opposition. But the never-to-be-erased record shows that Hussain had made the same mistake as his predecessor Len Hutton at the Gabba 48 years previously.

An oddity just preceding this controversial decision was that Hussain's wife had recently given birth to a son in, of all places, Perth, Western Australia. The natural exhilaration felt by the boy's father was soon dampened by events at the Gabba. He had already lost the services of Darren Gough, Andrew Flintoff and Graham Thorpe, and a spearhead bowler, Simon Jones, was about to sustain that horrific knee rupture in the outfield. "I was clever enough to realise, even in that first session," Hussain later wrote, "that the next 25 days of Test cricket were going to be absolute hell."

Even there he was not pessimistic enough, for Australia needed only 15 days to wrap up the first four Tests. Facing the threat of the first 0-5 green-and-goldwash since 1920–21, England bounced back at Sydney with that resounding victory, though Australia were missing the services of McGrath and Warne.

✼ ✼ ✼

As is now the established system, two Australia touring teams were chosen for the 2005 tour of England, first the one-day specialist party, which would later interchange with the Test match squad.

Darren Lehmann, 35, was the most disappointed exclusion, though he quickly signed up for media work on the tour, to be interrupted only by a possible return to Melbourne for the trial of the man charged with the manslaughter of David Hookes that terrible night in January 2004.

The fifteen selected for the warm-up act of NatWest one-day matches from mid-June to July 12 were (ages at July 21, 2005): **Ricky Thomas Ponting** (captain), 30, (Tasmania); **Adam Craig Gilchrist** (vice-captain), 33, (WA); **Michael John Clarke**, 24, (NSW); **Jason Neil Gillespie**, 30, (SA); **Bradley James Haddin**, 27, (NSW); **Matthew Lawrence Hayden**, 33, (Qld); **George Bradley Hogg**, 34, (WA); **Michael Edward Killeen Hussey**, 30, (WA); **Michael Scott Kasprowicz**, 33, (Qld); **Simon Matthew Katich**, 29, (NSW); **Brett Lee**, 28, (NSW); **Damien Richard Martyn**, 33, (WA); **Glenn Donald McGrath**, 35, (NSW); **Andrew Symonds**, 30, (Qld); **Shane Robert Watson**, 24, (Qld).

Four were due to leave after the one-day matches – Hogg, Hussey, Symonds and Watson – to be replaced by **Bradley John Hodge**, 30, (Vic); **Justin Lee Langer**, 34, (WA); **Stuart Charles Glyndwr MacGill**, 34, (NSW); **Shaun William Tait**, 22, (SA); and **Shane Keith Warne**, 35, (Vic).

The support team was: Steve Bernard (manager); John Buchanan (coach); Jamie Sissons (assistant coach and computer manager); Errol Alcott (physiotherapist); Jock Campbell (fitness adviser); Lucy Frostick (masseuse); Jonathan Rose and Belinda Dennett (sharing media manager duties). And to think that the Australians of 1905 had just one supernumerary, a manager, Frank Laver, who doubled – and very effectively – as a player in the party of 15 which was away from home for most of that year.

It was tempting, but rather too complicated, to add the counties served by many of the names above over the past half-dozen years. Their States are listed merely to confirm their hometown associations (allowing that Ponting now lives in Melbourne, Watson had a recent flutter with Tasmania, and Gilchrist and Katich have virtually swapped States).

The top Aussie names no longer play more than the very rare domestic match. The central contracts system eventually also adopted by England is a major factor in the emergence of their Test side from the doldrums. Fatigue can no longer be pointed to as a cause of under-performance (though the swelling amount of international cricket sometimes seems to be as exhausting as the county matches that used to keep a Test player in trim between the big matches).

As for the numerous full-season or part-season county contracts signed by Australians in recent years, one very important question remains unanswered: are the "foreigners" benefiting from this experience more than the English players who are now their temporary team-mates or against whom they are competing? The county game used to be cluttered with West Indians. Many of them returned to England with their Test teams and played in now-familiar surroundings almost as if engaging in a home series (and with loud support from legions of England-based West Indian fans, who latterly seem to have lost interest). It made little difference to Graham Gooch whether Malcolm Marshall was bowling a bouncer at him for Hampshire or for West Indies. Marshall had learned the right length to bowl in English conditions, and much else besides. It was like a finishing school. And if anybody in county matches spotted weaknesses in the techniques of Gordon Greenidge, Clive Lloyd and Viv Richards, they seemed incapable of exploiting that knowledge in the Test matches.

Who benefited more: Mike Hussey with his astonishing not-out treble-centuries for Northamptonshire against Essex at Northampton in 2001, at Bristol in 2002, and at Taunton in 2003, or his team-mates and/or opponents? Brad Hodge tried to get a message to Trevor Hohns and his fellow selectors with 302 not out for Leicestershire at Trent Bridge in 2003. It remained to be seen whether Australia's perception of county cricket – that anybody can score runs and take wickets in that environment – is now outdated. The establishment of four-day county cricket on usually sound pitches and with a first and second division is achieving its object. The only full-scale professional domestic competition in the world, the old County Championship is at last a true testing ground for both incipient and established talent.

When top dogs such as Glenn McGrath dabble in lucrative county cricket nothing is more certain than that they will not go and exhaust themselves. That wouldn't make sense, and Cricket Australia, as the Board now slickly calls itself, can be relied upon to guard against that risk anyway. Senior overseas players are doing it simply to bulk up the bank balance, stay in trim, and perhaps size up the enemy.

Shaun Tait was the most interesting selection in the Test squad. The big 22-year-old South Australian looked to be a raw and natural fast bowler on the evidence of a sighting in an Australian domestic one-day match. Yet his figures during his spell of county cricket with Durham in 2004 were a laughable 0 for 176 in first-class cricket off 18 overs. He had problems about placing his front foot in delivery and locating the stumps at the far end. Tait's early adventures had all the ingredients of Jeff Thomson's entry into the big-time. The world's fastest bowler – perhaps (and perhaps not) now a milli-second behind the likes of Brett Lee and Shoaib Akhtar – "Thommo" was secretly nursing a broken bone in his foot, and recorded figures of 0 for 110 against Pakistan at Melbourne on Test debut in 1972–73. He was discarded for two years. When he came back, he made up for lost time.

Tait, however, made the strongest of comebacks by taking 65 wickets in 2004–05, breaking Clarrie Grimmett's record for the State (63 in 1939–40, when the little spinner was 48 years old). Tait was, for the moment, in the front rank of Australia's likely next generation of internationals.

One Australian who was found "sleeping with the enemy" well into the 2005 season was the greatest wrist spinner of all time, the tabloids' personal favourite, Shane Warne. He first played for Hampshire in 2000, and returned four years later to utilise the captaincy skills that his misdemeanours had ensured he would never display as skipper of his country. (He had got as close as the Australian vice-captaincy. Ricky Ponting, another who had once broken the good-behaviour code, was rehabilitated and fairly quickly reabsorbed into the system;

with the crown now on his head he can afford to smile at his own aberrations.)

Of all the little sub-plots that emerge from cricket's vast canvas, one of the most intriguing has been the shared Hampshire dressing-room of Shane Warne and Kevin Pietersen – who even went out clubbing together some nights. It is not so much that they both have unusually throbbing egos. With Pietersen apparently destined to play a major part in this momentous Ashes series, who would have worked whom out more cleverly? Did Pietersen delight in repeatedly smashing his county club captain out of the nets? Did Warne sometimes spin and humiliate the batsman? Or (more likely) might he have withheld some of his variations for a future date? How many more deliveries remained in that magical right shoulder of Warne's after 34,438 serious whirls in Test cricket alone? It all added a delicious undercurrent to the series.

It all goes to show how attitudes have altered. In the 1950s the Australian cricketers in English county cricket were not current Test stars. They were mostly rejects who had prodigious talent but felt their chances back home were being denied. Cec Pepper, born in Forbes and a sensation with the Australian Services team, went to the leagues in Lancashire after upsetting the Australian establishment. His mighty hitting and clever leg-spin variations would surely have earned him some Test caps if only he had kept his opinions to himself. South Australia-born wartime commando Bruce Dooland was considered good enough to play for Australia only three times in the 1940s, yet for Nottinghamshire he spun out 770 batsmen in five seasons in the 1950s, at a time when his home country had only the fledgling Richie Benaud striving for Test wickets with leg-spin.

Left-arm spinner George Tribe, a Victorian, was given only three Test caps, like Dooland, without much success (in part because Don Tallon, the brilliant wicketkeeper, didn't always "read" him). So Tribe joined Northamptonshire and took over 1000 wickets for the county, baffling most of his opponents and bagging between five and nine wickets in an innings over 70 times. The brilliant Jack Walsh, another left-arm mystery spinner, played almost all his cricket, either side of the war, with Sir Julien Cahn's private team and with Leicestershire, and thought nothing of spinning out a dozen or more batsmen in a match. Tough Bill Alley from Sydney became a Somerset legend, winning matches even when in his 50th year.

Jack Manning (Northants), Jack Pettiford (Kent), Ken Grieves (Lancashire), John McMahon (Surrey), Alan Walker (Notts) and Jock Livingston (Northants) all settled for county cricket, realising that promotion to the Australian Test team was not a realistic option, even during the years of struggle between 1953 and 1958. Livingston in particular, a twinkle-toed little left-hander, was a better batsman than many who have Test caps in their wardrobes. He was once even sounded out as an England possible. The Australian Cricket Board of the day ignored them all, and there was evidence of resentment that they had chosen to emigrate, even when, in certain cases, it was a temporary move.

As years passed, some young Australians sought the further education to be found in the grind of county cricket. Greg Chappell and Kerry O'Keeffe at Somerset come to mind. But gradually the juicy contracts available in the English game became attractive to the established Aussie stars, and they to it. English cricket is divided, with the shadow of "Kolpak" darkening attitudes as the new century unfurled: players from South Africa and Australia with all sorts of European family backgrounds were free to offer their services to county clubs – without being classified as overseas players – under one of Brussels' European Union directives based on freedom of movement and freedom of employment. (Maros Kolpak, a Slovakian handball player, successfully challenged a ban on his playing in Germany. The European Court of Justice's ruling enabled any national from a country with an Association Agreement with the EU to work in Europe, subject to a work permit.) It seemed only a matter of time before county cricket, like premiership football, would consist of teams not only without any local lads in them but with not all that many British-born or even England-qualified.

Selecting a pool of England contract players may one day become less easy. Another reason for England, undoubtedly at or near a peak in 2005, to seize this glittering opportunity to compete very hard indeed for the Ashes.

❈ ❈ ❈

A reminder of the movement of people – involuntary movement in this instance – between Britain (and Ireland) and Australia came with Sky Television's brilliant pre-series trailer showing a fair-haired convict scowling down at the wharf as he is ushered aboard a sailing ship bound for the colonies. Among the authorities watching him go is a chap (David Gower) in a big naval officer's hat. He commands him to call out his name. "Warne!" comes the flat reply. And while the group, with Ian Botham bedecked in ship's chandler's leather apron, continue to glare at him from the keyside, the convict follows up with a sinister "I'll be back." Jump 200 years, and here he is, entering the room, spinning a cricket ball, and hissing, "I'm back!"

Not a bad day's work for £10,000.

But in the matter of omens, this unexpected Australian propaganda on British television ran the risk of backfiring, for one major celebration of events 200 or so years ago which was to glorify the whole year was the bicentenary of the Battle of Trafalgar, in which Horatio Lord Nelson (like the tough Edrich clan of cricketers, a Norfolk man), to this day the nation's premier warrior hero, was fatally shot as the fleet boldly demolished the French and Spanish opposition to avert invasion of England.

Two hundred years on, at Lord's right through to The Oval, as at Trafalgar, England expects that every man will do his duty.

This year also marks another major anniversary, of course, and one much nearer to ourselves: the 60th anniversary of the end of the Second World War, in which Britain and Australia were the closest of allies – apart from the occasional and inevitable little bout of verbal sniping – as the free world fought for its life. Emerging from it came a generation of cricketers who knew the difference between the authentic life-and-death struggle on the one hand and sporting combat on the other. The repetition in the obituaries became slightly tedious after a time, but it is worth recording once more the late Keith Miller's view of it all. Consulted about handling pressure on the cricket field, the ageing glamour boy, perhaps the greatest all-rounder produced by Australia, retorted: "Pressure? *Pressure*? I'll tell you what pressure is: it's having a Messerschmitt coming at your arse!"

Next time, batsman, old mate, that you face a series of mad bouncers to the background of a barrage of verbal abuse, or you, a bowler, get hit for three fours and a six in one over, remember if you will Keith Miller's words. As for the lamentable fact that much of today's cricket is played with the mouth: if only those pathetic sledgers would understand that their foulness is seen as a sign of a shortfall in physical skill and intelligence.

Ricky Ponting and his men crossed to France and visited a Western Front battlefield the day after landing in England. The previous Australian team had made a pilgrimage to Gallipoli along the way. That occasion had resulted in a cringe-making donning of Diggers' hats and posing in trenches, a routine apparently encouraged by Australia's then Army chief, General Cosgrove. The re-enactment of the cricket match played on "Shellfire Green" was more appropriate.

The 2005 tourists made it clear that they needed no persuasion to accept that the men who fought and fell at Villers-Bretonneux and all around in 1918 were the real heroes. There, for the first time, all five Australian divisions had gone into battle together, infantry, artillery, tanks and horses. It was a great victory, prompting the French Bishop to say in due course, "We bow to you, messieurs les Australiens, for the magnificent deeds you did . . . In the whole of history we cannot find an army more marvellous in its bravery." Stirring stuff. Some of the many Allied military cemeteries in France and Belgium stretch almost to the horizon. The purpose of the cricketers' visit was to pay respects to the fallen, along the countless rows of headstones, many listing teenagers, and perhaps to draw some inspiration. The streets of the village are named after

Australian suburbs, and there is a prominent kangaroo logo. So there was no play-acting on this occasion. Having beheld the Australian war memorial park in Fromelles, young Queenslander Shane Watson, for one, said it made him proud to be Australian.

The hope is that the young men of today will never have to go through those horrors, coupled with a further hope that cricket writers will abstain from martial metaphor. One particular Yorkshireman-turned-Australian used to be obsessed with writing how, during a torrid Test match, "it was like the Somme out there". Sports-writing obscenity.

❊ ❊ ❊

England would not win the Ashes in 2005 merely because it is about time and because such a victory would be a huge tonic for Ashes cricket. Why did I blurt out my prediction in Sydney in January? Perhaps the conviction owed something to the phenomenon of superstition. It is inherited from my mother: salt over the shoulder, black cats, avoiding walking under ladders, and all that nonsense. If I drive through this next roundabout without having to apply the brakes I'll get a fifty this afternoon. That sort of thing.

So, searching for further omens, I have come up with things that happened 50 and 100 years ago. It is always a treat to look at pictures of the old-timers and to read about the cricket they played. There were some great names involved in the 1905 Ashes series, and some even more freshly remembered – many, indeed, still alive – in the 1954–55 series.

If anything "guaranteed" an England victory in 2005, these were the pointers.

2

Jacker and Joe

With the possible exceptions of Andrew "Roy" Symonds, who seemed to have a large tarantula stuffed under his cap, and Jason "Weird Al" "Dizzy" Gillespie, with his award-winning biblical dyed black mane and facial foliage, Ricky Ponting's team looked a fairly clean-cut bunch as they landed in England on June 5 – although Michael Kasprowicz's lower face is prone to thick stubble, the sort of covering that many older men use as disguise for a double chin and compensation for a thinning thatch. (Shane Warne added to his album of headlines when it was revealed a few days later that he was having treatment for hair loss – or, as he insisted, the *threat* of future hair loss.)

This flashback is inspired by the search for omens for the 2005 Ashes series. If, for the good of the game, the Ashes are to change hands this year, will the theory of the 100-year cycle be effective? Quite obviously I still don't know, but by the time these words are read, the writer will appear either a fool or a lucky prophet.

My handy book of quotes offers two that are appropriate and worth considering at this moment. One of my major non-cricketing heroes, Winston Churchill, said: "I always avoid prophesying beforehand, because it is a much better policy to prophesy after the event has already taken place." Well, we all know people like that, do we not?

A fellow named Thomas Fuller, however, wrote in the early eighteenth century: "He that would know what shall be must consider what hath been." Spot on, Thomas. It's not so much a familiarity with history that gives insights. It is the belief that there are often cyclical patterns. My conviction concerning the 2005 series is based in part on that theory.

❊ ❊ ❊

One hundred years ago, the Australian cricketers disembarked at Liverpool, met up in London with their captain, Joe Darling, who had travelled independently, and then they were all filmed at Lord's, where Frank Laver's jocular V-sign almost into Warwick Armstrong's nostrils became the first such vulgarity to be immortalised by that wondrous and fairly new contraption, the cine-camera.

As the Australians of 1905, in their tight green caps and with Armstrong wearing a polo-neck sweater, trotted out from the Trent Bridge pavilion for the first Test match, Lionel Lunn, the commentator in *That's Cricket*, the 1931 Australian film which embodied this precious footage, remarked that the cricketers all seemed to have left their razors behind.

He really ought to have looked more closely. While Edwardian fashion dictated that a good set of whiskers was no bad thing, the only Australian cricketers to sport even a moustache were skipper Darling and wicketkeeper Jim Kelly (who both cultivated Rod Marsh walrus moustaches), Charlie McLeod, Reg Duff, Bill Howell, and Syd Gregory. About the same proportion of their England adversaries had hairy upper lips.

The figure towering from the home pack in this summer of 1905 was F.S.Jackson. By the end of his life he was Colonel the Honourable Sir Francis Stanley Jackson, PC, GCIE, and he had stamped his name on an Ashes series. "Jacker's" golden-brown moustache was of the clipped military style (that's intended to be the last word on moustaches). He was a man of good humour, Yorkshire-born, youngest son of Lord Allerton, educated at Harrow, where the boy

F.S.Jackson, the most successful captain England has ever had in terms of all-round success in an Ashes series.

David Frith Collection

Winston Churchill was his "fag" (a junior whose task it was to wait hand and foot on the senior, and sometimes to cop a flogging if his performance fell short of requirement: young Winston was also Archie MacLaren's fag).

While at Cambridge University, Stanley Jackson established a reputation as a batsman and intelligent medium-fast bowler, and as captain he had the foresight to award young Ranjitsinhji his Blue in 1893.

That was the summer when undergraduate F.S.Jackson made his England debut. In his first Test innings, in a drawn match at Lord's, he stroked 91 against Jack Blackham's Australians, Turner, Trumble and all. In the next Test, at The Oval, W.G.Grace said to Jackson: "With all these batsmen I don't know where to put you!" – much as Ricky Ponting might have said to Simon Katich 112 years later. The young man shrewdly replied: "Anywhere will do." So Jackson went in at No.7 and made a serene 103 in 135 minutes – hoisting his century with his last-wicket partner in. The blow off Giffen hit the pavilion. Then Jackson's partner, Arthur Mold, ran him out.

Before the final Test of 1893, at Old Trafford, Jackson declared himself unavailable. He preferred to play for Yorkshire against Sussex in a match which sealed the Championship for the white rose county, who won 18 and lost three of their 28 matches. It was not a unique decision among amateur cricketers of the day. Test matches were important, but not all-consuming as in our time.

It was at Lord's three years later, again in a Test against Australia, that gentleman cricketer Stanley Jackson displayed the chivalry associated with the Golden Age of cricket. Approaching his fifty, after Australia had been bowled out for 53 by Tom Richardson and George Lohmann, Jackson lofted a ball to the midwicket boundary. Joe Darling went for the catch but was impeded by the spectators on the grass and the chance went down. So Jackson played exactly the same stroke to the next ball, and Darling held the catch, the whole episode applauded appreciatively by the 30,000 spectators who had crammed the ground. One observer described it as a "pretty piece of quixotism". Hard-headed old Wilfred Rhodes claimed years later that Sir Stanley, like any sensible batsman, amateur or professional, would never be so misguided as to throw his wicket away like that. But such was the over-riding spirit of the age. We may wait in vain for something as chivalrous to occur 100 years later.

In that 1896 summer, just before the Lord's Test match, Jackson had been struck by a bouncer from the rough-and-ready Ernie Jones when the Australians played against Lord Sheffield's XI at Sheffield Park, Sussex. The impact cracked a couple of Jackson's ribs, but he still managed to finish with an unbeaten 95.

Later that season he opened for Yorkshire against Warwickshire at Edgbaston and scored 117. This, the best of the four centuries in the innings, was supported by 210 from Bobby Peel, 126 from Ted Wainwright, and 166 from the captain, Lord Hawke, and the visitors went on to a total of 887 in two days. It was proof that Anglo-Australian rivalry was acute even in those days, for Yorkshire's stated objective was to top the existing world team record, currently held by the 1893 Australians, who gorged themselves against Oxford & Cambridge Universities Past & Present with a total of 843 at the United Services ground, Portsmouth.

When Australia next toured England, in 1899, F.S.Jackson, now recovered from a fall from his horse while riding with the Bramham Moor hunt, scored another Test century, 118 at The Oval, where he opened with Tom Hayward and posted a then record 185 for the first wicket as England marched on to 576, showing up the absurdity of staging Tests over a mere three days when both sides boasted such an array of top-class batsmen.

Jackson had been perfectly happy to play for England under the command of his junior, Archie MacLaren, acknowledging that his fellow Old Harrovian, already having toured twice, had more extensive knowledge of the Australians. After the first Test MacLaren had succeeded the bulky W.G.Grace as captain, the Great Cricketer having acknowledged that at last, at the age of 51, Test cricket was a bit beyond his physical capabilities. At Lord's it was MacLaren's misfortune to run into Ernie Jones at top pace (10 wickets in the match) and Hill and Trumper in top form (135 apiece) as Australia took the only outright result of the summer. Jackson, who failed so very seldom, scored 73 and 37 in the losing cause.

Three years on, in 1902, he batted well enough to make half-centuries in the first two Tests and 128 at Old Trafford in the thrilling encounter which had been kicked off by a pre-lunch century by Trumper and won by Australia by three runs. Then, at The Oval, Jackson made 49 in his customary calm manner. Had he failed on that famous last day, then Jessop would not have had the chance to launch his immortal assault to snatch a one-wicket victory.

In 1903, Jackson, MacLaren and Ranjitsinhji successfully opposed the demand for a widening of the wicket. Their objection was based on the conviction that the high scoring of the day was to some considerable degree caused by poor fielding. There should be a campaign, they thought, to encourage improved work in the field before any further move was made to broaden the stumps.

In the following season, Jackson captained the Gentlemen against the Players in the showpiece match at Lord's (some spectators even preferred it to the occasional Test matches), when the amateurs passed 400 in the fourth innings to win the match. He contributed 80, and said later, with a smile: "To put it mildly, my batting was very 'streaky'. I was missed at slip when 33, again when 53, and in addition was confidently appealed against for a catch at the wicket." This last remark leaves us to wonder whether "Jacker" merely survived an appeal which he knew to be unwarranted or was actually a non-walker – which would be a major surprise in such a Corinthian sportsman.

Stanley Jackson's military and political career curtailed his appearances in big cricket, and it was a cause of much regret that he was never available to tour Australia, where his clean-cut cricket would have been much admired, even if by some a little grudgingly. He would have liked to have toured.

Commissioned into the 3rd Battalion of the King's Own Royal Lancaster Regiment, he served in the Boer War (and was repatriated for a time with enteric fever – typhoid) and then, briefly, in the First World War, when, as a lieutenant-colonel, he commanded the 2/7th (Leeds Rifles) Battalion of the West Yorkshire Regiment.

Having entering Parliament, Jackson became chairman of the Tory party and eventually Governor of Bengal (1927–32).

Near the end of his term in India, a female student tried to kill him in Calcutta, five bullets missing their mark from close range. Jackson, who refused to allow the incident to disturb him, continued his speech, saying later that he had made the quickest duck ever. The vice-chancellor was grappling with the young woman as Stanley Jackson resumed his address. She later gave her motive for the attempt. She had been "impelled by my love of my country, which is being repressed". Some of the Australian cricketers in 1905 might have harboured similar dark thoughts about the England captain.

Stanley Jackson was chairman of Test selectors in 1934, when the acrid smoke generated by Bodyline was slowly drifting away. Without Jardine, Larwood and Voce, England bowed before

Bradman and Ponsford. Australia regained the Ashes, and for once there was nothing F.S.Jackson could do about it.

His house in London was bombed in 1940, but he lived on into 1947, the last survivor from England's 1896 Lord's Test match. The shock and after-effects of a road accident hastened the end of a life of enormous achievement. It was one thing to hook and duck the fizzing bouncers of Ernie Jones and Tibby Cotter but quite another to absorb the impact of a speeding taxi.

❋❋❋

Joe Darling, Australia's captain in England in 1899, 1902 and 1905, was also a politician later in life, in the Legislative Assembly of Tasmania. Amazingly, he was born on the very same day as his 1905 adversary F.S.Jackson – November 21, 1870 – so if ever there was a portent of something special when they lined up their players for the Ashes series, this was it. (Ricky Ponting and Michael Vaughan were born 52 days apart in 1974, but an eerie connection is to be found even here: Ponting is from Tasmania, where Darling died; Vaughan is a Yorkshire batsman, like Jackson. To broaden further the package of coincidences, a high-scoring left-hander of a later generation, Justin Langer, was born precisely 100 years after Darling – and Jackson – on November 21, 1970.)

Joe Darling was a stocky, aggressive left-hander who took no nonsense from anybody. One English newspaperman described him as a "plain, blunt man, despising finery and effeminacy". His first Test innings lasted one ball at Sydney in 1894 when Tom Richardson drilled a quick one through his guard. Few might then have guessed that he would go on to captain Australia in 18 Test matches, which remained a record until Don Bradman passed it.

The son of Scottish migrants, Darling was a six-hitter (the ball needed to he heaved right out of the ground in those days) and a five-hitter (clean over the boundary fence or railings would do, though the batsmen then had to change ends). He was a champion who had shown his worth early with an innings of 252 for Prince Alfred

College in the annual match against St Peter's College at Adelaide Oval when he was a day short of his 15th birthday. The lad's hands were blood-streaked after this monumental feat, for he wore no batting gloves, and the twine around the bat-handle was coarse.

His three centuries against England were all posted in the 1897–98 series, won 4-1 by Australia under Harry Trott's leadership. In the final Test, at Sydney, Joe Darling thundered to a 91-minute century which is still, over 100 years later, the fastest for Australia against England (surely something of which Adam Gilchrist should be made aware).

Darling was now, in 1905, seeking the special triumph of a hat-trick of victories on English soil. He had led the Australians to a tight victory (1-0) in 1899, the first five-match series (three-day Tests), when the tourists won at Lord's, though the captain had a moderate series himself. Then in 1902, Australia held on to the Ashes after as thrilling a series as has ever been played. At Old

Joe Darling, Australia's captain in England 100 years ago: third time unlucky.

David Frith Collection

Trafford the fourth Test was won by Australia by three runs to secure the little urn, and at The Oval, Gilbert Jessop smashed a 75-minute century and George Hirst and Wilfred Rhodes got England home by one wicket after bravely finding 15 runs for the 10th wicket (and most definitely not "in singles"). It probably didn't occur to the stunned Australians to shrug off that reversal at The Oval as a matter of "dead-rubber syndrome".

They may have lost the series, but England sent into the field, for the opening Test match of 1902, at Edgbaston, what is still regarded as probably their strongest-ever Eleven. Some say it was their strongest-ever *batting* line-up, but on a rain-affected pitch they did bowl Australia out for 36 (Victor Trumper 18; next-highest scorer Bert Hopkins with 5; Rhodes 7 for 17, Hirst 3 for 15). The batting order in this first of Birmingham's Test matches read: A.C.MacLaren, C.B.Fry, K.S.Ranjitsinhji, F.S.Jackson, J.T.Tyldesley, A.F.A.Lilley (wicketkeeper), G.H.Hirst, G.L.Jessop, L.C.Braund, W.H.Lockwood, W.Rhodes.

From that embarrassing 36, the Australians endured another nightmare in their fixture against Yorkshire. With Hirst's swinging left-arm pace at the other end, F.S.Jackson bowled the tourists out for 23, having Hill stumped by David Hunter and then taking four wickets in an over. He finished with 5 for 12, Hirst 5 for 9. Australia by now must have been developing a Jackson complex comparable with that suffered by Kim Hughes and his players in the 1981 series when Ian Botham toyed with them.

In the final stages of that memorable summer of 1902, Jackson unfurled his strokes at Scarborough in an attractive 72. Cricketers must be judged by their performances against the best, and Australia, then as now, were the best.

A year later the first English Test tour of Australia to go under the flag of MCC, with P.F. "Plum" Warner as its captain, won back the Ashes after four series in which Australia had dominated. It was a creditable victory, for Australia were strong: Trumper, Reg Duff, Clem Hill, Warwick Armstrong, Syd Gregory, M.A.Noble as batsmen or all-rounders (Darling was unavailable and sorely missed), lanky Hugh Trumble still picking up bags of wickets in his final series, and Tibby Cotter blasting his way onto the scene. England won three of the first four Tests. Defeat in the fifth was no dead-rubber syndrome. They were simply caught on an impossible pitch after rain. That was the only problem with unprotected pitches (apart from the revenue lost when play could not continue or resume): the better side was not always assured of a fair chance of proving that it was. Against skilled bowlers, slow or medium-pace, batting became a lottery when hot sunshine began to firm up a sodden surface.

England sprang two major surprises on Australia in this 1903–04 series. R.E. "Tip" Foster, tall, elegant and moustachioed just like F.S.Jackson, scored 287 on Test debut in the opening encounter at Sydney. His tenth-wicket stand of 130 with Rhodes was still a record for either country as the 2005 series began. A spell of 5 for 12 at Sydney by Bernard Bosanquet secured the series victory for England in the fourth Test. The tall Middlesex amateur was bowling his erratic back-of-the-hand spinner, the googly, the wrong'un, the Bosie. Other bowlers had played about with it, but he was the first to apply it seriously in big cricket, despite occasional ridicule and even unwelcome accusations of deceitfulness in those years of lofty ideals in sport. The 1905 Australians would be seeing a good deal more of Bosanquet.

❋ ❋ ❋

Temporarily led by M.A.Noble, the 1905 Australians played some matches in New Zealand, and there were some fireworks from Hill and Trumper against a non-Test New Zealand side at Wellington before the voyage to England was resumed. How many cricket-lovers are aware that Trumper once scored 40 in Fiji?

The Australian cricket team being a democratic (and profit-sharing) bunch of men, they now formally voted Joe Darling in as captain again, and settled into their London headquarters, the Inns of Court Hotel. Arrangements had been made with the Midland Railway company for a special carriage to be set aside for the players as they rumbled from one part of England to another. A photo-shoot of the visiting cricketers, similar to that of today, was organised, with two dozen cameramen clicking away on their cumbersome equipment. Player-manager Frank Laver later wrote that they were astonished to see themselves cavorting on the silver screen when they went to the Palace Theatre to watch some moving films. The newsreel showed the cricketers' "antics" and "we were highly amused . . . our movements looked particularly funny". That V-sign was no doubt a key distraction.

By today's standards it was not a very commercial age, but the Australians soon became impatient with photographers who were making money out of their images, selling photographs and postcards to the public without any prior financial agreement. Eventually a Mr Bolland was given sole rights. They went on to play the Test matches, of course, in unadulterated cream/white shirts and flannels, wearing only the proud Australian green cap (not yet quite a baggy) with coat of arms, or a sunhat. Not a commercial logo in sight.

Before the first Test match, Darling and his men, between the preliminary matches, enjoyed the social whirl – as did the several wives who accompanied them. They heard Dame Nellie Melba sing *La Traviata* at Covent Garden, and met the Prince of Wales (the future King George V) and his sons (two further kings-to-be: Edward VIII and George VI). In the opening match, against W.G.Grace's side at Crystal Palace, Reg Duff scored a nine when Plum Warner and Gilbert Jessop threw wildly. And the enchanting continuity of cricket's eternal links was to be found in a casual par in the magazine *Cricket* which told of the young Surrey newcomer Hobbs scoring four off "Sailor" Young of Essex off his first ball in first-class cricket. Jack Hobbs, much loved on his tours of Australia, and who was to finish just short of 30 years later with a supreme tally of 61,237 charming first-class runs and 197 centuries, was run out for 94 in Surrey's match against the Australians shortly afterwards.

A strong MCC side were flattened at Lord's (Armstrong 248 not out), and when mighty Yorkshire were overthrown in smoky Sheffield (Laver 8 for 75, Penrith off-spinner Bill Howell 6 for 38 in

Yorkshire's second innings of 78) England knew that the forth-coming Tests would be tough. F.S.Jackson fired a signal with 42 good runs here in the first innings, and predictions for the Tests became more excited when news came through that George Hirst had hit a record 341 for Yorkshire at Leicester.

For the Australians, Lancashire came next, 149 from Clem Hill and 10 wickets in the match by Charlie McLeod setting up victory against a strong county side, sending the tourists into the first Test in good heart. In his book on the tour, Frank Laver harked back to the accommodation problems endured by the 1899 touring team. This time they had taken the precaution of booking hotel rooms in Nottingham well in advance. Ricky Ponting and his men take travel and accommodation arrangements for granted. A large Cricket Australia staff takes care of all their needs, and to four- or five-star level as well.

A serious back injury to Victor Trumper prevented Australia from salvaging at least a draw at Trent Bridge in the first Test. The touring team's star attraction, who had charmed his way through the previous tour of England in 1902 with 2570 runs, 11 centuries and an average of almost 50, tore a muscle in his back while going for a catch at slip and had to retire hurt for 13 in the first innings. He was in too much pain and restricted in movement to bat in the second when the tourists were fighting to save the match. Inexplic-ably, Trumper, regarded – at least by Australians – as the best and most attractive batsman in the world, was to struggle throughout this 1905 tour, managing only two centuries in other matches and a top score in the five Tests of only 31. It was almost beyond belief.

The Tests were all set down for three days' duration, and Stanley Jackson won the toss for England all five times. (This was less of an advantage than might be supposed, for in three of the Test matches Australia, batting second, had the better of conditions. In all the other matches the Australians won 20 out of 35 tosses.) Jackson was also to top the batting and bowling averages for either side, and he stood out as an immaculate, almost infallible leader of a strong unit.

There was an irregularity about this first toss. Instead of the home captain spinning the coin as per tradition, Joe Darling suddenly flipped a coin of his own. Taken off-guard, Jackson called heads and earned choice of innings, but as he walked back into the England dressing-room he was still slightly bemused at the liberty taken by his opponent. "Archie," he said to MacLaren, "Darling ought not to have tossed." His friend agreed, and they idly considered the possibility that the Australian might lose all the remaining tosses.

With today's Test match referees hovering close by such irregularities are a thing of the past.

Here at Trent Bridge in 1905 there was an early wobble for England. Cotter and Laver swept aside Tom Hayward (5), A.O.Jones (4), Archie MacLaren (2) and Jackson himself (0, bowled via his bat-handle by Cotter) to leave England 49 for four before the skilful Lancashire professional Johnny Tyldesley rescued them, together with some stout tail-end support. Cotter was a rarity. At that time truly fast bowlers were few and far between.

Darling's men had had some good victories before the Test series started, and they were clearly threatening to regain the Ashes so recently lost. Frank Laver, now more the player than the tour manager, returned the best figures, 7 for 64 with his medium-pacers, as England managed to reach 196. Never again in the series were they to be under serious duress.

Australia replied with 221, Hill and Noble making fifties, Tibby Cotter clouting 45, and Armstrong lifting a ball from Bosanquet over one of the stands. Jackson counted his opposite number, Darling (0), among his five wickets as he made his first major mark on a series that forever would bear his name. In one of the most sensational overs in Ashes history, Jackson's smooth action, pace-changes and knowing use of the seam brought him the wickets of Noble (caught behind off the first ball), Hill (bowled by the fourth), and Darling (caught at slip by Bosanquet off the sixth). They were champions all, and Jackson's feat vied with Jack Hearne's great hat-trick against Australia at Headingley six years previously.

England's second innings then took the game away from Australia. They amassed 426 for five before Jackson declared, when he himself was 82 not out and MacLaren had made a majestic 140. In

An Australian Cricketer on Tour Laver claimed that MacLaren should have been given out early in his innings, and went on to complain about what he saw as a general hometown bias in the ranks of English umpires, nearly all of whom were poorly-paid old pros. With equal disdain Laver condemned the absence of sightscreens on English grounds, particularly when unthinking – or perhaps mischievous – club members turned the pages of their newspapers, or rose from their seats just as an English bowler began his approach to an Australian batsman. As for uncovered pitches, although as a bowler he often derived benefit from them after rain, Laver condemned the practice. He felt, as did so many others, that it too often gave one side an unfair advantage.

What he didn't chronicle, probably because he was out of earshot at the time, was that MacLaren was so fired up before going in against the tearaway Cotter second time round that he paced up and down the balcony snorting: "Cotter! I'll bloody well Cotter him!"

The competitive temperature soared steeply during this opening Test at Trent Bridge when, as England built a commanding lead, starting with MacLaren and Tyldesley's 145 for the first wicket, not only did Charlie McLeod bowl negatively wide of off stump but Warwick Armstrong, the big, blunt Victorian, bowled leg-breaks outside leg stump, with most of his fieldsmen on the leg side. His 52 overs cost 67 runs. Most became bored with this, and the bowler was barracked as MacLaren contemptuously kicked the ball away and sat on his bat when not facing, watching as Tyldesley sometimes skipped to leg and banged the ball through the off-side spaces, rather as Don Bradman did when facing the leg-side deliveries from Harold Larwood in Australia less then 30 years later, a fusillade coming at almost twice Armstrong's speed. With Cotter earlier in the match having upset the crowd by bowling a lot of bouncers at MacLaren and Tyldesley, the Australians were not Nottingham's favourite visitors.

Jackson finally left Australia to score a highly improbable 402 in 4½ hours, and this time it was the mystery spin of B.J.T.Bosanquet which proved conclusive. As in Australia just over a year previously, Bosie, who occasionally reverted to fast bowling, was sometimes ludicrously erratic before managing to slip in an apparent leg-break on a length which fizzed back from the off. Today he took a spectacular 8 for 107 in his 32.4 overs.

The light was dreadful towards the end, and batsman Charlie McLeod walked towards the pavilion to call out to his skipper on the balcony. Should he appeal against the light? Darling looked at the broad expanse of dark sky above Trent Bridge and shook his head. England had played well enough to deserve victory. This story has been disputed – by, among others, Bosanquet, who wrote that McLeod did appeal – but since there is no videotape evidence we have the choice to accept it or otherwise. Most of us, I think, prefer to believe that it happened.

At the fall of the ninth wicket, the pathetic figure of Trumper was seen to stagger as far as the gate, but the agony of his back injury forced him to give up all hope of batting. The match was England's by 213 runs, and they were one up with four to play. The absence this season of Ranjitsinhji, R.E.Foster, who played little, and S.F.Barnes, now selling his skills to Minor County Staffordshire, seemed hardly to matter.

Five minutes after Bosanquet had completed his rout the rain began to fall. It persisted all evening.

*** *** ***

England's newly-established Board of Control had taken the unusual step of asking four players to make themselves available for all five Tests in that summer of 1905. They were not quite guaranteed selection, but there must have been some anxiety that one of them might suddenly choose to help his county rather than play a Test match. It was the nearest thing to an international central contract 100 years ago. F.S.Jackson, of course, was willingly committed as captain. Dick Lilley of Warwickshire was the outstanding wicketkeeper, with all the nous that captains seek from that position. MacLaren was another obvious name from which the Board sought full-scale commitment. The other was the multi-talented C.B.Fry, who had been forced to miss Trent Bridge after a youngster damaged one of the great man's fingers at the nets. But he showed up at Lord's and scored 73 and 36 not out.

It had rained over London for days beforehand, and there were nightly thunderstorms, so it was a wonder that they got two days' play in before a further spoiling downpour ruled out any play on the final (third) day. Still, there had been some individual performances of note.

Having won the toss again, Jackson took first innings for England, who made 282 and then bowled Australia out for 181. Darling's superb 41 was top score in difficult conditions. Three Yorkshiremen did most of the damage, left-arm spinner Wilfred Rhodes opening with the faster right-arm slinger Schofield Haigh, and Jackson recording the best figures with 4 for 50. Notably, he bowled poor Trumper with his first ball as he shaped to cut after a whirlwind opening stand with Duff of 57 in 35 minutes – Hayden and Gilchrist stuff. Trumper's 31 was to be his best score of the entire series, in stark contrast to his glittering feats on the 1902 tour. He, like Clem Hill, was thought by some to have been too ambitious, too dashing, too careless during this 1905 series.

Sensibly, Jackson temporarily made over the captaincy to MacLaren whenever he decided to bowl. He once reflected that Archie was more a partner than a lieutenant.

Jackson had missed Yorkshire's recent match against the touring team, when a fast bowler named Billy Ringrose took 9 for 76 with swerving deliveries. How many who spot the grey-haired gentleman in a suit standing on the end of those between-wars photographs of Yorkshire teams might be aware that the club's official scorer had once had such a memorable day's cricket against the mighty Australians?

F.S.Jackson had captained MCC in the Australians' next match, but it was another rain-wrecked affair. However, the eerie pattern was sustained: Jackson won the toss again and made runs again, 85 of them, in 165 minutes of battle on a damp and difficult pitch before Darling caught him on the leg side. When the Australians batted, there was time for only one ball before further weather interruption ended the match. With it, J.T.Hearne bowled the unfortunate Reg Duff.

Before this rain-ruined Test match at Lord's, senior members of the Australian party had been invited to meet MCC committee members to discuss the state of Anglo-Australian cricket. The Englishmen revealed that they had no confidence whatsoever in the newly-formed Board of Control (Cricket) in Australia. Their chief objection was to the fact that the new organisation seemed not to represent the true interests of all parties (South Australia were in dispute with it, and soon Melbourne Cricket Club and the Victorian Cricket Association were tearing each other's hair out). MCC would therefore not be sending a team to Australia in 1906–07.

Under the existing arrangements, Australian teams would continue to be welcome in England, although there was an awkward stipulation that for the 1909 tour Australia would be required to agree to play in a triangular tournament (including South Africa, the only other Test-playing side in the world). F.S.Jackson helped to alleviate the situation. No triangular was attempted until 1912, and for various reasons it was a complete flop.

Thus England added an extra element to the rumble that soon became a roaring earthquake in Australian cricket as players took on the would-be totalitarian Board, many of whose members were compensating for their former deficiencies as players with reckless use of their new-found administrative power. It has been a recurring theme throughout cricket's history, once painfully evident in Australia, but in the 21st Century elsewhere too. Joe Darling relayed MCC's views by cable, and naturally enough the NSW Cricket Association were affronted by England's apparent attempt to interfere in Australian cricket's affairs.

❊❊❊

The quest for the Ashes had become an uphill struggle for Joe Darling and his warriors. Before rain washed out the final day at Lord's, England had established a handy lead on a pitch which was losing its top. The innings of the match was MacLaren's 79, to add to his first-innings 56.

But with the match abandoned, the series still stood at one-nil to England, with three to play. The after-match chat concerned not only Armstrong's further negative bowling and the defiant innings of Jackson, who fought for almost an hour and a half for his 29, but England's exaggerated caution. They batted through 140 overs to reach 282. In the *Daily Express* C.B.Fry gave as many as eight reasons for the slow scoring.

Although Australia had fallen well short on first innings, the fighting manner in which they tried to overcome probing bowling on a difficult surface won them many plaudits. Trumper and Duff had rocketed to 57 in little more than half an hour. Perhaps feeling the need to restore his country's honour, MacLaren had engineered

England batting ace A.C.MacLaren's high backlift is dramatically portrayed in S.T.Dadd's sketch of the action in the 1905 Lord's Test. Australia's wicketkeeper is Jim Kelly.

David Frith Collection

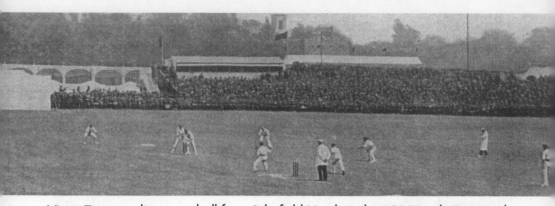

Victor Trumper digs out a ball from Schofield Haigh in the 1905 Lord's Test match.
David Frith Collection

a similarly fast start to England's second innings. But Fry (already with two double-centuries, two centuries and a 98 in his huge first-class aggregate to date) was bogged down. Jackson was bowled first ball by Armstrong. Had the wicket flattened out, given an extra day or two the tourists might have sprung a surprise victory.

In his book, Frank Laver's plea for longer Test matches made abundant good sense, though he countered his own remarks by acknowledging that the length of time a major cricket match takes "in this age of progress and bustle" was far too great. How might he have felt 100 years later, when, even in an age of batting supremacy, so many Test matches finish in three or four days (some in two), and in our own frantic society – in which progress is supposedly many times greater and the hectic pace of life makes the Edwardians seem almost to be going in slow motion – the newer cricket followers seem to be demanding shorter and shorter games?

Slightly confused Laver may have been – aren't we all? – but he was astonishingly prescient in stating that "life is too short for long contests" and in wondering if cricket might be a better game if the second innings were to be abolished. Had he lived well beyond his short span of just under 50 years, he would, in turn, have been appalled at the Test matches in the 1920s and 1930s in Australia and South Africa which stretched over anything up to 10 days; but he would surely have delighted in the revolutionary late-twentieth century format of limited-overs cricket, and perhaps – just perhaps – even the Twenty20 variety.

As it was, the overs in 1905 were often grievously limited by rain. But not enough to deny Essex a thrilling 19-run win over the Australians at Leyton, the touring team's only reversal outside the Tests. They had just enjoyed a quick trip to Dublin, and when Laver took 6 for 49 to send Essex back for 118, everything seemed fine. Then the Australians were bowled out for 100, Essex passed 200, and the final target of 222 proved just too distant. Syd Gregory suffered a pair, and *six* Australians played the ball onto their stumps in this second innings, which ended with F.L.Fane's breath-taking catch on the boundary to dismiss Laver. Claude Buckenham took 12 wickets for the county and pace partner Bert Tremlin took eight, giving the England selectors further names to consider, though across the nation there was bowling talent to spare. Tremlin, who bowled through both Australian innings in this match, took a further 10 wickets when the tourists played a return fixture.

Darling's men cheered themselves up by thrashing Warwickshire in the next match, where it was apparent that pace-man Tibby Cotter (7 for 76) was at last coming into his stride. While in the Midlands, Frank Laver and some other players visited the Rover motor car factory. Laver was so impressed that he ordered a vehicle and took delivery a few weeks later. He had previously ridden a Rover bicycle. Now it would be the fast lane for him and team-mate passenger Algy Gehrs as they drove across Europe after the cricket tour ended, and then embarked at Naples on the ship that would take them and Laver's shiny new automobile home.

Herein lies another oblique connection between 1905 and 2005. One hundred years after Laver's call at the Coventry works the esteemed MG Rover company, midst heated controversy, slid into liquidation.

Young Tibby Cotter had had to settle for a noisy motor horn, with which he scared the wits out of unwary people. For his own amusement he crept up behind them and squeezed the horn. His team-mates soon found it all a bit wearying, and somebody stuffed bread-crumbs into the mouth of the horn. Still it emitted a funny noise when activated, so the rubber squeezer was finally fatally punctured with a pin. Every tour has its tiresome prankster. For Cotter read Hughes, M.G.

Trumper, with some relief, crafted an even-time 108 against Gloucestershire at Bristol, and the Australians sailed past 500 before Armstrong spun his way to 7 for 16 (including Jessop for a duck). In the Australians' innings it was Bert Hopkins who had batted like the typical Jessop, hoisting three balls from spinner George Dennett out of the ground during his 70-minute knock of 93. In his book Laver remarked on the orphanage built just outside the Bristol ground by the Prussian, George Muller. Other Australian eyes 100 years later were to fall on that rather sombre-looking building as Ricky Ponting's team came to grief in a one-day match that had been intended as a positive step in the build-up to the main events of their tour.

Rain interruption or not, confidence had returned to the 1905 touring team, and England were going to be pushed hard at Headingley in the third Test – where, strange to reflect, neither side had an out-and-out fast bowler. Yorkshire had four representatives, including David Denton, whose place might better have been taken by Gilbert Jessop, the hurricane hitter and brilliant fieldsman.

There was soon a problem for Australia, and it was becoming all too familiar. Put simply, F.S.Jackson blocked their path. Three wickets for McLeod helped embarrass England in the first hour or so. Jackson had won the toss yet again and the pitch looked good. So when the score stood at 64 for four, with Hayward, Fry, Tyldesley and debutant Denton gone, the captain had a sizable repair job on his hands. By close of play he had hauled his team up to 301, having made an admirable century himself. The first-ever Test century at Headingley and a captain's innings if ever there was one, this 144 not out took Jackson 260 minutes and contained 18 fours, nearly all from stylish strokes, the ball purring across the grass. It was the highest of Jackson's five centuries against Australia, and if there should be any doubts that the crowd got their money's worth, the Australians bowled their overs at a rate of 22 per hour.

Next morning the England captain, light-blue Cambridge scarf around his waist, led out his team on his home ground, and soon Arnold Warren, the Derbyshire fast bowler, was enjoying his hour of glory. In his only Test match he took 5 for 57, with Trumper, Noble, Armstrong and Darling among his scalps. By the second evening England were practically unbeatable, 275 runs ahead with eight wickets in hand, and when Johnny Tyldesley advanced to a fine hundred on the third and final day, again having had to deal with Armstrong's leg-side tedium and McLeod's off theory, Jackson declared. The little Lancastrian had been more resourceful than his fellow batsmen in dealing with Armstrong's stultifying leg-side bowling. Charles Fry's original mind and his obstinacy (the latter quality on a par with even Armstrong's) persuaded him simply to exist at the crease. It was, after all, Australia's need to win this match if they were to come back into the series. (A fortnight later, as captain of Sussex, Fry instructed his bowlers to deliver daisy-cutters along the ground in protest when Lancashire batted on beyond 600.) As for bully-boy Armstrong, he took all five wickets to fall in this Leeds Test, but put down catches off consecutive balls at slip off Noble's bowling

Now came another coincidence, this time within the 1905 series itself. Here at Headingley, at precisely the same time as at Trent Bridge (12.45 pm) Jackson declared, setting Australia exactly the same target (402) as at Trent Bridge. Trumper was not injured this time, but instead he was caught at slip by Hirst off Warren for a duck. Noble held the innings together with 62 before he lost patience against Bosanquet and was stumped, but the draw was duly earned, though it would probably have been denied to Australia if England had held their catches. Hayward missed Hill early in the innings, and the highly-strung "Charlie" Blythe's caught-and-bowled miss off Noble proved quite expensive. This time Australia certainly did appeal against the light and the match ended at 6.20 pm, 10 minutes before the scheduled close, with Australia 224 for seven. England one up with two to play.

While the Australians took the train down to Southampton for the Hampshire match, Frank Laver and Charlie McLeod had a break. They went to the Henley Royal Regatta and then Wimbledon, where they watched the English champion, little Laurie Doherty, beat the Australian left-hander Norman Brookes in the men's final. "The styles of Doherty and Brookes," wrote Laver, "resembled the styles of their respective countries in the Test matches; Doherty was safe, Brookes brilliant." There was no comment on the ladies' final, in which May Sutton (USA), pioneering the daring half-sleeve blouse, broke the long English stranglehold on the title by beating Dorothea Douglass. The contestants' flowing ankle-length white skirts would have surprised today's Wimbledon aficionados, who are accustomed to seeing female players looking as if they had just emerged from the shower.

※ ※ ※

More contrasts: the 1905 Australians, regrouping before the vital fourth Test, trounced Hampshire, with Hill, Noble and Gregory making centuries and Trumper 92, Cotter mowing down nine wickets in the match. But then they struck trouble during the Derbyshire match at Derby. Bert Hopkins cut a finger on some broken glass and Syd Gregory went down with sunstroke. To worsen matters, players from both sides were mildly poisoned by the pigeon pie.

It was a relief to get to tranquil Bath, in the light, warm air of the West Country, where Warwick Armstrong heaved an unbeaten 303, taking the Australian record in England from his team-mate Trumper, whose 300 at Hove in 1899 had been the first treble-century on such a tour. The Australians scored 609 for four declared at about 100 runs per hour (Armstrong got slower the longer he was in), and the doughty Len Braund, who took 1 for 142 off 34 overs of leg-spin, then opened the Somerset innings and scored 117. All-rounder Braund was sometimes England's answer to Armstrong, bowling leg-spin outside leg stump and either enticing mis-hits caused by frustration or bringing the game almost to a standstill.

The Somerset match was drawn, thanks to brilliant wicketkeeper Harry Martyn's stop-go 130 not out, his only first-class century, and another big effort by Braund (62). It was further evidence to demonstrate that good players on a perfect pitch needed more than three days to effect a genuine result. Tom Richardson, once the world's leading fast bowler, played as a guest for Somerset, but, bloated at 35, he was a spent force. It was the last first-class appearance for a titanic fast bowler who 10 years earlier had bowled Joe Darling first ball at Sydney on the left-hander's Test debut.

Hundreds more miles were travelled by train for two matches in Scotland, where the enthusiastic attendances were gratifying. At Edinburgh the Australians renewed on-field acquaintance with Gregor MacGregor, who had kept wicket for England in Australia on the 1891–92 tour and in home Tests either side, and was currently captain of Middlesex. A big drinker, MacGregor must surely have joined the colonial lads for a noggin or two after hours. The Glasgow match, against a Scotland Fifteen, was drawn after further weather interruption. Had global warming seriously begun?

As for Australia's fitness parade, Syd Gregory was now struggling with a leg strain, incurred in a rare spell of bowling, and Laver had a similar problem and needed to wear an elastic bandage for the remainder of the tour. Grinning and bearing the fatigue and strains as best they could, the Australians took it out on the waiters who served them in their hotels. Many were foreign, and the cricketers teased them with orders for such unlikely dishes as possum soup, roast bustard on kangaroo tail, and emu wings with lizard sauce. Laver records that the obliging servants often replied: "Yes, sir . . . sorry – no more; it is just off."

Australia were soon in trouble again when the fourth Test match began at Old Trafford on July 24. England were strengthened by the return of MacLaren and Rhodes, and by the successful Test debuts of R.H.Spooner and boastful amateur fast bowler Walter Brearley, both from Lancashire.

By now Joe Darling, fed up with the vagaries of their travels (their sleeper had finally brought them to Manchester at 5.30 in the morning), must have wondered if the formality of the toss was worth the trouble when Jackson again earned England first use of the slowish pitch. The home side cruised to 446, F.S.Jackson making another century (113, with a dozen fours, 225 minutes), Hayward a three-hour 82, and the newcomer amateur Reg Spooner, the youthful Cardus's joint favourite batsman (alongside Trumper) and like Jackson a veteran of the Boer War, scored 52 in his maiden Test innings. Spooner, crooned Neville Cardus years later, "told us in every one of his drives past cover that he did not come from the hinterland of Lancashire, where cobbled streets sound with the noise of clogs and industry; he played always as though on the elegant lawns of Aigburth". With his captain, Spooner added a decisive 125 for the fifth wicket.

Spooner became one of McLeod's four wickets that day, to which he added Jackson's on the second day, caught by Cotter at mid-off, to give the Victorian medium-pacer 5 for 125. "Jacker" had reached his hundred just before the close of the first day. It was his fifth century against Australia in 19 Tests and 31 innings, all achieved in England. Not until Geoff Boycott, a very different kind of Yorkshireman, ground out 137 at The Oval in 1981 did any England batsman equal that performance of five home hundreds against the old enemy. Nine of Jack Hobbs's 12 centuries were compiled on Australian grounds, as were seven of Wally Hammond's nine, five of David Gower's nine, six of Herbert Sutcliffe's eight, and four of John Edrich's seven. One might add, before the 2005 Ashes series begins, that all of Michael Vaughan's three hundreds against Australia to date have been made "away" (he had yet to face Australia on his home patch). It will be a mighty batsman indeed who passes the five home Ashes hundreds which rest against the names of F.S.Jackson and G.Boycott.

Some observers reflected on how many (or few) England might have made had "Demon" Spofforth been bowling for Australia, or "Terror" Turner or Hughie Trumble, just as 15 years from now Australians will be lamenting the absence of Glenn McGrath and Shane Warne as the opposition grinds out a huge total.

Old Trafford was almost full for the first two days, and the crowd was expectant of some fireworks on the second day after overnight rain. It was just the Australians' luck to start their innings as the sun was beginning to tease out the hidden evil in the turf. Brearley got Trumper and Noble cheaply, and Hill was bowled by Ted Arnold for a duck. If England's fielding and catching hadn't been so erratic, Australia would have been in even deeper trouble. It was also thought that Jackson missed a trick by under-using Wilfred Rhodes, whose slow left-arm seemed perfect for the conditions.

Captain Darling easily topped the score, hitting gamely for 73 in under an hour and a half. The power of his driving was awesome. All but one of his 13 fours came from drives. But he was dropped at least three times. Still, Australia's innings was wrapped up for 197 and they followed on.

This time Reg Duff was reunited with his legendary partner Victor Trumper at the top of the order. At one stage in the match, with rain about, Duff had been seen on the Australian players' balcony sporting a sunhat, his trousers rolled up to the knees, and pretending to search for the elusive sun, holding two empty soda-water bottles to his eyes as if they were binoculars. This was the self-effacing fellow who used to describe his opening-batting role as "Vic taking me for a walk", pre-dating Jack Fingleton's rueful remark that he didn't so much "bat with" Don Bradman as "run for him".

Duff top-scored with 60 in what was to be his penultimate Test appearance. Just over six years later he was dead. Towards the end Arthur Mailey had spotted him around Sydney's Haymarket area, his straw boater battered, his aura that of a hopeless inebriate. Such are the highly variable possibilities of tomorrow.

There were complaints at the laxity in observing the prescribed hours of play. The match started not at 11.30 am but 10 minutes later; the players' lunch break lasted 50 minutes instead of the 45 set down; and the tea interval stretched to nearly 30 minutes. On the second day, the interval between innings was over 20 minutes instead of the regulation 10 minutes. Such carelessness today would give the International Cricket Council cause to issue volleys of Press releases and to fine, censure or sack everybody concerned.

By the second evening at Old Trafford, working in easier conditions now that the pitch had rolled out evenly, Australia were 118 for the loss of Trumper. Sydney's genius was leg-before to Rhodes for 30. Many years later the old Yorkshireman made the remarkable statement to the author that he was sometimes frustrated when bowling to the Australians. "I wanted to get at Victor Troomper," was his surely exclusive remark. The rationale was that Joe Darling and Clem Hill, being left-handers, were disadvantaged to a lesser degree on a sticky wicket when facing Rhodes's wily left-arm spin than was Trumper. For many years yet the ball needed to have pitched strictly between wicket and wicket for a bowler to obtain an lbw decision.

To general amazement, the Manchester Test was decided in a mere 80 minutes next day. Australia's dreadful luck with the weather continued when rain fell, and since only victory now could preserve their chances of recapturing the Ashes, they had to try for a miracle. Abandoning all caution, they played into England's hands. Nine wickets fell for 51 runs. Brearley, regarded as England's fastest bowler that summer, came away with four wickets in each innings, fuel for his claim in later years that he could throw his hat faster than present-day so-called fast bowlers such as Harold Larwood.

An England XI probably as strong as that Edgbaston team of 1902 thus secured the Ashes for another series, and their captain, according to the *Yorkshire Post*, believed it was the strongest-ever England team. He also thought that no England side could ever have fielded as badly as here in the first innings. And the wonder of it all is that Jackson pulled off this handsome victory with no official personnel whatsoever backing him up. Compare this with the people supporting Michael Vaughan in 2005: head coach, assistant coach, analyst, chief medical officer, physiotherapist, physiologist, sports psychologist, vision experts, operations manager, massage therapist, and media relations manager, to say nothing of the covey of players' agents and personal managers and Professional Cricketers Association representatives who hover in the vicinity.

Just as the Honourable F.S.Jackson's stocks could not have been higher, all of Joe Darling's hopes had ended in frustration. Now the Australians almost lost to Surrey. The Browncaps needed only 41 to win, with eight wickets in hand and 45 minutes remaining.

Armstrong duly bowled negatively from around the wicket, and the batsmen did not play very sensibly. A mixture of resentment, panic and stupidity caused those eight wickets to go down in 40 minutes, leaving the Australians winners by 22 runs (Armstrong 6 for 25).

In an age of broader compassion and understanding between the two nations (Australia, a federation for four years, was no longer a "colony"), it was with no tongue in cheek or sense of condescension that these remarks were published in *Cricket* magazine in midsummer 1905: "It would be the very worst possible thing which could happen to the game if Australian cricket were to begin to show signs of falling off. One could almost wish to see the Test match, next week, end in favour of our visitors – it is quite certain that no Englishman would, under the circumstances, grieve very much if they were to pull off the match. But it looks as if they will want a great deal of luck if they are to do so."

Paraphrased in reverse, might there have been one single Australian in 2005 prepared to extend a similar sympathy towards England?

* * *

Against Sussex at Hove the touring team ran up another huge total (556), M.A.Noble making 267, Darling 93, and the best bowling for the county coming from an Australian named Dwyer – well, actually, John Elicius Benedict Bernard Placid Quirk Carrington Dwyer. He took 6 for 178 (Trumper included), and if his father – who clearly was a man of some humour – was still alive he would have been very proud of his boy. Here C.B.Fry, by far the season's leading run-scorer, reached 2000. All he needed now was a century in a Test against Australia to show the world that he could compete with the very best.

The loss of the first day to foul weather prevented the Australians from crushing Worcestershire, who simply had no idea how to cope with Cotter's pace. He took 7 for 15 and 5 for 19, including seven wickets among the brothers Foster. Four of them were playing, including the great R.E., and Cotter got three of them in both innings and W.L. in the second. R.E. Foster, star of England's recent tour of Australia for his 287 at Sydney when on debut in the first Test, made 31 of Worcestershire's pitiful 78 in the first innings. For the county, George Wilson dismissed Noble (who made another century here, as did Trumper) and bowled Gehrs and Laver with his next two balls to secure a proud hat-trick – almost made four in four when his next ball just missed Cotter's stumps.

There can surely have been no more enchanting spectator experience than watching Victor Trumper's innings of 110 against the backdrop of Worcester Cathedral.

A major inconvenience had been inflicted on the Australians before this match. The county club would not agree to a later start, which left Darling and his men no option but to rise at 4.30 on the morning of the match in order to get from Brighton to Worcester on time. (Imagine the tour management of today giving in to that one!) It might have infused Cotter with a little extra motivation, as modern players call it.

(There was an uncanny echo of that 4.30 am Brighton wake-up call 100 years later when Ricky Ponting's Australians, abed in the Lumley Castle Hotel in Durham, were roused from their sleep – those, that is, who weren't staring into the darkness, spooked by the resident ghost – by a rogue fire alarm at precisely that time: half-past-four. Shane Watson had already requested a change of room. Hearing of this, Darren Gough pretended to scare Watson in mid-over, pulling a spooky face and wiggling his fingers. The Queenslander must have thought he was mad.)

A strange match against South Wales in Cardiff, where the pitch was moved a foot nearer the pavilion after the first day, was followed by victory over Middlesex, with Noble's masterly form continuing and Armstrong bagging another big haul, 8 for 50. Albert Trott, the Australian outcast now serving Middlesex, caught Trumper in both innings, but could only but dream of repeating his unique and stupendous hit over the Lord's pavilion off Noble six years before. Armstrong now got him in both innings, and he finished with 11 wickets in a match where the most memorable ball was that which one of the Beldam brothers hit straight at a sparrow, with fatal results.

Frank Laver had a few further gripes about touring conditions. The dressing-rooms at some of the grounds were not up to scratch. They had insufficient pegs for the hanging of clothes, and "shower-baths – an Australian's delight – were conspicuous by their absence in the majority of grounds". Even worse: there was no privacy in some inadequate dressing-rooms, and women sometimes peered across at the Australian cricketers as they were pulling on their flannels. How Shane Warne would have disapproved of that! Laver complained, with good reason, about the scoreboards, most of which gave so little information (scorecards were a major source of revenue for the counties). And he attacked the social divide which placed English amateurs in a separate zone to the paid profession-als. Bound by the prospect of a £100 fine should an Australian player write for a newspaper, he was understandably bitter that several England cricketers were earning extra cash by doing so.

All these grievances had long been laid to rest by the time Ricky Ponting's 2005 Australians landed in England. What Ponting's and Darling's teams did have in common was the problem of deciding which of the cascades of dinner and social invitations they should and could accept. While much of the moderns' time is taken up with sponsors' events, it would still be interesting to know if the huge inflow of gifts, as recorded by Frank Laver, has been maintained.

A further friendly observation from Laver's pen: "The behaviour of the crowds, except on three or four occasions, was very fair. Though not so demonstrative as an Australian crowd, who give an English team a very flattering reception upon entering the cricket field, they are perhaps fairer in their treatment of erring players. They do not unmercifully attack players, to my knowledge, for having missed catches, or for having fumbled the ball. They do not tell delinquents to 'get a bag', or 'get off the field' and 'give somebody else a show' &c, as the Australian crowds do. But then it is generally our own players who get the gruelling."

Now *that* marks a most significant behavioural change over 100 years.

***

Could the visitors now claw something back in the final Test? Already Kennington Oval was established as a lucky ground for England. They had won seven of the previous 10 Tests at the drab old venue in south London and lost only the fateful 1882 encounter, when Australia, fired up by Spofforth, stole victory by seven runs. Out of that sensational event emerged the Ashes.

The match at The Oval, like all the other Tests in the 1905 series except for the one at Lord's, began on a Monday. And Jim Phillips, the no-nonsense Australian who had led the campaign on chuckers, stood as umpire for the fourth time in the series.

Tibby Cotter, with his long, easy run-up, began a stint that was to bring him the best return – 7 for 148 (five of them bowled) off 40 overs – in all of his 21 Tests. His arm was lower than Brett Lee's but the bowling of fierce bouncers and searing yorkers was an enjoyment common to both of them. Cotter broke many stumps and bones. This popular young fellow, who was to lose his life in the Australian cavalry charge at Beersheba in 1917, had the sort of physique, slightly low-slung, that enabled him to remain steady when bowling flat-out even on slippery turf.

MacLaren, Tyldesley and Fry were the gems in Cotter's collection that day, but he didn't get Jackson. The England captain fell to Laver for 76. It was not his most attractive effort of the series but it was still second-top score in the innings of 430. C.B.Fry secured a long-awaited and supremely satisfying century, 144, this polymath's only three-figure score against Australia after so many doubts had been expressed about his ability to score from the best bowling. Cutting vigorously, he put on 151 with Jackson, his skipper, in little more than two hours to get England to a solid total. Bathing in sunshine, the Ovalites delighted in a scoreline of 381 for seven at better than a run a minute.

The England and Australia cricketers at The Oval in 1905, a cordial integration unlikely to be emulated in today's demonstrably "competitive" age. Back row: Ted Arnold (E), Phil Newland (A), Bert Hopkins (A), Bill Howell (A), Warwick Armstrong (A). Standing: Wilfred Rhodes (E), Arthur Jones (E), Victor Trumper (A), Tom Hayward (E), Charlie McLeod (A), Walter Brearley (E), Frank Laver (A), Dick Lilley (E), Algy Gehrs (A). Seated: Charles Fry (E), Monty Noble (A), Stanley Jackson (E), Joe Darling (A), Archie MacLaren (E), Clem Hill (A). In front: Tibby Cotter (A), Reggie Spooner (E), Jim Kelly (A), Johnny Tyldesley (E), George Hirst (E), Syd Gregory (A). Of the Australian tour party only Reg Duff is missing.

David Frith Collection

That Australia managed to get within range of England's 430 by scoring 363 owed most to Reg Duff, who (unknowingly at the time) closed his Test career with a game 146 (200 minutes), which was the highest score by either side in the 1905 series, but the only hundred by an Australian. Losing his renowned partner, Trumper, early – he played on to Brearley, who was soon claiming him as his rabbit – Duff had that bit of luck to which all centurions are entitled when

MacLaren and Hirst collided in moving to catch a high ball over slips. Duff was then 78. The bare scorecard fails to reveal the support he got from Noble, whose 25 took him 100 minutes.

Duff had begun his Test career with a century at Melbourne in January 1902, batting at No.10 after Darling had rejigged the order to counter a tricky wicket after rain. These hundreds made a handsome pair of brackets for a career which, like his life, was all too short. Duff was unable to take his place in the field or bat on the final day of this Oval Test. Influenza was the official explanation. One can but wonder if he had overdone it in celebrating his century.

On the third day England suddenly found themselves threatened. Nightwatchman Arnold had been bowled by Cotter the evening before, and now Armstrong got MacLaren and Hayward. With Lilley unlikely to bat (the wicketkeeper had a badly cut finger), was this Australia's chance to post a last-minute victory in this difficult series?

At 48 Fry went. But Tyldesley and Jackson then steadied the ship, and after the captain's departure, bowled by Cotter for 31, there was a bright stand between the Lancashire batsmen Tyldesley and Spooner. Soon the match was safe. In fact Jackson declared in the long-shot hope that a surprise victory could be sprung. But Australia finished 124 for four, safe at last, and the captains began drinking each other's health in the Oval pavilion.

Years later Charles Fry looked back to this golden period and wrote: "We all admired and liked the Australians of those days" – with the somewhat predictable postscript: "but, by Jove! we did like beating them."

Frank Laver had been none too impressed with the umpiring in the later stages of this fifth Test match. "What should have been, under ordinary circumstances, a victory for Australia," he groaned, "ended, owing to bad decisions, in a draw . . . Tyldesley hit the ball and was caught behind but given not out. Immediately afterwards Spooner got his leg in front of a straight ball, but though everybody in a position to judge thought he was out the verdict was adverse."

It might have comforted Laver if he could somehow have known that a century later, with unimaginable technological advances available "upstairs", the umpires continue to misread lbws and edges (or misses). They could perform to perfection – and the game would be more just and fair – if only the authorities had the brains to provide them with a link to *all* of the findings of the probing television lens.

Darling's boys vented their disappointment over the Test series with innings victories against Northants, Lancashire (at Liverpool) and Kent, and it was during this last match, at Canterbury, that Laver noticed how forward were the local womenfolk: "Ladies of title, and their daughters and friends, spoke to one of our side whenever he went near enough to them in the outfield. Some made eyes; others smiled. Two beautiful daughters of one of the Peers of England waited, after the game was over, to have a few words with two of the Eleven. Introductions were at a discount. Ladies in their carriages bowed and smiled as they drove past, some pulling up to speak. From one of the most prominent young ladies at the match, one of us received a characteristic letter enclosing her photo; and this was not the only letter of the kind that reached us."

In this Kent match, Joe Darling top-scored with 114, his first century for three months, and in the next he was caught in the deep for 99 against Gloucestershire, who scraped a draw when Jessop, of all people, blocked for over after over against the fire of Cotter and Howell's buzzing off-spin. The last pair just held out.

The next match was equally thrilling. At the pretty Bournemouth ground the Australians played "An England XI" captained by 57-year-old Dr W.G.Grace, and once again it came down to the tenth wicket. With Howell and Gehrs together, the tourists nine down and the scores still level, as they had been when the eighth and ninth wickets fell, a leg-bye was scrambled as the ball bounced away to old WG. It would surely not have happened had F.S.Jackson been in charge.

It became three thrillers in a row when the second Essex match ended as a draw with the last two Essex men at the crease. With five lbw appeals being turned down in the final minutes the Australians' mood can be readily imagined.

And so to the penultimate match of the tour, and the reappearance of the man of whom the Australians must already have seen more than enough: "Jacker" himself. He was leading C.I.Thornton's XI at the holiday venue of Scarborough. But when he went to meet Joe Darling in the Australians' tent he froze at the sight which greeted him.

Stanley Jackson's own words have been chronicled: "When I got there I was received with jeers and cheers. Some of the Australians shouted out, 'Come on, he is ready for you!' I told them I was not at all afraid, and that I was certain to beat him again. But they said, 'He is much stronger than you are.' 'Stronger than I am,' I wondered! 'Never mind; come inside,' they said, and imagine when I did so finding Mr Darling stripped to the waist with a Union Jack round his waist, waiting for me with his arms crossed! He looked at me and said, 'Now we will have a proper tossing, and the one who gets on the top wins the toss.' I said 'All right, we will have it that way if you please.' And I called to George Hirst and said, 'Georgie, you come and toss this time.' On that Darling said, 'All right, then, we will toss in the old-fashioned way.'"

Hirst, the valiant Yorkshire and England all-rounder, was even broader of shoulder than Darling. Jackson, of course, won the toss for the seventh time in his seven spins against Darling that summer. The Yorkshireman was, after all, the seventh child of his parents, a smoker and drinker who steered clear of both "vices" during a match.

Rain had seeped under the tarpaulins and batting was so difficult that nobody in Thornton's XI scored more than 24 – except, almost inevitably, F.S.Jackson. Cautious to start with, he moved up a gear and put together a wonderful 123, his third century against the 1905 Australians. If anything, Clem Hill's 181 in reply was an even more stirring performance, but Jackson was at the wicket again when the home team, well on the back foot by now, held out for a draw as a storm broke over the ground.

Jackson's final run tally against the Australians in the eight matches in which he faced them was 776, at an average of 70.55, with three centuries: all this in a wet summer on uncovered pitches.

Nor did any one Australian bowler have a hold on him, for six of them shared in his 11 dismissals. He was surely the world's leading all-rounder that summer. There might even have been an irrational temptation to take into account his ability at tossing the coin.

Joe Darling was among the many who cordially hoped that Jackson would lead the next England team to Australia. But it was not to be. A career in politics beckoned. Jacker had played his last Test match. So, for that matter, had Joe Darling.

During the customary convivial banquet held during the Scarborough match – this one in honour of Lord Hawke's 25 years with Yorkshire – Jackson made a graceful speech praising his England team – apart from their poor showing in Australia's first innings at Old Trafford – and reverting humorously to the guest of honour by remarking on how Hawke always seemed to enjoy positioning himself in the deep, near the ladies enclosure. Jackson expressed appreciation to the Australians for the sportsmanlike manner in which they had contested the series. It was a theme no less crucial to cricket's unique standing among games 100 years later.

Not that there weren't private rumbles of discontent. Years afterwards, Joe Darling felt free to compile a litany of bad umpiring decisions seen during his five tours of England. It was prompted by Lord Harris's recent complaint about two decisions which went against England at Adelaide in 1924–25, a Test won on the seventh day by 11 runs by Australia. Darling went into the Australian dressing-room and enquired, and sure enough the local players honestly agreed that Patsy Hendren and Roy Kilner had suffered poor decisions. As if to ease his conscience, Darling then proceeded to write about many dodgy decisions against the Australians. And one of them was in this 1905 match at Scarborough.

The batsman was none other than F.S.Jackson. "He was run out before he had scored 50 runs, but the umpire gave him 'not out'. Reg Duff did a fine piece of fielding at cover point and threw Jackson's wicket down. Jackson was out by yards and had no possible chance of getting home. The umpire, who was a former player, gave Jackson not out. This was bad enough, but what disgusted all of us was the fact that Jackson turned to the umpire, who was standing at square leg, and told him it was a good decision. In other words, Jackson told him he approved of him giving not out when everybody on the ground, spectators and all, knew that he was clearly run out. Jackson went on to score 148 not out."

At this, counsel for the defence would have jumped in and challenged Darling's memory, for Jackson was caught for 123 that day. Nonetheless, the tale leaves us to wonder. Perhaps Jacker was, after all, human like the rest of us.

The weary Australians moved on to their final match, the 38th (counting the three which were not first-class). It was at Hastings, and typically in this damp summer the first day against South of England was washed out. Mr & Mrs Vic Trumper had already departed on their short European holiday, and thus Australia's greatest batsman missed out on the last of the many matches W.G.Grace played against Australian opposition. To mild amazement, WG made a sweet gesture as the match ambled towards an inconclusive end. *Wisden* could not conceal its disgust: "The play at the finish was a travesty of cricket. Grace declared the innings closed and when the Australians went in again Armstrong was given balls to hit in order that he might complete the double feat of scoring 2000 runs and taking 100 wickets."

Warwick Armstrong joined select company. This double had only ever been achieved by WG himself, C.L.Townsend, George Hirst (twice), and Gilbert Jessop. Armstrong, like Shane Warne in 2005, would "be back" to create big problems for England's best in 1909 and 1921.

On the voyage back to Australia Joe Darling was found one evening leaning on the ship's railings, gazing at the sea. "Looking for the ashes?" an enquirer ingenuously remarked. "No," said the Test skipper with a smile, "unfortunately we left them behind us. That dampens our homecoming, as otherwise we had a most successful tour."

A man usually of few words but always of strong opinion, he opened up a little. He lamented Trumper's back injury, which he believed cost Australia victory at Trent Bridge, and nominated Australia's 181 in extremely difficult conditions at Lord's as the best performance in any of the Test matches. The loss against Essex was explained away with fatigue after their all-night boat journey from Ireland. Acknowledging the "right royal" treatment extended to them during the tour, he also claimed that the Australians were more popular with the crowds than the Englishmen, "simply, I suppose, because they liked fast scoring".

He went on: "This team was the happiest lot of fellows ever I travelled with. There was absolutely no kicking over the ropes, and no disagreements either on or off the field."

Even in death Darling was slightly bested by Jackson. They had been new-born babies within hours, perhaps minutes, of each other on that momentous day in November 1870. The Australian died on January 2, 1946 following a gall-bladder operation. He was 75. Jackson outlived him by just over a year. His life ran out on March 9, 1947, when he was 76.

❊ ❊ ❊

Fifty years later, all but a few weeks, England again won the Ashes. The captain this time was Len Hutton, *who was a Yorkshire player like F.S.Jackson and Michael Vaughan*. I nearly wrote "Yorkshireman", but Vaughan was born in Manchester. To offset that, however, on his mother's side he lays claim to a family relationship – admittedly somewhat remote – to J.T.Tyldesley. Little JT, of course, batted so well in the 1905 series, scoring centuries at Headingley and The Oval.

Hutton had recovered the Ashes in 1953, in a celebrated contest at The Oval, after Australia had held them for 19 years. Allowing for the loss of the war years, this didn't quite compare with England's recent failures to win back the urn, which stretch through eight series back to 1989.

Hutton then took a strong side to Australia in 1954–55, despite the absence of Laker and Lock, the spinners who had sewn up the famous Oval victory. With classy young batsmen like Peter May and Colin Cowdrey on board, and the wily spin of Johnny Wardle, and the dependable all-round skills of Trevor Bailey, Hutton decided that Australia could be beaten this time by pace bowling, with the over rate held as low as decency and the umpires would allow.

Winning the first Test of any series has dubious value. In 1997 England won at Edgbaston only to be crushed thereafter. So it was at Brisbane in 1954 when Hutton put Australia in and they made 601 for eight before rolling England over twice. Arthur Morris scored 153, Neil Harvey 162.

Two major developments sprang from that debacle. Alec Bedser, the giant who had carried England's bowling on his broad shoulders ever since Test cricket resumed in 1946 after the war, was placed in abeyance, and Frank Tyson, the 24-year-old express bowler, banished his gruesome figures at the Gabba from his mind, shortened his marathon run-up, and, either side of a knockout blow to the back of the head from a Ray Lindwall bouncer, took 10 wickets to win the Sydney Test.

"Typhoon" Tyson they named him, and he demolished Australia again at Melbourne, taking 7 for 27 on a cracked pitch on the last day. Then in the fourth Test, at Adelaide, England retained the Ashes. Australia had a mixture of under-baked youngsters and experienced players who were just losing their edge, and fast bowling can sort out batsmen from whom the bloom of youth has departed.

The struggle continued in England in 1956, when off-spinner Jim Laker's amazing deeds brought him 46 wickets in the series at 9.60 on responsive pitches. It was not until 1958 that Australia were finally revivified under the new-wave leadership of Richie Benaud.

Fifty years ago, then, just as 100 years ago, England won the Ashes, and the superstitious author now uses these facts as a foundation for his omen-based belief that the health of Ashes cricket will be restored with another England success in 2005. Fifty and 100 are surely the landmarks that matter? These are the points at which a batsman raises his bat in acknowledgement of the congratulatory applause – these, and the fifty breaks which follow (in Brian Lara's case a wearying 10 times all told when he constructed his 501 not out for Warwickshire in 1994).

There will be those who would ask why the 75th anniversary of Don Bradman's magical tour of England should not serve as a favourable omen for the 2005 Australians. Well, maybe it should, though more than any other batsman Don would have had no reason to raise his bat when reaching 75, a figure he passed on 13 occasions during that memorable tour. And what about 25 years ago? Best forgotten. While the celebration of 100 years of Test cricket in England in 1980 was highly enjoyable for the presence of so many Ashes Test veterans, and for Kim Hughes's thrilling strokeplay (Trumper redivivus, some said), the celebration of the Lord's Test match was muted. The weather was awful and so was the umpires' refusal to resume play because there was still some slight dampness in the outfield.

No, the events to examine are those that took place a century ago and a half-century ago, and for Vaughan's England those distant Ashes series – whatever they know of them – should serve as inspiration.

There is nothing terribly clever about predicting another emphatic win by Australia. From recent history and in the mood preceding the start of the 2005 tour such apparently safe forecasts were akin to saying that there were bound to be further increases in taxation, or that the weather was bound to change.

So there it is: all these omens and portents (if you chose to adopt them as such) – 1905 and 1955 – are either valid or they would soon be exposed as fallacious. (Even Frank Laver was superstitious, keeping his pads on during luncheon intervals.) I was about to find out. If I'm misguided and am proved wrong, it will actually bring relief, for the ever-haunting burden of superstition will have been lifted forever.

Naturally, I'd remain disappointed for the sake of the competitive balance in Ashes Test cricket. But that abandonment of superstition would be a monumental relief. Imagine never being susceptible to portents and omens ever again. Free at last!

3

The Prelude

The first omen appeared to favour Australia. Brett Lee dismissed Stephen Fleming with the first ball of the tour in the Australians' 20-overs jaunt against the so-called PCA Masters at Arundel on June 9, a showpiece won by the tourists by eight wickets with a ball to spare.

But it was no omen at all in reality, for Fleming, brilliant player that he is, is a New Zealander. Michael Clarke took another step towards full recognition as an all-rounder by taking a hat-trick, but if one propaganda blow was landed it was the cheap dismissal of England's brightest new hope, Kevin Pietersen (6), who slogged and was caught. As Adam Gilchrist and Matt Hayden thrashed 131 for the first wicket, the fast and accurate bowling of the tall Hampshire man Chris Tremlett was heartening for England's selectors, while the bowling of the ageing Devon Malcolm (3-0-38-0) and Chris Lewis (2-0-17-0) brought an unexpected reminder of some of England's frustration during the 1990s. Australia's openers might have been rusty after the weeks of no match play, but most of the rust flakes peeled away at Arundel, the loveliest ground in the land.

ARUNDEL, June 9, 2005
PCA MASTERS 167 for 6 (20 overs) (D.L.Maddy 70*, P.D.Collingwood 38, M.A.Ealham 39; M.J.Clarke 3 for 36);

AUSTRALIANS 170 for 2 (19.5 overs) (A.C.Gilchrist 53, M.L.Hayden 79, R.T.Ponting 31*). *AUSTRALIANS WON BY 8 WICKETS.*

In the next fixture too, a one-day bash with Leicestershire on June 11, all went well – apart from the miserable theft of some valuables from the touring team's dressing-room. Hayden became the Australians' first centurymaker of the tour, and Damien Martyn (85) and Andrew Symonds (92 not out off 59 balls) came close as 321 runs were torn from the 50 overs. Jaunty Brad Hogg's left-arm wrist-spin then accounted for three wickets, McGrath gave nothing away, Lee swung the ball at great speed, and a welcome if overdue sense of ease enveloped Ponting's camp.

In defiance of the old wisdom that snap judgments should never be made so early in a season, the papers were all saying: "Here we go again". The first big shock was only 24 hours away.

LEICESTER, June 11, 2005
AUSTRALIANS 321 for 4 (50 overs) (M.L.Hayden 107, D.R.Martyn 85, A.Symonds 92*); LEICESTERSHIRE 226 for 8 (50 overs) (H.D.Ackerman 38, P.A.Nixon 43, O.D.Gibson 50; G.B.Hogg 3 for 56). *AUSTRALIANS WON BY 95 RUNS.*

On the same Saturday, an England one-day team overwhelmed Hampshire, who were led by Shane Warne. A few weeks hence Warne would relinquish his county commitments and become an Australia Test player again. Many could hardly wait. Here, at the Rose Bowl, Hampshire were 20 for seven wickets at one point, Simon Jones having gingered things up before Darren Gough took a hat-trick which included Craig McMillan, the Kiwi, and John Crawley, the former England batsman. Tremlett's 21 dragged the county up to 85 all out, 153 runs short of an England XI score which rested mainly on Andrew Strauss's 85 and Pietersen's 77.

✻ ✻ ✻

If it is stretching matters to call any 20-overs result a "shock", it was Australia's loss of seven wickets for eight runs that unarguably had to be noted down as something beyond imagination and prediction. Even allowing that there might still have been some residual rust on the machine, this was horrible, laughable, just about incredible. It certainly caused the host nation to sit up and consider further possibilities.

The Rose Bowl on Monday, June 13 was full, with 15,000 there to see English cricket's latest creation, the Twenty20 format, dignified by international status. Here it was at long last: Brett Lee cantering in and flinging down the cherry at over 90 mph, Trescothick solid at the other end. Choosing to bat first, England ran up 179 for eight in their 20 overs in 78 minutes. If this frantic, miniaturised format has anything to recommend it, it is that if you turn to speak to your neighbour you'll almost certainly miss a six, a four or a wicket. The merciful feature is that it's all over so quickly.

Leicestershire's Darren Maddy has almost mastered this new quick-as-a-flash format, and his analysis says it all: "It's almost like being a kid again – not worrying about technique or keeping wickets in hand and just going out there and looking for boundaries."

As usual some of the bowling figures made grotesque reading: Lee 0 for 31 off three overs, Gillespie 1 for 49 off four, though McGrath got away with 3 for 31 off his four, and the mean Symonds 2 for 14 (including Michael Vaughan, caught first ball) off three. Assisted by a number of uncharacteristic Australian misfields, Marcus Trescothick anchored England with 41 (37 balls), Pietersen blasted 34 (18), and Paul Collingwood, the unobtrusive but sometimes brilliant three-way rubicund all-rounder, ensured a decent score with 46 (26) at No.6.

Australia had 23 on the board when Gough began the carnage. Gilchrist and Hayden were caught by Pietersen off consecutive balls. Gloucestershire's 29-year-old Jon Lewis, on international debut (but not entitled to a cap), found the edge of Clarke's bat and then had Symonds chipping to Pietersen at square leg. Gough got

Mike Hussey via a slip catch, and Lewis took two more big wickets, Ponting caught at cover, then Martyn. It was now 31 for seven, and in 20 balls seven world-class batsmen had been dismissed while a sickly eight runs were made. The Geordies, Steve Harmison and Collingwood, administered the final rites, and Australia's total of 79 (defeat by 100 runs) sent people home quite stunned. For their money they had seen no more than 34.3 overs in total, yet every one of them would say in years to come, "I was there!" Some of the more whimsical had yodelled to the Australians: "Are you Bangladesh in disguise?"

ROSE BOWL, SOUTHAMPTON, June 13, 2005

ENGLAND 179 for 8 (20 overs) (M.E.Trescothick 41, K.P.Pietersen 34, P.D.Collingwood 46; G.D.McGrath 3 for 31, A.Symonds 2 for 14); AUSTRALIA 79 (14.3 overs) (J.N.Gillespie 24; D.Gough 3 for 16, J.Lewis 4 for 24, P.D.Collingwood 2 for 8). *ENGLAND WON BY 100 RUNS.*

Of course, should England go on to win the two 50-overs tournaments, this 20-overs bash would be relegated almost to meaninglessness. And if they should then win the Test series – indeed, even if they do not – well, all the limited-overs success will be put in its rightful place: that's to say, on history's bottom shelf.

❋ ❋ ❋

Two days after the Twenty20 upset, there was another. Against a Somerset side shored up by the formidable left-hand presence of South Africa captain Graeme Smith and Sri Lanka's Jayasuriya, Ponting's men lost again. The Australians' 342 for five was a huge total from 50 overs, even allowing for Taunton's batsman-friendly ambience. Hayden, one of his blows having reached the River Tone, retired for 76, Ponting for 80 (it was, after all, a practice match), and Clarke and Hussey passed 50. Somerset's bowling figures were gruesome.

Then, however, Smith and Jayasuriya launched the chase with an explosive 197 for the first wicket, both making centuries, and with the ground fielding again found wanting, the middle order of local lads hung on to clinch the match. There were actually three overs and a ball, and four wickets, to spare. As might be expected, McGrath was not unduly beaten up, but Michael Kasprowicz's figures were ugly (0 for 89 off eight) and Shane Watson's were little better (1 for 72 off 8.5).

TAUNTON, June 15, 2005
AUSTRALIANS 342 for 5 (50 overs) (M.L.Hayden 76, R.T.Ponting 80, D.R.Martyn 44, M.J.Clarke 63*, M.E.K.Hussey 51); SOMERSET 345 for 6 (46.5 overs) (G.C.Smith 108, S.T.Jayasuriya 101, J.C.Hildreth 38*). *SOMERSET WON BY 4 WICKETS.*

The only previous occasion on which Somerset had beaten the Australians was in a first-class match at Bath in 1977, when young Ian Botham had a rewarding match under Brian Close's captaincy. Skipper Greg Chappell stroked a century for the tourists, and in their second innings David Hookes hit an 81-ball hundred. Botham, then 21 years old, took five wickets in the match and smashed 59 before ushering his county to a seven-wicket victory with 39 not out. Ten weeks later he made his Test debut and kicked off his ultimate collection of 383 wickets with that of Chappell. England regained the Ashes at Headingley in the fourth Test of 1977. Now, in 2005, Botham is dispensing wisdom on Sky Sports. Ponting, like Chappell, has worn a Somerset cap. More links. More omens?

Demonstrations of premature English triumphalism were not attractive. "Is this the worst Australian touring side ever?" asked one newspaper, presumably in all seriousness, while there were some ripe cartoons. In time, the ingenious work of headline writers produced such taunts as "Kangaruins" and "Scare Dinkum". Not that similar excesses are unknown from Australian sources. I suppose one has to cling to that wonderful old credo uttered by the

Great Britain Rugby League player of the 1960s, Derek Turner: "Tha's to give it an' tek it and not t'groomble."

Ricky Ponting was finding it more difficult now to shrug away this chain of setbacks. "I'm pretty embarrassed. We'll sit down and talk about why we weren't able to defend a total of 342. We weren't smart enough or good enough. We'll have our work cut out against Bangladesh on Saturday the way we're playing." How prophetic.

❉ ❉ ❉

We were hearing that the Australians were being torn apart in some of their newspapers back home and that Ponting had ripped into his players after this defeat, probably as a boxing trainer/coach/manager does between rounds when his man seems to be cruising and losing ground. I've noted over many years that the English and the Australians deal with defeat very differently. The English wring hands, dissect, agonise, cogitate, apportion blame and enter into countless post-mortems, the tabloids mocking while the quality papers embark on rounds of navel-examination and the tiresome old "what's wrong with English cricket?" debates. Australians, faced with failure on the field, usually simply pretend it didn't happen. Forget it.

As for myself, I have now started to feel a touch of shame at getting so intensely excited about the 2005 Anglo-Australian battle. This agitation really goes against my natural code, for I've known full well for many years now that all frenzy evaporates, everything becomes history, calm history.

After Taunton, with disarming frankness, the Australia captain spoke of how unimaginatively his bowlers had operated. "The lengths didn't change," lamented Ponting, "the lines didn't change, the ball was in the perfect hitting zone every time." His mood cannot have improved when he read that victorious Somerset lost their next match, a 45-overs league game. Nor was the loss to a strong county side. The county's adversaries were Scotland.

What made the Australians' defeat by Somerset seem all the worse was the event the next day across at The Oval. Held up only by Aftab Ahmed and Mohammad Rafique, England had rolled Bangladesh over for 190 in the first of the NatWest triangular series and knocked the runs off within 25 overs without losing a wicket. Trescothick, in his 100th one-day international, added 100 not out to his 194 and 151 in the two recent Test matches, once deliberately uppercutting a short ball outside off stump down to *long leg*. His touch would have amazed the Australian bowlers, such as McGrath, who had been so accustomed to the Somerset left-hander standing leaden-footed and poking or slashing at anything outside off stump.

He was reunited with his successful Test match partner of the past 12 months, Andrew Strauss, who threw off his stumbling start to the season with 82 not out. Jon Lewis had a successful full ODI debut, Geraint Jones held four catches, and Steve Harmison looked genuinely dangerous. Wearing a plastic wristband in support of the anti-bullying campaign, he blasted out the middle order with pace and steep bounce. It was reassuring for England fans, too, to see Flintoff bowling close to his best after the heel surgery early in the year. The poor early-season form of almost all of England's top names could now probably be put down to subconscious relaxation after a tough winter tour in South Africa.

THE OVAL, June 16, 2005
BANGLADESH 190 (45.2 overs) (Aftab Ahmed 51, Mohammad Rafique 30; J.Lewis 3 for 32, S.J.Harmison 4 for 39); ENGLAND 192 for 0 (24.5 overs) (M.E.Trescothick 100*, A.J.Strauss 82*). Match award: M.E.Trescothick. *ENGLAND WON BY 10 WICKETS.* E 6pts, B 0.

While excitement was rising as the first 50-overs clash between England and Australia loomed at the weekend, Australia first took on Bangladesh at Sophia Gardens, Cardiff. It was to be an historic match. The shock result was dubbed by some as the greatest upset in Australia's cricket history, and by Ponting as the greatest in the history of the *game*.

In 74 completed one-day internationals against Test countries (excluding Zimbabwe: they don't count any more, having been partially delisted) Bangladesh had lost 72, and not one individual century had graced their records. Australia were therefore almost unbackable.

The ball moved around when the World Cup champions batted, for the pitch had sweated under covering for the best part of two days. Gilchrist was leg-before to Mortaza for a duck (the ball would have gone over the bails) and Ponting went lbw to Tapash for 1. Martyn then helped Hayden take the score to 57 before young left-armer Najmul Hossain ended Hayden's latest quest for a long and fluent innings. Again Martyn was left to shore up the innings, which he did with a string of ones and twos. Michael Clarke eventually settled, and advanced to a pleasant half-century. With both these gone, it fell to left-handers Hussey and Simon Katich to build some sort of fortress, and at 249 for five, Australia, after certain discomforts, ought to have been safe.

There followed an astonishing performance by Mohammad Ashraful, a 20-year-old from Dhaka with two Test centuries to his name already (one on debut, at Colombo, when he was only 16). It is hardly necessary to point to his diminutive size since all of Bangladesh's batsmen seem to be around Gavaskar's or Tendulkar's height, mostly without the chunkiness. I was reminded of what a journalist wrote during the deciding Test match at Melbourne in 1936–37 while Ross Gregory and Jack Badcock, both small men, were piling on the runs against England: "They were the nearest things to two pixies seen in a cricket field".

Ashraful was daring, and outwardly unaffected by the overpowering reputation of his adversaries. The mid-innings bowling admittedly was not all that challenging, but when McGrath returned, Ashraful hit him as if he were a part-time bowler. With his captain, Habibul Bashar, he created 130 runs for the fourth wicket. And when Habibul was run out the 19-year-old Aftab stayed with him to add a further 25, with Ashraful seemingly overwhelmed by delirium with the arrival of his precious century. Then he got out, and was inconsolable. Of course, it had all been an impossible dream.

But it wasn't. Aftab and Rafique made sure of seeing Bangladesh to their target, with four balls from Gillespie to spare, and people were lost for coherent words. Not for long, however, as this was declared the shock result to top all recent shock results. And it pays to bear in mind that at least one of those previous shock results was investigated by the ICC's Anti-Corruption Unit.

SOPHIA GARDENS, CARDIFF, June 18, 2005

AUSTRALIA 249 for 5 (50 overs) (M.L.Hayden 37, D.R.Martyn 77, M.J.Clarke 54, M.E.K.Hussey 31*, S.M.Katich 36*; Tapash Baisya 3 for 69); BANGLADESH 250 for 5 (49.2 overs) (Mohammad Ashraful 100, Habibul Bashar 47). Match award: Ashraful. *BANGLADESH WON BY 5 WICKETS.* B 5pts, A 1.

After this upset in Cardiff, Ricky Ponting admitted that he was "close to pressing the panic button". Frowning, he said: "If you lose to Bangladesh, you should be a little bit worried." Maybe Australia's cunning plan was to sink so low that they some day soon would rise again with all the force of a volcano, pouring revenge upon the critics and other doubters.

An absentee from this match was Andrew Symonds. Aussie coach John Buchanan had stated the all-rounder had a "niggle" somewhere about his person; then he had flu; but the full truth was that the Queenslander had stayed out beyond official curfew – perhaps helping Shane Watson celebrate his 24th birthday, perhaps not – and the management had to bring some punishment to bear. For all we know, Symonds's two-match suspension and fine was the key factor in this colossal upset by Bangladesh.

That morning I had flippantly closed an email to a friend in India with the excuse: "Must dash now. Got to watch Bangladesh thrash Australia." That fellow, of course, could not have detected the jocular tone. He now thinks I have extra-sensory perception – that would be rather useful – and he swung his opinion on the Ashes series in an instant, deciding that England were now certainties to win.

And the dancing in the dusty streets and paddocks of Bangladesh, with its population of 140 million, continued.

It was a fateful weekend. Next day, a very hot Sunday, Australia came out determined to show who they were and to banish all memory of these nonsenses of the past six days. Now, surely, was the time to find their stride, hit their straps, get in the groove. The opposition was England, the venue Bristol, and the team bus entered the ground through the wrong gate, exposing the Australian players, Symonds in particular, to much ribaldry as they made their way to the pavilion. The locals seemed to have forgotten how brilliantly the Birmingham-born Australian had batted for the county 10 years ago.

For some time now English cricket followers' dreams had been that the sharpest weapon available, Steve Harmison, the world's premier bowler in the official rankings not so long ago, would be unsheathed at Australia's throat. At Bristol it happened. Ponting won the toss and chose to bat. Gough and Lewis were given the new ball, but when Harmison loped up and banged it down from the eighth over, the game tilted. Gilchrist thin-edged him, Ponting was too late on the next ball, which thudded into his pads, and two balls later Martyn brashly flicked high into third man's hands. In his next over Harmison gave Hayden the chance to cut/slash, a perceived weakness in his game, and the Queenslander would have had four for the shot had not Collingwood taken off to hold a one-handed catch seemingly twice his height above ground level: 63 for four. Stupendous effort; interesting scoreline.

Mike Hussey made one of his treble-centuries for Northamptonshire on this Bristol ground, and he now worked hard for an 84 (83 balls) that gave Australia something more solid to defend. Michael Clarke contributed 45 (71) to a crucial stand of 101 mainly against soft bowling (Simon Jones and Ashley Giles were both sidelined because of injuries) and Shane Watson did his bit with 25. Harmison returned and bowled Hussey, and although Flintoff was fast and tight, Australia managed to haul themselves up to 252 off their ration of 50 overs. Five sixes were hit, but the addition of Bert Hopkins's three big hits in 1905 would have come in mighty useful on this congenial batting strip.

When England were six down for 160 in the 38th over, not only did Australia seem to have it won, but the inflatable kangaroo draped in England's cross of St George, noticed among the 15,000 spectators, seemed not only impertinent but slightly ridiculous. Openers Trescothick and Strauss were both bowled by McGrath, and although, to the great relief of his camp, Vaughan passed 50, the ship seemed to be sinking, especially when the polished No.8, Vikram Solanki, was thrown out by Gilchrist as he hesitated about a run. That made it 214 for seven: 39 needed off 7.2 overs, and the No.9 at the crease, the steady Jon Lewis.

The key was the man at the other end. Kevin Pietersen had by now crashed his way to 60, having survived an extremely close run-out appeal. Now he was intent on finishing the match with little ceremony. If his hits didn't make it into the crowd (four did) then they screamed over the rope (eight fours). In a mere 65 balls he did a Gilchrist. Pietersen's 91 not out was an heroic, match-turning knock, one to rouse Jessop's ghost, an awesome effort that saw him engaging with Watson (teasing him over the recent break-up with fiancee Kym Johnson: my, how word travels) and punching the ball with his bat and the air with his fist repeatedly as he plundered 61 from his last 26 balls. Pietersen's one-day average for England now stood at 162. And as ever in these circumstances, credit deserves to be recorded for his supporter, Lewis, who finished 7 not out.

BRISTOL, June 19, 2005

AUSTRALIA 252 for 9 (50 overs) (M.L.Hayden 31, M.J.Clarke 45, M.E.K.Hussey 84; S.J.Harmison 5 for 33). ENGLAND 253 for 7 (47.3 overs) (M.P.Vaughan 57, K.P.Pietersen 91*, G.B.Hogg 3 for 42). Match award: K.P.Pietersen. *ENGLAND WON BY 3 WICKETS.* E 5pts, A 1.

There were actually 2½ overs, and three wickets, to spare after all. Captain Vaughan told everyone that Pietersen's effort was one of "genius". Ponting's men looked thoroughly fed up. They had, after all, now lost *four* one-day matches in a week. This was not through carelessness alone, nor could it be attributed to rustiness, or even bad luck. Gillespie's face was a picture of grief, so badly had his bowling been treated, while the look on Ponting's face was one that I had never seen before. The *Sun*, reliable as ever in echoing the mood of the masses, depicted the Australians holding floral handbags and being comforted by Dame Edna Everage.

Invincible, that sacred word latterly coined in respect of Bradman's 1948 Australians, came into the reckoning. "Invincible" was something Ponting's team were not. Bill Brown's "unbeaten" prediction had now gone down the spout four times over in one extraordinary week. The odds on the Ashes were shortening, and made people like me regret that they had not plunged at the betting shop months ago. During a call from Ashley Mallett, the Australian off-spinner of the 1970s and 1980s, he not only asserted that Gareth Batty was England's best spinner and Durham's Phil Mustard was their best wicketkeeper, but he was tipping England to win the Test series 3-1. Nobody so far in my hearing had been quite that bold.

❅ ❅ ❅

Something from beyond the boundary cast a further pall over the Australian camp. Shane Warne's latest misdemeanour was splashed all over a Sunday tabloid paper. A 25-year-old woman told of an involvement with the cricketer, whose marriage as a consequence was once more in jeopardy. Soon his wife Simone and three children, Brooke, Jackson and Summer, were on their way back to Melbourne after an announcement that the couple were separating.

A short time later Warne, in his newspaper column, assured everybody that he would not be deflected from his cricket aims and responsibilities. Cricket Australia had instructed his county club to rest him from the domestic Twenty20 competition because of a sore spinning finger, so he spent time in Spain, collecting his thoughts. The remarkable upshot was that this player, who recently had at long last notched a first-class century (previous best 99 in a Test against New Zealand at the WACA in 2001–02) now added another, again for Hampshire, the county he captained, this time at Southgate, against Middlesex. There have been instances of cricketers performing well at a time of personal upheaval, even when undone by grief. It added a further dramatic undercurrent to the 2005 Ashes series.

England dutifully thrashed Bangladesh in the next NatWest Series match at Trent Bridge, roaring almost to 400 after a reassuring 152 by Strauss, 85 by Trescothick and 112 not out by Collingwood, whose seam mixture then returned him 6 for 31, the best-ever figures by an England bowler – and all-round performance – in ODIs. Five times Paul Collingwood cleared the ring, to go with 10 fours. A 94 by Ashraful stole some of his thunder. Only the most mean-minded would have begrudged the little chap a century to go with the one he had just taken off Australian bowling. He was endowed with good fortune as well as much talent, for his first ball was jabbed into the ground and bounced onto the bails, which refused to move. It would have given Tremlett a hat-trick.

TRENT BRIDGE, June 21, 2005
ENGLAND 391 for 4 (50 overs) (M.E.Trescothick 85, A.J.Strauss 152, P.D.Collingwood 112*; Najmul Hossain 3 for 83); BANGLADESH 223 (45.2 overs) (Javed Omar Belim 59, Mohammad Ashraful 94; C.T.Tremlett 4 for 32, P.D.Collingwood 6 for 31). Match award: P.D.Collingwood. *ENGLAND WON BY 168 RUNS*. E 6pts, B 0.

Two days later, at Durham's Riverside ground, Australia came back into the picture with a 57-run win over England. Symonds was back, as was Lee after a slight injury. Naively put in by Trescothick, deputising for Vaughan (groin strain) as captain, the visitors moved steadily to 266 for five off their 50 overs, then blew the top off the

England innings. Martyn coolly steered Australia with another unbeaten contribution, this time 68, and Symonds clouted 73. Ashley Giles, fit again after a hip injury, wheeled away accurately without causing alarm, but that was to come in rapid episodes as Strauss played on to Lee, and a scoreless Trescothick got a thin edge to McGrath, who then persuaded Collingwood to play on.

This time there was no revival by England after being three down for 6. Muscular forties came from Flintoff and No.10 Gough, but the hopes naturally attaching to Pietersen were this time soon dashed: he smacked Symonds to Hussey at deep midwicket when 19. The victory cheered Australia up and sobered up those who had so jubilantly celebrated earlier setbacks by Ponting's bedraggled army. There was just the quiet assertion from Giles, interviewed after the match, that "we know we can beat them".

RIVERSIDE, CHESTER-LE-STREET, June 23, 2005
AUSTRALIA 266 for 5 (50 overs) (M.L.Hayden 39, D.R.Martyn 68*, A.Symonds 73); ENGLAND 209 for 9 (50 overs) (V.S.Solanki 34, A.Flintoff 44, D.Gough 46*). Match award: A.Symonds. *AUSTRALIA WON BY 57 RUNS*. A 6pts, E 0.

Australia flexed their muscles every bit as efficiently that Saturday. At Old Trafford they simply flicked Bangladesh aside. Out went the minnows for 139 in just over 35 overs, and Gilchrist and Hayden coasted home by 10 wickets in a mere 19 overs. Yet the spectators could not but help admiring, above all, little Ashraful once again. He was really the star of the day as he skipped around and whacked 58, having survived some vicious deliveries from Lee. The fast man again seemed to get carried away, one over costing 20, with Ashraful taking him for two brave if only partially controlled sixes. It took the slow men, Symonds and Hogg, to confound Bangladesh, whose last eight wickets fell for 26 runs.

And the shadow-boxing continued with a provocative heading to Michael Atherton's newspaper column: Mr Nice Guy [Ricky Ponting] Leading Aussies Into Decline.

OLD TRAFFORD, MANCHESTER, June 25, 2005
BANGLADESH 139 (35.2 overs) (Shahriar Nafees 47, Mohammad Ashraful 58, G.B.Hogg 3 for 29, A.Symonds 5 for 18); AUSTRALIA 140 for 0 (19 overs) (A.C.Gilchrist 66*, M.L.Hayden 66*). Match award: A.Symonds. *AUSTRALIA WON BY 10 WICKETS*. A 6pts, B 0.

Andrew Symonds, for the second time in two matches since his suspension, was Man of the Match. It is his misfortune to have been classified as strictly a one-day cricketer. Ten years ago, when he was playing for Gloucestershire, he was voted by the Cricket Writers Club as England's Young Cricketer of the Year. At the CWC dinner at the end of the 1995 season he asked me, not without anxiety, if he was expected to make a speech. There was no need, but I teased him all the same, saying it would be good practice for when he became captain of Australia one day. The tease was a double one, for selector David Graveney, standing alongside us, could only splutter, "Aw, steady on!" Soon, Symonds had to decide this serious twin-nationality question once and for all, and after days of agonising and phone calls to father Ken back in Queensland he relinquished the offer of a place in the England A team and threw in his lot with Australia, saying repeatedly and dogmatically thereafter that he was "dinkum". It must be wonderful to have a clear mind on such a complex matter.

Michael Vaughan continued to rest a slight groin strain and Trescothick again led England in the next match, against Bangladesh at Headingley. Bangladesh upheld their pride and were no pushover, though the contest always had an inevitability about it. Javed Omar batted stubbornly for a 150-ball 81, and the experienced Khaled Masud also appreciated the absence of Harmison (rested) by carving an unbeaten 42. England seemed not completely switched on at times, from the embarrassing four consecutive leg-side wides with which Simon Jones began his effort to the four catches grounded. Flintoff, though, was on song, and should have had a hat-trick had not the normally reliable Aleem Dar turned down an apparently spot-on leg-before shout against Habibul.

Tremlett bowled well as a junior member of England's huge squad of fast bowlers, and Giles was tight, and when the chase began, Trescothick was rampant. Strauss, though, continued with his smart run-gathering against this particular opposition (as opposed to the other: Ponting's lot), and, having just hit a six, he was bowled for 98 having a hoick when the scores were level. This victory would keep England at the top of the final table, with Australia in no peril of not qualifying for the final.

HEADINGLEY, LEEDS, June 26, 2005
BANGLADESH 208 for 7 (50 overs) (Javed Omar Belim 81, Tushar Imran 32, Khaled Masud 42*; A.Flintoff 4 for 29); ENGLAND 209 for 5 (38.5 overs) (M.E.Trescothick 43, A.J.Strauss 98; Manjural Rana 3 for 57). Match award: A.J.Strauss. *ENGLAND WON BY 5 WICKETS*. E 6pts, B 0.

The tempo heated at Edgbaston on June 28, when the next NatWest match began in bad odour after an unpleasant accusation in a newspaper against Matt Hayden. It was apparently unsubstantiated, and it stirred the accused. He was said to have sworn at a youngster in the guard of honour past which the players trotted onto the field at the start of an innings. He vigorously denied this. One thing that had been noticeable in previous matches was that some of the Australian players sidestepped away from the line of youngsters in order not to run beneath the England flags. One wonders whether the cricketers had cotton-wool in their ears as well, so as to deaden the sound of *Jerusalem* as it boomed across the ground.

In the sixth over Hayden played a ball back to bowler Simon Jones, who, off-balance, threw clumsily at the wicket in a run-out attempt as the batsman followed through. The ball bounced and hit Hayden in the chest. Instead of shrugging it off and accepting the bowler's instant apology, the burly batsman glared, uttered a few hot words, and advanced towards Jones. Collingwood was the first outsider to join the fray, and as umpires and captain Ponting converged on the scene, there was a sizzling tension in the air. Edgbaston is probably the most noisy and patriotic of England's cricket grounds, and most of the 15,000 had their say before play was mercifully allowed to proceed.

The last man Hayden would have wanted to pick up his wicket now was Jones, but he did, lbw. Gilchrist, Ponting and Martyn were also gone by the 28th over, with 123 on the board, Martyn to a turf-level diving catch by Pietersen at third man which was not seen as a clean catch until television playbacks more or less confirmed it. The only Birmingham-born player in the match, Andrew Symonds, top-scored with 74 (75 balls) before live-wire Collingwood ran him out. Mike Hussey again impressed with 45 (42), and Australia climbed to 261 for nine in their 50 overs. Was Darren Gough now a spent force? Figures of 3 for 70 off nine overs left the question open.

England thus had a tall task that evening, before rain fell, sending the mathematicians to consult the Duckworth-Lewis scale to ascertain the revised target. When play was resumed, Strauss clocked a few fours off McGrath (booed as a key Mr Punch "hate figure" was surely overstating it) before being caught, and then a storm put paid to proceedings. The dress rehearsal for the final had been inconclusive.

EDGBASTON, June 28, 2005
AUSTRALIA 261 for 9 (50 overs) (R.T.Ponting 34, D.R.Martyn 36, A.Symonds 74, M.E.K.Hussey 45; D.Gough 3 for 70); ENGLAND 37 for 1 (6 overs). *NO RESULT*. A 3pts, E 3.

On June 30, Australia had their last pre-final match to play: against Bangladesh at Canterbury, before a crowd which hearteningly included hundreds of schoolchildren. The famous ancient lime tree which had crashed down during the winter had now been replaced with a sturdy sapling, leaving us to ponder on what cricket will look like 100–150 years from now. Perhaps better not.

Again Bangladesh showed courage. Nineteen-year-old Shahriar Nafees ground out 75 after the first three wickets had fallen for 19, and Khaled Mashud (an unbeaten 71) helped him make 94 for the sixth wicket. Australia were set 251 to win. The tension point was 83 for three. Gilchrist's dismissal was the curiosity of the day, perhaps of the season. He drove hard at Tapash Baisya, the ball floated into slip's hands, and away the batsman trudged to the pavilion. But the ball was shown to have landed in the rough and cut away without touching the bat. Mr Sporty's reputation was enhanced.

It was Michael Clarke's turn now to display his talents. After Ponting departed for 66, the glamorous Sydneysider stroked a reassuring 80 not out and, with the ever-reliable Symonds, saw Australia home. The eager scrutiny persisted. Which of the Australians looked past it, who now were the real threats, which of them seemed still dangerous yet somehow vulnerable?

CANTERBURY, June 30, 2005

BANGLADESH 250 for 8 (50 overs) (Shahriar Nafees 75, Habibul Bashar 30, Khaled Mashud 71*; S.R.Watson 3 for 43); AUSTRALIA 254 for 4 (48.1 overs) (A.C.Gilchrist 45, R.T.Ponting 66, M.J.Clarke 80*, A.Symonds 42*). Match award: Shahriar Nafees. *AUSTRALIA WON BY 6 WICKETS*. A 5pts, B 0.

The final of the NatWest series, an all-day match played at immaculate Lord's, produced an Anglo-Australian's dream result. It was tied. Nothing looked less likely when England were five down for 33 in reply to Australia's humble 196, but a couple of fellows were about to become heroes.

Put in to bat, Australia was saved again by Mike Hussey. In at No.7, the 30-year-old left-hander batted sensibly to gather 62 priceless runs after an explosive start (Gilchrist and Hayden 50 in 6.5 overs) had been countered by some smart bowling by England's pace quartet of Gough, Jones, Flintoff and Harmison which left Australia lurching on 93 for five. (Harmison finished with 15 wickets in the series, clear of the field.)

England's early collapse was even more stark and sickly than Australia's. Marksman McGrath picked three off early and Lee, swinging the ball at top speed, took two wickets. The toll looked good on Australia's strategy board back at headquarters: Trescothick 6, Strauss 2, Vaughan 0, Pietersen 6, Flintoff 8. But Paul Collingwood and Geraint Jones then resisted through the next 34 overs, frustrating all that Australia could hurl at them. Having for the second time this week held five catches behind the stumps (one a flying take off a Ponting leg glance), Jones now cleared the rope three times in a stirring hand of 71 that did much to silence the critics who constantly complained that his wicketkeeping was not really up to scratch. Collingwood was alert but more considered in his 53, and their partnership of 116 brought England back from the slippery edge of oblivion.

With both gone, and Simon Jones bowled by Hussey for a single, the match swung back to Australia. Twenty-nine balls remained, 35 runs needed (nobody, surely, was thinking in terms of 34 to tie), and only the lumbering yeoman Giles and burly, florid Gough to get them, with Harmison to come.

Nineteen were needed off two overs. Then 10 off one – not easy against McGrath, who, like Curtly Ambrose, is a master of the dot ball. He was also master of the cool gather and lob at the stumps, which ran out Gough. Nine down now, three to win, only one ball remaining. It was unlikely to be a no-ball or a wide.

McGrath cantered in, whipped one down just outside off stump, and Giles jabbed at it. There was an appeal, a screaming, desperate appeal. Umpire Bowden, in contrast to the bowler, reckoned Giles had made contact. The ball sped towards third man and two fieldsmen converged on it as the batsmen ran as if a bomb had exploded in the vicinity. Turning automatically for a second run that would save them from defeat, they were relieved and probably amazed to see Brett Lee fumble. Had he picked up cleanly and thrown, Australia must have won by one run.

LORD'S, July 2, 2005
AUSTRALIA 196 (48.5 overs) (M.E.K.Hussey 62*; A.Flintoff 3 for 23, S.J.Harmison 3 for 27); ENGLAND 196 for 9 (50 overs)

(P.D.Collingwood 53, G.O.Jones 71; G.D.McGrath 3 for 27). Match award: G.O.Jones. *MATCH TIED.*

So the captains, shortly afterwards, were photographed with one hand apiece on the trophy, and Andrew Symonds clutched the Man of the Series prize. Much had been learned during these preliminary sparrings, and conjecture went on regenerating itself. One certainty was that this was the perfect conclusion for anyone who had a foot in each camp – as well as for the rare free-minded sporting type unblinded by excessive patriotism. The memory of Australia's 14 successive one-day defeats of England before that Champions Trophy semi-final at Edgbaston in 2004 now seemed to be safely buried in English cricket's refuse bin for nightmares. That just left the Ashes to be sorted out.

❊ ❊ ❊

The ideal would have been for the campaign now to move into top gear with the start of the Test series. Instead, we had to watch three more 50-overs matches which would rake in further gate money, sponsorship revenue and television-rights income. The series just finished had been near to perfect, with thrills and highlights galore. That should have been the end of it. Who could recall Rod Marsh's chilling theory some years ago that the time could well come when Tests slide into obsolescence, and countries would face each other only in series consisting of 15 one-day matches?

Still, the four clear days between the two limited-overs series gave everybody some opportunity to reflect, analyse, predict. England coach Duncan Fletcher told a Press gathering that Flintoff and Harmison had rattled the Australian batsmen: "They do not like facing them and it is pleasing to see." He noted, too, that Ponting in the field often seemed to be making decisions by committee, clearly a suspected weakness.

The anticipated response soon came from John Buchanan, Australia's coach: "It would be interesting for Duncan to reflect on how Trescothick, Strauss and Vaughan got out through the series." Later, after the match which followed, he itemised the play-and-miss fortunes of England's two openers. Sixteen times had they been beaten, only to survive. Quite. And there had been a few instances of batsmen playing into their stumps as well.

The first of the three one-dayers was set down for Headingley on Thursday, July 7, a day which dawned happily and expectantly only to be plunged into grief, anger and terrible distraction. It was the day of the terrorist bombing in London's bus and Underground rail system in which over 50 innocent lives – from several nations – were terminated.

Even here, in this cavern of horror, there was to be a coincidence. It soon emerged that one of the perpetrators identified by the police and forensic people had been a student at Leeds Metropolitan University, and had played cricket in the Headingley area, close to where England and Australia were playing this match on the very day of the outrage in London. Three of the suicide bombers had lived close to Leeds.

There was an almost identical sense of shock and agitation on that November day in 1963 when news of President Kennedy's assassination swept around the world. That morning I held to my plan to watch New South Wales play the South Africans at the Sydney Cricket Ground. During an eerie two-minute memorial silence the only sound that could be heard was the pigeons fluttering among the roof struts over the stand. There followed an anaesthetic century for the tourists by Peter van der Merwe.

The hundred scored by Marcus Trescothick at Headingley on July 7 was the opposite of anaesthetic. Bar the Australians, perhaps, everybody who watched was supremely grateful for the distraction from the horrors of London that day, though all the news channels had on-going coverage of developments. Through the day the cricketers knew what was going on.

Yet again the game of cricket served one of its key purposes as an ever-available shelter and source of solace, there to help transport a man or a woman from sadness and the brutal daily realities into that other world, a world where cricketers play this beautiful game in a spirit of joy and sportsmanship, properly grateful for the talent granted and the opportunity given to them. Do all players acknowledge this truth?

These three one-day matches gave both sides further opportunities for tactical observation and points-scoring. Who was rising to the challenge? Whose weaknesses were being exposed? Who was fully fit and mentally calm? Where were the chinks in players' armour? Which bowler was especially targeting which batsman? And how the devil do the new rules regarding substitution work?

The start was conventional. With the ball deviating sharply through the air and off the turf, Gilchrist (42, with a couple of sixes and five fours) and Hayden had 62 on the board when Gilchrist was caught behind off Harmison in the 16th over. A subdued Hayden (17) skyed Flintoff, Ponting (14) lobbed a catch to Pietersen to give Collingwood the first of four wickets, and with Martyn (43) standing firm yet again, Symonds, Clarke and Watson all went for next to nothing. Once more a batsman who was not part of Australia's Test squad recorded the highest score. Hussey intelligently buttressed the innings, his unbeaten 46 coming from 52 balls, with Lee's 15 not out helping the cause. Australia hauled themselves up to 219, something to bowl at after all.

This time, though, England jumped boldly out of the traps and got away with it. Trescothick and Strauss made 101 for the first wicket before the Middlesex man was caught by Gilchrist after trying a reverse-sweep against Brad Hogg. Trescothick went on to 104 not out, constructing another century stand with his skipper and finding the immense relief that came from a maiden century against Australia after 36 innings. Vaughan, having been in fairly desperate need of runs himself, finished 59 not out. For the Australians the major worry remained the bowling of Gillespie. The old bite simply wasn't there. As for that crucial factor, luck (as well as bad fielding and catching, which are too often mistakenly classified under "luck"), England enjoyed plenty of it. Gilchrist dropped

Strauss on 1 and almost immediately afterwards Trescothick was "caught" at deep third man off a Lee no-ball.

If Australia had any source of comfort for such a decisive loss, their heaviest for two years, it came from the fact that this toss was unduly influential on the result. Vaughan won it and Australia had to cope with conditions favourable to bowlers, the ball doing dangerous things late in flight and off the track. By the time England batted, the pitch had calmed and, in literal terms at least, the skies were blue again.

HEADINGLEY, LEEDS, July 7, 2005

AUSTRALIA 219 for 7 (50 overs) (A.C.Gilchrist 42, D.R.Martyn 43, M.E.K.Hussey 46*; P.D.Collingwood 4 for 34); ENGLAND 221 for 1 (46 overs) (M.E.Trescothick 104*, A.J.Strauss 41, M.P.Vaughan 59*). Match award: M.E.Trescothick. *ENGLAND WON BY 9 WICKETS*.

This was the first international to be played under the new "power-play" and player substitution rules. It is an attempt to relieve the tedium which often afflicts the middle section of a limited-overs innings. The "super-sub" manoeuvre was immediately seen to favour heavily and unduly the captain winning the toss. He can bowl first, then replace a tail-ender bowler with a good batsman. If his super-sub is a genuine all-rounder or a bowler, then he can bat first and if things go well he can utilise the super-sub as an extra bowler later on.

Here at Headingley, Australia made enigmatic use of the substitute rule. Hogg came on as sub for Hayden (and bowled six overs), yet Hayden remained on the field as substitute for the injured Watson. These manoeuvres shifted the game of cricket even further away from the vision of its original designers, who saw 22 yards as the best length of pitch, three stumps as the best target, and eleven players per side as the best formula in that less complicated age.

The new mobility of choice for two five-over sequences of fielding restrictions to follow the mandatory first 10 overs – the "powerplay" – seems actually to have cluttered a game which thrives on simplicity.

So July 7, a date never to be forgotten for reasons beyond an England victory at cricket over Australia, left people dazed and wondering. Security would be tightened even further at Lord's and The Oval for the remaining two matches in the series. Life in London town had to go on, as it has after so many assaults over the years.

There was a minute's silence before the start at Lord's, respecting the memories of the variegated souls who died in the Underground and bus bombings. Both teams' flags were at half-mast above the pavilion, MCC's likewise atop the impressive grandstand, and the players wore black armbands. And now a cricket match was played which conformed more to what had been recognised under the old order.

World Cup holders Australia beat England with some comfort. Put in to bat, England never got into any sort of stride. Strauss (11) became tucked up in a cut and played on to Kasprowicz's first delivery; Vaughan (1) was given out lbw to McGrath, though the ball would have gone over; Trescothick (14) touched one to the keeper off "Kasper"; Pietersen (15) reached to drive Lee and fetched the ball into his stumps: 45 for four and the sound of SOS echoing.

Trescothick had been fortunate that the umpire turned down a shout for a catch behind in the opening over. The ball clicked a pad buckle on the way through, and the batsman could not logically have complained had it been thought to have touched the bat. It was baffling that a batsman at this level should leave himself vulnerable with this protrusion of an outside buckle.

Flintoff and Collingwood made a game of it, adding 103, sighs of relief coming with Flintoff's first fifty off Australian bowling. His 87 included two hits high into the ranks of the spectators, reminding the elderly of Jack Robertson's defiant gesture after a sinister German V1 flying bomb had just missed the square at Lord's in July 1944. Having gathered themselves up from the prone position on the turf, adopted of necessity when the deadly machine's engine cut out, the cricketers continued playing, and Robertson hit the next ball, from Bob Wyatt, clean over the boundary. Who did Mr Hitler think he was kidding?

Geraint Jones stroked 27 but Ponting's diving one-handed catch at extra cover when Giles drove Lee seemed to be a symbol: Australia were in command, and it was going to stay that way.

Chasing 224 to win, the tourists suffered no great anxiety. Hayden was absent, resting a slightly damaged shoulder, so Katich went to the middle with Gilchrist, who slammed 29 of the first 36 runs before Flintoff found the edge. England's frustration grew when Gilchrist was bowled by a rare beauty from Gough, only for the cry of no-ball to nullify the outcome. The rest of the innings was a portrait of Ricky Ponting at his best. The old spark was back. Strokeplay fit to sit alongside any that the great old ground had ever seen creamed from his bat. Facing Gough he wore a cap in preference to a helmet. His 111 was not only his first three-figure innings at Lord's but also his 18th one-day century for Australia, equalling Mark Waugh's record. And, as so often before, Martyn, a kind of reliable man in grey flannel suit, stayed with his skipper until victory was in the bag – by seven wickets with 5.4 overs to spare.

LORD'S, July 10, 2005
ENGLAND 223 for 8 (50 overs) (A.Flintoff 87, P.D.Collingwood 34; B.Lee 5 for 41); AUSTRALIA 224 for 3 (44.2 overs) (S.M.Katich 30, R.T.Ponting 111, D.R.Martyn 39*). Match award: B.Lee. *AUSTRALIA WON BY 7 WICKETS*.

Many eyes moistened that afternoon when the Battle of Britain Memorial Flight – a Lancaster bomber, a Spitfire and a Hurricane – flew low over Buckingham Palace and, very soon afterwards, over Lord's itself, to a rousing, heartfelt reception. Beyond the British onlookers, there must have been many old RAAF Bomber Command pilots, navigators and wireless operators at that moment sitting thoughtfully in armchairs in night-time Australia whose minds were jerked back to a different time, a different London, a different world. Four thousand Australians lost their lives while serving with the RAF in Europe between 1939 and 1945.

❊ ❊ ❊

It was just what Barnum and Bailey would have desired. England and Australia had a win apiece, which made the final one-dayer at The Oval a virtual cup final. Whoever won it would go into the upcoming Test series with a slightly more cheery grin than the opposition. Unless, of course, it was another tie.

The popular David Shepherd took his position as an international umpire for the final time after standing (and hopping) in 172 one-day internationals and 92 Test matches. Prince Philip and John Howard led the file of tributes to the genial rolypoly from Devon.

And it was Australia this time who raised their game and glowed once more as champions. Ponting put England in and controlled them so well on a pitch conducive to movement that all they could manage was 228 for seven. McGrath started with four maidens, though he was to pay out heavily (29 runs) from his final four overs. After the scoreless Trescothick lofted a catch to third man (Lee's 200th ODI wicket) there were two dropped catches. Gillespie put down a sitter off Vaughan at long leg, and Gilchrist made a mess of a steepling top-edged pull from Strauss.

But Vaughan then lost out on a suicidal single when Ponting threw down the stumps from gully. Strauss fought through 16 overs before touching Kasprowicz to the keeper with a nondescript dab. The big wicket of Flintoff came with something similar. Collingwood hit a catch to cover to give Gillespie a drought-breaking wicket, a moment commemorated by a frenzy of hair-mussing. Geraint Jones became the second to fall to a third-man catch.

All this left England 93 for six, at which point Vaughan gambled with his super-sub. Vikram Solanki came into the eleven and paceman Simon Jones left it, never having stepped into the field of action. The move succeeded in the short term without being a totally convincing manoeuvre.

Kevin Pietersen had gone in at No.4, and once more displayed his extraordinary self-belief, rescuing the innings. For a time his shots seemed to find fielders everywhere, but then the thunder and lightning began: even balls outside off finished up crossing the leg boundary. He later told of the remarks aimed at unsettling him. "This is Test match cricket!" the fieldsmen hissed at him. "Can you hack it?" (It *wasn't* Test cricket actually, and as it transpired he could "hack" it – whatever that means.) The catch of the summer (matching that one by Collingwood at least) unfortunately turned out to be no such thing as a leaping Kasprowicz clutched the screaming ball high above him only to be taken by the cannonball force well past the rope. Pietersen's second six was the least classical that The Oval can ever have seen. He trotted out to Gillespie, who dug the ball in short when he saw him coming. The batsman simply swung baseball-fashion and sent the white ball into the bleachers. Soon afterwards he was deceived by Gillespie's slower ball. But he had revived the match with his 84-ball 74, and his stand with Solanki, who finished with a smooth 53 not out, was a new limited-overs record for England's seventh wicket, passing the mark set by Tony Greig and Alan Knott in 1977. More importantly, Pietersen had left the England selectors, David Graveney, Geoff Miller and Duncan Fletcher (no Rod Marsh now) with a compelling case for selection in the first Test match.

Giles, benefiting from a diving miss by Hussey at deep cover, added a sensible 25 not out to help drag England to 228 for seven, but any hopes England had of making early inroads into the Australian line-up were very quickly dispelled. Adam Gilchrist's idea of playing himself in is to twiddle his club – that's to say bat – as he strides out through the gate. He and Hayden slaughtered the white-ball offerings, especially Gough's. In five overs 45 runs were blasted, and there were 10 fours in Gilchrist's 42-ball half-century. His hundred, celebrated with what was conceivably a new world high-jump record in pads, came off 81 balls and was his 11th in one-day internationals. It takes a mighty batsman to overshadow Hayden (31 in their opening stand of 91) as he did.

The question returns: how do you bowl to Gilchrist? The best scheme might be to persuade the administrators, who always seem so keen to change everything, that in these days of batting ascendancy it might be worth experimentally returning to cricket's framework in the time of William Lambert and Lord Frederick Beauclerk, when there was no such thing as a wide. Bowling a metre outside leg stump might actually contain Gilchrist, though there can still be no certainty. Then, as Lambert did to His Lordship, the peeved batsman might suddenly be taken fatally by surprise with a straight one. Then again, there was the great Silver Billy Beldham's ruse on the old Lord's ground in 1806. He stuck some mud and sawdust on the ball and bowled Beauclerk with a delivery that probably did as much as Warne's incredible ball to Gatting 187 years later.

So Australia romped to an overwhelming victory, Ponting making a pretty 43, again tauntingly preferring a cap to a helmet when facing Gough, Martyn again dutifully hanging around till the finish, and Gilchrist for once finding himself still at the wicket at the end, 121 not out, off 101 balls, with two sixes and 17 fours. Importantly, Steve Harmison had to suffer some fearful punishment. We hear much about targeting. The Australians know how fragile Harmison's confidence can be, and a prime aim in this particular encounter was to send him into the first Test with a demon or two inside his cap. "Harmie" knows that Gilchrist in particular seems not to know the difference between a Test and a one-day match. And the left-hand slaughterman will be appearing in the middle order, by which time the score might be . . . oh, it's anybody's guess.

THE OVAL, July 12, 2005

ENGLAND 228 for 7 (50 overs) (A.J.Strauss 36, K.P.Pietersen 74, V.S.Solanki 53*; J.N.Gillespie 3 for 33); AUSTRALIA 229 for 2 (A.C.Gilchrist 121*, M.L.Hayden 31, R.T.Ponting 43). Match award: A.C.Gilchrist. *AUSTRALIA WON BY 8 WICKETS.*

We've been guessing all summer during this nerve-racking lead-up to the Ashes Tests. Which of England's several fast bowlers should have the new ball? Should they pack the first Test team with batsmen in order to play out the match on their hoodoo ground, Lord's? A setback there would make their mission so much more difficult. Are Australia as brittle as so many of these preliminary contests have suggested?

It wasn't long before the biggest question of the Test match summer so far was answered. On July 14, England's twelve was named: Michael Vaughan (captain), Marcus Trescothick, Andrew Strauss, Ian Bell, Kevin Pietersen, Andrew Flintoff, Geraint Jones, Ashley Giles, Matthew Hoggard, Simon Jones, Steve Harmison, Chris Tremlett.

One of the fast bowlers was sure to be omitted on the morning. The big name missing was Graham Thorpe. The Surrey left-hander was approaching his 36th birthday, with only 73 as a season's top score to date, and a few recent errors in the field and fitness doubts hanging in the air. He therefore seemed to have played his last Test against Australia, off whose bowling he scored a memorable 114 not out on debut at Trent Bridge in 1993. It was England's great misfortune over recent years that of the 100 Test matches played by this smart little toiler only 16 (out of a possible 30 since his debut) have been against Australia. In those 16 Tests (four won, nine lost, three drawn) he averaged 45.74 and made three centuries, but his absence through injury and domestic problems from 13 of the most recent 14 Ashes Tests was one of the severe handicaps England have had to bear. It was a difficult choice for England, but Thorpe's omission seemed a positive move. They could have played safe and held the bold young Pietersen or the serene Ian Bell back. A recall for Thorpe now seemed unlikely, but he planned to join New South Wales as player-coach at the end of the year, by which time he would have retired from Test cricket. If any lingering words of Graham Thorpe were to assist England's cause it would be his contention that you should never fear failure.

Kevin Pietersen, aged 25, was thus at last given his chance in international white flannels. His record showed 21 first-class centuries in his 78 matches, an identical number of appearances to that of Bell, aged 23, who had made 13 centuries. Their first-class experience in match terms is greater than the average Australian at a similar age, and their respective temperaments seemed to be on a par with that of the archetypical unflappable Australian. All was about to be revealed.

Meanwhile Michael Vaughan, England's captain, gave a sort of state of the union Press conference. That wide-brimmed hat that he places so centrally on his head when fielding gives him a prim and solemn appearance. This is completely misleading, and yet the set of his facial features, which might easily be those of a bible-clinging preacher, allied to the flat voice, with its unfortunate inclination to hop over the letter t, support that misconception of the man. He is, for that matter, a good bloke.

Under the current system these chaps have an approach to end-of-match interviews and presentations that excludes the unpredictable remark, and would be of assistance to anybody who might have nodded off during the afternoon's play. Probably the result of keen instruction and coaching, the captains' responses tend to be in keeping with the parrot spiel of the master of ceremonies on these groundhog occasions. The delivery is sort of sans punctuation and comes out at well over 100 words to the minute: "It-was-a-good-toss-to-win-and-we-played-well-but-they-came-back-at-us-well-and-it-was-full-marks-to-Freddie/Adam-for-turning-the-innings-round-and-bringing-us-back-into-the-match-with-the-help-of-Geraint/Shane-and-when-we-got-their-openers-early-we-got-on-top-and-managed-to-stay-there-by-fielding-well-and-bowling-well-and-catching-well-and . . ."

No point in expecting profundity. Mike Brearley was sometimes almost too much anyway. Bob Willis usually glowered. David Gower tried to amuse but usually failed. Allan Border was conscientious and you usually left feeling he had given his all at the group interview just as he had out in the middle. Graham Gooch was deadpan and often sent you away slightly depressed. Steve Waugh gave the impression that there was something he wasn't prepared to divulge – maybe keeping it for his next book. And there was Mike Atherton, letting question after question pass over his off stump, reticent and mono-syllabic as captain, in complete contrast to the fluent talker who emerged when he threw away his cricket gear and became a media merchant.

Perhaps the auto-response is the best way after all.

"Vaughany" was certainly good value as he summarised England's position on the eve of the series. The team needed to be calm and level-headed, he said: "We mustn't get too drawn into the emotion of playing an Ashes series, because if you do that, it might get the better of you." As it does some over-keen authors perhaps.

He surely spoke for everyone when he said: "I think that both sets of players are sick and tired of talking about it." Hear, hear! "Every game we have played over the last year people have been asking, 'How will this effect the Ashes?'" He referred to England's second place in the world Test standings and said it had been well earned. As for one-day cricket: "If you'd said a year ago that we'd compete with Australia in that form of the game, I would not have believed you."

Vaughan recognised that Test cricket was very different, and he divulged a portion of England's doctrine by saying that "we must not look too much at the bigger picture [but instead] break the Test down into small parts, as we always do."

It might almost have been F.S. Jackson speaking when he said: "We are actually looking forward to what is a massive challenge. What a great opportunity it is for all of us." He also believed that this was essentially the side which would play in Australia late in 2006: "We could certainly have the same Eleven playing" – a subtle hint, perhaps, that the 2005 Australians are a great team which inevitably is very close to dismantlement because of ageing.

Then an immaculate summing-up from Vaughan: "We've got to play consistent cricket. If you have bad days against Australia they can hurt you really badly, because they play a faster form of the game than most. But 60 wickets will win it for us if we get them fast."

Suddenly, though, 60 wickets seemed an awful lot either to blast or tease out.

❋ ❋ ❋

There was one final loosener for the Australians, a three-day match against Leicestershire. Andrew Symonds had signed for Lancashire and spectacularly made his one-day debut for them – a C&G quarter-final at Old Trafford – completely his own. Clad in garish red now, he smashed 101 (team-mate Flintoff fell for 5) and enforced victory over Sussex by taking two wickets, holding four catches, and completing a run-out.

Another of those released from Australia's touring squad did rather well too. Playing in a custard-coloured shirt for Hampshire, though still unfit to bowl, Shane Watson helped his side to an amazing victory over Surrey (who were still coached by former Australia wicketkeeper Steve Rixon) at The Oval. Chasing 359 in their 50 overs, they won with some ease, with Watson hammering 132 off 115 balls. There was no questioning that not only did Australia still have talent to burn but the English game was probably approaching saturation as far as Australian involvement was concerned.

It even showed in the Leicestershire match, the last before the Tests began. Chris Rogers of Western Australia saved the county on the final day with a magnificent 209 after the Australians had piled up nearly 600 to go 365 ahead on the first innings. Anticipating a short third day, feet up, watching Tiger Woods win the British Open Golf Championship at St Andrews, the tourists instead had to endure a full, hot day in the field. Rogers, a compact left-hander, and Darren Robinson, ex-Essex, posted 247 for the first wicket, the highest-ever opening stand by a county against an Australian side, some achievement when the number of matches over 127 years is counted up.

Stuart MacGill was the touring team's most successful bowler, though he conceded almost a run a ball. Gillespie and Kasprowicz both failed to impress in what was really a contest to establish which of them would win preference for the opening Test match. The resurrected, accurate, speedy Brett Lee had ominously struck with the first ball of the match, trapping Robinson lbw, and later broke John Sadler's collarbone. "Bing" Lee finished with four wickets and made sure beyond all doubt that, after missing Australia's last 17 Tests, his name would be among the first to be scribbled down when the selection panel shaped the Test team. Justin Langer hit the first century of the innings, a reassuring contribution, and Ponting and Martyn filled their boots too, making it all look so easy.

Rogers, 27, who spoiled the party, extends the web of coincidence. His father, John, played for us alongside Adam Gilchrist's dad, Stan, in the Paddington first-grade team in Sydney in 1963, and later for New South Wales. And the omen-detector came up with yet another odd connection during this Leicester match: just when it seemed that Gilchrist (entering at 451 for five) might swiftly propel the touring team to a total of 1000, he was bowled (via the bat) for 26 by a towering 19-year-old named Broad. This Stuart Broad was the baby son Chris Broad left behind in 1986–87 to register three centuries for England on the triumphant Ashes tour of Australia. Broad junior had recently advanced his game with a season in Australia, playing for an outfit called Hoppers Crossing in Melbourne. Cricket in the blood? There has to be something to this theory. The potency of omens? We are about to find out.

LEICESTER, July 15, 16, 17, 2005
LEICESTERSHIRE 217 (C.J.L.Rogers 56, B.Lee 4 for 53) and 363 for 5 (D.D.J.Robinson 81, C.J.L.Rogers 209, S.C.G.MacGill 4 for 122); AUSTRALIANS 582 for 7 dec (J.L.Langer 115, M.L.Hayden 75, R.T.Ponting 119, D.R.Martyn 154*). *MATCH DRAWN.*

4

First Test

At long, long last the waiting was over. Lord's was just about full, latecomers still queuing to have their bags searched. At the Nursery end, the media centre, that suspended Space Age gherkin, Cherie Blair's lips, to quote the more uncouth, was overflowing with writers, photographers and broadcasters, and the babble was intense. And out on the pitch before the start, which was set down for the unearthly hour of 10.30am so that television schedules could be met, stood what was probably a record number of people, 35 of them, dark-suited, with badges dangling from their necks, and carrying cameras and clipboards. I had a flash vision of a well-known picture of Lionel Tennyson and Warwick Armstrong ready to toss before a 1921 Test match. They both wore business suits and Homburg hats, and smoked pipes. Standing by the boundary, the two captains were alone apart from the cameraman. The late cricket historian Derek Birley's insistence that cricket of this modern age has become a vibrant branch of show business (vaudeville, perhaps?) is reconfirmed.

Nobody envied the captain who won the toss on this particular morning. There was something about this Lord's pitch, even through binoculars, that suggested liveliness. This impression was coupled with a batsman's view of the sky, which spawned apprehension, for it was thick with cloud. Ricky Ponting, having correctly predicted the fall of the special gold coin, thus made the strong-minded decision to bat, suppressing any temptation to get England in on a fresh pitch in overcast conditions, with Glenn McGrath ready to roll.

Most of the players from both sides seem to be writing newspaper columns, and Justin Langer had expressed in his latest piece great excitement about this much-vaunted Ashes contest. The keen little left-hander's stated ambition in an Australian Cricket Board handbook a few seasons ago was to become a "famous" writer. "I can't tell you how excited I am about this series," he now gushed, "facing Harmison, Flintoff, Jones. My toes are tingling just thinking about it."

Well, within the first hour three of the Australian batsmen were not so much tingling in the toes as around the elbow (Langer), the head (Hayden) and the cheek (Ponting) as missiles from the lively Harmison pierced their guard. There were hold-ups each time, pauses during which it was uncomfortably noticeable that the England players kept their distance. This, we soon found, annoyed the Australians, who claimed they had been hoping for a renewed rapport between the two teams. It was said that England's previous captain, Nasser Hussain, had ordered his men not to socialise with the opposition. Another grievance emerged concerning England's fieldsmen hurling balls back to the wicketkeeper, just missing the innocent batsman.

Now these moans were slightly laughable. How much importance did Steve Waugh attach to the social side? And didn't Allan Border suddenly transform himself – in the perceived interests of his struggling team – into an uncommunicative adversary, refusing David Gower's and Ian Botham's doubtless abundant invitations to wine and dine, and, on the field, even denying the parched Robin Smith a drink of water?

As for the pinging of the ball needlessly back to the keeper, this annoyance so upset a chap named Frith back in January 2001 that the following appeared in his match report for *Wisden Australia* of the Australia v West Indies Test match at Sydney: "Australia's frustration showed, not least in the over-aggressive firing of the ball at the wicketkeeper, sometimes causing the batsman to take evasive action." Nor is it by any means a new expression of irritation and intimidation. Some of the Australians during the 1932–33 Bodyline series sometimes threw hard in the general direction of the English batsmen because it was their only physical, albeit desperate, means of reacting to the bouncers they were copping from Larwood and Voce.

Understandably, the recently successful England team under Vaughan have been eager to demonstrate that this is a new, tough, uncompromising side. But they might have benefited from seeing a photograph taken at Adelaide Oval during the Bodyline series of 72 years ago. Australia's Bert Oldfield took a serious blow to the head (no helmets then) while batting against Harold Larwood, and every single member of the England team – including the ruthless captain Douglas Jardine – gathered around the stricken player, with Gubby Allen signalling urgently to the dressing-room. Jardine not only sent a consoling telegram to Oldfield's wife. He arranged for a pair of Shirley Temple dolls to be delivered to the couple's little daughters.

Maybe the Englishmen of July 2005 had been destabilised by having to walk to the ground from their hotel. With so much corporate hospitality planned for Lord's, there was no room for the players' cars. Taxis were not prepared to venture into the clogged traffic around St Johns Wood. So the cricketers were seen walking – *walking* – to the ground with their newspapers tucked under their arms. Maybe now they can appreciate the stamina of mighty Tom Richardson, the Harmison of the 1890s, who used to walk many miles, with his cricket bag on his shoulder, from Mitcham to The Oval and then home again, often having bowled through much of a sweltering day. Not that Andrew "Freddie" Flintoff would shirk the opportunity. I'm sure he'd be up to it.

Let's believe, then, that had an Australian batsman in this 2005 series been as seriously hurt as Oldfield, then the opposition would have displayed due and genuine concern. If there's to be any hope of holding secure what remains of the precious Anglo-Australian bonds, the cricketers of both sides must never forget Keith Miller and his Messerschmitts.

❈❈❈

FIRST DAY. Thursday, July 21, 2005

Steve Harmison's physical hits occurred with the second ball of the match (Langer), on Hayden's helmet shortly before he was out, and in the 11th over when Ponting tried to hook him. The wound to the captain's face later required eight stitches. Up on the Australian balcony sat David Boon, now a Test selector. He must have thought back to the time when he captained Durham in the late 1990s and helped promote Harmison through the ranks. This was the Harmison who had demolished all before him until his difficult recent tour of South Africa. He is very fast and accurate and makes the shiny new ball bounce steeply. His record against Australia is poor. Now he set about making spectacular amends.

Matthew Hoggard laboured at the Nursery end. He prefers the pavilion end, as do most fast bowlers at Lord's, but he had to cede that preference to England's heaviest gun. The blond hangdog Hoggard can bend his outswinger at a nifty pace, and he can equally have spells of the most patent blandness. In the off-season he had worked on obviating his no-ball habit by running in at net practice with his eyes closed, just as Dennis Lillee once did – worth a try, perhaps, so long as you didn't disembowel yourself on the stump. The Yorkshireman now produced a beauty to swing back and bowl Hayden (12), the first wicket of the series.

He then had Ponting (0) missed two-handed at gully by Pietersen, and there was English frustration at seeing Australia's fifty come up off only 67 balls. Langer had made 31 of them in this his first Test at Lord's. Doubtless unaware that he was born on the exact centenary of both Joe Darling and F.S.Jackson, of 1905 fame, he proudly raised his 1000th run against England, a quarter of which had come in that marvellous innings at Melbourne in the last Ashes series, the eighth-highest score ever made for Australia against

Steve Harmison, displaying all the hostility that England had hoped for on the opening day at Lord's, bowls Shane Warne after his useful contribution of 28.

England (four of the eight, not surprisingly, having come from Don Bradman's bat) in the 128 years of competition. Old Joe would have been proud of little "Alfie" Langer.

Ponting's was the second wicket to fall. Harmison found the edge as the captain (9) played defensively, and Strauss clung to the catch at third slip. After seven challenging overs Harmison now made way for Flintoff, who was about to bowl against Australia in a Test match for the first time. He hit the bullseye with his fourth ball. Langer (40) attempted a hook but merely spliced a looping catch. Simon Jones came on for Hoggard next over and struck with his first ball: Martyn caught at the wicket by the other Jones for 2 off a spot-on delivery. Clarke joined Katich.

The ground had rocked with excitement as England dealt these early blows. It was the perfect stage for the entry of the most glamorous and uncomplicated of Australia's players. The triviality of this next connection perhaps needs forbearance, but Michael Clarke hit his first runs at the Home of Cricket to the exact spot where Doug Walters got off the mark in his first match here in 1968. The ball raced through backward point to the Tavern boundary. One could only wish Clarke better fortune in the years ahead than Walters experienced on his four unfulfilled tours of England.

There was more success to come for England in this opening session. With lunch pending, Jones breached Clarke's defence. The electronic assistance so readily available through slow-motion television play-back showed that contact was slightly high. Nonetheless umpire Koertzen gave Clarke (11) out lbw. It was a blow. When Australia went to lunch they were 97 for five, Katich a measured 7, Gilchrist a restrained 8.

Jones and Flintoff resumed the attack, and in the sixth over after the break Gilchrist (26), having sliced and banged six fours – and for once no sixes – touched a ball to the keeper. Flintoff, the jolly Lancastrian with a fresh crew cut, celebrated in an uncharacteristic frenzy, eyes bulging, mouth open wide after striking a second very important blow.

While Katich held on staunchly, moving well across his stumps in both defence and rare attack, Shane Warne fended a Flintoff bouncer over slips and then clubbed him to the Grandstand in the manner of the confident centurion he had recently become. (His 72-ball hundred for Hampshire was still the fastest of the season.) Soon he was falling backwards to avoid a fierce throw from Vaughan, rolling, stretching out and rebounding upright just like a Cossack dancer.

The tension tightened again with the return of Harmison, who immediately had Warne (23) missed at gully by the leaping Strauss. Straight after drinks, with the saving partnership worth 49, the highest of the innings, Warne (28) had his leg stump plucked out by a rare full-length ball from Harmison: 175 for seven. In the same over Katich (27) touched to Geraint Jones, a dismissal echoed in Harmison's following over when Lee edged him to Pietersen's stomach at gully (the chance went begging) and then to the keeper off the inside edge, easily held. In his next over – it was only the 41st of the innings – Harmison had Gillespie (1) leg-before to seal a spell of 4 for 7 off 14 balls, and to claim his first-ever five-in-an-innings against Australia. It had been the start dreamt of by England for many, many months: the world champions all out for 190 at the first time of asking.

Then it dawned that Mr McGrath from Narromine was ready to test this pitch for size.

It was mostly sunny now, almost as if England had control of weather conditions too. A nudge to the third-man boundary by Trescothick (he alone among the England players had taken part in the 2001 Lord's Test, whereas there were eight Australian survivors here) put the first runs on the board. Four leg-byes came via Strauss's left shoulder, and England were 10 without loss at tea.

With his first ball after the interval from the pavilion end Glenn McGrath's long-held dream became delightful reality. Trescothick (4) propped forward, edged to Langer at third slip, and the bowler had his 500th Test wicket. It had taken him 109 Tests plus 19 balls

Marcus Trescothick edges Glenn McGrath to Justin Langer, and the long-legged New South Welshman has his treasured 500th Test wicket.

in this one, and the cost had been a mere 21 runs per wicket. He followed Warne, Muralitharan and Walsh across the half-thousand threshold, and later stated that he had an ambition to reach 600, mocking the murmurs in English ranks that he must be on the very brink of retirement. His boot suppliers were ready with a special pair touched with gilt and with "500" shining from the uppers, memorabilia which McGrath was later generous enough to hand over to MCC on loan for the Museum at Lord's. With Don Bradman's boots already there, and Victor Trumper's cap and blazer, to say nothing of the recent portrait in oils of Shane Warne, everything in the world of Anglo-Australian relations seemed after all to be as cordial as ever.

How much additional damage might McGrath now inflict? Captain Vaughan received an unsavoury verbal reception in the middle from his opposite number and others, and the news grew worse when Strauss (2) played defensively against McGrath only to edge a low catch to Warne at first slip. In came Ian Bell, the classy 23-year-old from Warwickshire with the freak average of 297 after three Test matches. He would not have been human had he not felt acute pressure. It was noticed that his eyes were open very wide.

At 18 the third wicket toppled. Vaughan, hesitant about playing forward, was bowled for 3 as he hovered just inside the crease. McGrath, pitching accurately, as ever, and seaming the ball sometimes, but not always, sharply down the slope, had to be resisted. But what should be played and what should be left alone? It was a batsman's nightmare. McGrath had taken 8 for 38 at Lord's in the 1997 Test, and eight wickets in the Test four years later. It seemed to be his personal patch of ground. The England and Wales Cricket Board thus allowed the series to commence in generously favourable conditions for the visitors.

Clunk! McGrath struck again in his next over when Bell (6) touched the ball into the leg stump. In his next over McGrath dispatched Flintoff for a fourth-ball duck in his maiden Ashes innings, and England were in the rarely embarrassing situation of being five down for 21 and racing to oblivion. Could they climb up past the infamous 52 all out against Bradman's men at The Oval in 1948? Wasn't McGrath ever going to tire? His spell, 5 for 2, had swung the match, and placed his name alongside the likes of S.F.Barnes, who, one morning at Melbourne in 1911–12, shattered a high-class Australian top order with a dazzling 5 for 6 in 11 overs. Barnes nearly didn't play in that Test match. He was ill the night before, and it was only a bottle of whisky that revived him. The sweet part of the tale is that the bottle of restorative was taken to him in his hotel room by none other than Syd Gregory, a member of the opposition team. Whatever repeats itself in this glorious game of cricket – and so much does – there can surely never be a repetition of this incident. Imagine McGrath feeling off-colour the night before the Test, and one of the England squad, say 12th man Chris Tremlett, tending to his needs. An underlying point is that Sydney Barnes was 38 at the time, two years older than McGrath, who may yet be around for ages to come. England had better work out a way of dealing with him.

Complete humiliation was averted, chiefly by Kevin Pietersen, who at last had reached the Test crease at the fall of the third wicket. After almost half an hour he had hit his first boundary, a cut off Jason Gillespie, who was the weak link now that his form had so obviously slumped. Geraint Jones, Papua-New Guinea-born and Queensland-raised, drew deep-throated cheers when he smoothly cut McGrath for four and drove Gillespie down the slope for another. In McGrath's 13th and last over, he cut him to the rope again – and was then almost sliced in half by a ball which snarled back.

Another of Jones's copybook square-cuts sent a long-hop from Gillespie to the boundary, and he punished him further to raise the half-century stand. Then Warne came on. It was the 34th over, and he was bowling to his Hampshire club-mate Pietersen. The first ball rapped his pad. The appeal was ear-shattering. Pietersen survived. How helpful would all those Hampshire nets be now, and how beneficial might prove all the Englishmen's practice against "Merlyn", the bowling machine that spins the ball?

In the next over Jones was out. Brett Lee was steaming in in his first Test since January 2004, 17 Australian Tests ago, when he had conceded almost 300 runs in the match against India. Now he was very fast and a good deal more accurate, and a nasty lifter clipped Jones's helpless bat and lobbed to Gilchrist. Jones (30) had held the fort for almost an hour and a half, but England, six down, were still 111 adrift on first innings.

Ashley Giles is determined, but he is equipped no better than any other No.8 to deal with anybody as fast as Lee on a surface such as this. He played him through the slips, was nearly killed by the next ball, which he spooned for a catch (a weaker batsman would not necessarily have been relieved at the shout of no-ball), then courageously on-drove for four. A few minutes later, however, Lee forced Giles (11) back again, and as he trod on his leg stump the catch down the leg side finished in Gilchrist's outstretched gloves: 92 for seven as stumps were drawn.

The normally aggressive Pietersen had held firm all this time. He had made 28 in two hours, and had clearly decided to hold back any attempt at counterattack until the last three tailenders were in. He had recently told a Press conference that he thought the crowds at Lord's gave England less support than at other grounds, such as Edgbaston, but he can have had no legitimate complaint on this unforgettable day.

Giles, like a number of others, now went to a quiet corner to write his newspaper column. He would claim that this had been the most draining day he had ever experienced. And he hadn't even bowled. What he now desperately needed was a cup of tea and a "kip". He was not alone in that.

Steve Harmison, aglow from his 5 for 43, was interviewed after close of play in the cosy environs of the MCC Museum. "I don't care if a player gets hurt," he said by way of policy statement. "It's all in the game. It's my job. I'm six-foot-five." When someone innocently referred to the reception given him by the "old boys in the Long Room", Harmison caused surprise by revealing a compassionate trait: "Old boys? Don't call them 'old boys'."

In his fading baggy green cap, Glenn McGrath could not stop grinning after this illustrious day. He explained how he had almost come off earlier in that opening spell, but wickets kept clattering. (Fourteen of the 17 this day fell to bowling from the pavilion end.) He agreed that there was variation in the pitch, and with a fuller length he had made the ball go down the slope more than usual. With so many members of his family at Lord's, he had experienced the first butterflies in the stomach at breakfast, when he first rekindled thoughts about that 500th Test wicket. He was asked if the pitch was really that helpful to bowling? Having made 10 not out at No.11, he was emboldened to quip: "I felt comfortable out there batting!"

"I'm probably feeling younger than I have done," he beamed. It would have encouraged him further, perhaps, if he had known that S.F.Barnes – assuming he had heard of the man who took 189 wickets in 27 Tests – could still bowl effectively at the age of 60, and lived on into his 95th year.

* * *

Over in Australia, television viewing figures suggested that nearly three-quarters of a million people had shared the excitement of this hard-fought day's cricket through the SBS coverage. The minority channel had bought rights for $2-million and already booked $3-million in advertisement revenue. I couldn't help but picture my relatives and mates dragging bleary-eyed off to work after the nocturnal vigil. A couple of them had telephoned when news of further bombings in London had circulated. In the Lord's Press-box typically yet inexplicably conflicting reports had been drifting in throughout the day of further bombs. Eventually it became clear that none had actually gone off, only the detonators. One had been placed at Shepherds Bush, west London, through which I had passed much earlier that day, on the way to BBC Radio 4, whose listeners I urged to believe that D.R.Jardine's reputation was being re-evaluated. He was a man ahead of his time, just as

Bodyline was merely a partial precursor of the prolonged and dangerous four-prong West Indian fast-bowling blitz of the 1980s. Although Bodyline must be ready to recede in significance and allure all these years on, it simply refuses to fade away.

The perspective following this day of sensations in the Test match at Lord's was reshaped yet again when I received news that an old friend, an acceptably grumpy cricket-lover who had been a wartime airman, had collapsed and died in the Tavern Stand on this first morning of the Test match. I'd chatted with John MacDonald at the Guildford county match only the day before. He was relaxed and, by his standard, happy. It was so sad to reflect that if England were to prevail in their desperate mission, John would not be around to savour it.

SECOND DAY. Friday, July 22, 2005

The sky was grey again, and most England fans were further distracted by the fate of Graham Thorpe. Overnight the Surrey and England left-hander had announced his retirement from international cricket. It looked like a decision based on pique. Some thought he should have been selected for this Test in place of young Bell. Others felt that his form was so ordinary and his age and his fitness of such concern that this would have been higher risk than staying with Bell. There was also the matter of subconscious wind-down now that he had announced his impending retirement, with a season for New South Wales coming up. Nonetheless, when England were one for 10, two for 11, three for 18 and so forth, Thorpe would have been most people's choice as the man in the middle, braced to turn the innings around yet again. He looked good at Guildford the day before the Test as he worked his way to 95 against Kent. His non-selection here was a further mark of the selectors' determination to look ahead positively and unblinkingly.

Warne to Pietersen from the Nursery end launched the day's play, friends again transformed into temporary enemies. Ball strikes pad and bowler appeals with all the impassioned theatricality of a bulky Mick Jagger. These umpires need strong minds.

Pietersen found McGrath a problem. The batsman pulled away for some reason, the bowler couldn't stop, and the resultant rocket had the off-balance Pietersen toppling over. McGrath went down to him and displayed a welcome friendliness as he lay on the ground. Pietersen showed his appreciation by tipping him over the slips for four.

England's hundred came up, a landmark yesterday seemingly beyond them, but Hoggard, having survived a nose-high bouncer from McGrath, and still without a run, touched Warne to slip, where Hayden reacted smartly enough to pocket the catch on the rebound. The Yorkshireman has often usefully taken root in recent Test matches, but not today. Perhaps he still had his eyes shut at the crucial moment.

Harmison came in ahead of Simon Jones. Had he not top-scored for England with 42 from the No.11 spot at Cape Town in January? How precious such a contribution would be now. Pietersen, of course, knew that it was time for him to go after the bowling.

McGrath didn't know what hit him. First Pietersen slugged a cross-batted four straight to the pavilion. A slower ball was tried. Pietersen spotted it and drove it high into the pavilion. A serene cover-driven four followed, then a delicate touch for a single to third man to keep the strike. He was now 51, eyes ablaze.

Warne was next to feel the heat. Pietersen cracked him for six into the Grandstand. If he could somehow choose the right ball to punish and use only the meat of his bat, there was no telling where this might end, or what sort of lead England might finish with. Again he heaved into Warne, and up went the ball towards the same place. This time, though, there was a little less meat on the shot. Would it beat Martyn to the rope? The Westralian was running like a centre three-quarter for the try line. And he threw himself at that imaginary try line, perfectly timed, to gather the catch as his chest slid across the ground. It was a stirring ending to a stirring maiden Test innings. For an hour and a half Pietersen (57) had tried so hard to haul his side up to Australia's 190. Now they were nine down and the deficit in this bowlers' match was still quite vast: 68.

Simon Jones reduced that figure, swinging his bat like some Welsh blacksmith: two off-side fours and a three when Lee returned for one over; a four over the slips off McGrath. Harmison drove Warne for an exquisite four and then Lee returned and sealed off the innings for 155. England were 35 behind. It could have been so much worse.

In the dozen overs before lunch Australia lost Langer (6), whose dive at the bowler's end failed to beat Pietersen's underarm throw after an athletic pounce on the ball. Hayden (34) looked more his old self, until he under-edged a pull against Flintoff, and if some of Jones's rapid leg-cutters had been slightly redirected Australia might have been in serious trouble. Ponting became the eighth Australian batsman to reach 7000 Test runs, but he looked jumpy at times when facing Harmison, and Martyn's uppercut to the third man boundary belatedly brought a fieldsman into position there. It was the 28th over before the third wicket fell.

The hundred had just come up when the Australia captain cut Hoggard chest-high to substitute James Hildreth, a 20-year-old Somerset all-rounder who will never forget the moment. Ponting's 42 had stabilised the innings, and – subject to England errors – the advantage was now to grow in parallel with Australia's grip on the match.

Hoggard's leg-stump half-volleys – the traditional penalty for slightly misdirecting the full-length outswinger – were milked happily by the Australians, and when Giles came on for his first bowl of the match after 35 overs, the watchful Martyn soon concluded that there was hardly any turn, even down the slope. Harmison couldn't bowl indefinitely, much as Vaughan might have wished, and he went into the outfield to recharge his batteries after bowling 12 overs for 20 runs.

Now came England's peripeteia. Michael Clarke was 21 when Jones returned to bowl at the pavilion end. Clarke hit the first ball waist-high towards cover, to the right of England's best fieldsman, Pietersen, who unaccountably grounded the catch. Had he held it, Australia would have been 139 for four, only 174 ahead, with the match still anybody's. As Clarke went on to make a further 70 runs, the error grew in dimension until it matched something at Headingley in the 1997 Ashes series. There, Graham Thorpe spilt a first-slip catch from Matthew Elliott when the left-hander was 29. Other errors followed. Mike Atherton and Mike Smith also blew chances from Elliott, who went on to make the first score of 199 in Ashes history. This was also the match in which Ricky Ponting scored a century on Ashes debut, and Australia won by an innings.

The sun shone at last as the two Australians, Martyn and Clarke, strolled off for tea with the score 140 for three, their team holding the advantage, and their Prime Minister beaming in the entertainment box of MCC President Tom Graveney. Providing a kaleidoscopic background to the action out in the middle, alongside

Michael Clarke came so close to the glory of a century in his first Ashes Test match, making 91.

John Howard sat John Edrich, who scored 120 on this ground in his maiden innings against Australia 41 years earlier, and near them sat three players from Don Bradman's 1948 team of "Invincibles". Left-hand batting star Neil Harvey, symbol of youth, is now an improbable 76, Sam Loxton, 84, and Arthur Morris, another centurion on this ground, 83. Close by sat Alan Davidson, who took 5 for 42 in Australia's 1961 Lord's victory. Marylebone Cricket Club and its members may think they own this ground, but perhaps they ought to have a good look at the title deeds, for it so often seems to belong to Australia, whose wartime Prime Minister John Curtin's words – "Australia will always fight for those 22 yards!" – uttered after a visit to Lord's, are apparently taken by Australian cricketers a little too literally.

And they went on fighting, Martyn and Clarke. There was still something in the pitch for the bowlers, but the pair selected the ball to hit with unusual care. Martyn fell backwards in pulling Jones to extend Australia's lead past 200, and Clarke played a pedigree straight-drive off Giles, persuading him to switch to bowling around the wicket. It made no difference. Clarke's half-century came off only 64 balls as he placed fours through midwicket and then through Flintoff at cover. There followed a comic delivery when Martyn stole a single to cover off a Giles no-ball and Pietersen missed the stumps with a sharp and justifiable throw. The upshot of that tap by Martyn was six runs. Soon he was 50 (108 balls), a milestone he celebrated with a subdued little flick of the fist, and soon afterwards his 4000th Test run came up.

An experimental over of Bell's innocent medium-pacers failed, and Hoggard, with seven off-side fieldsmen, looked almost as harmless until Clarke impatiently drove, only to inside-edge into the stumps. He was nine runs short of that rare distinction of a hundred on Ashes debut, an honour roll which includes the names of three of his team-mates, Ricky Ponting, Adam Gilchrist, and the chap at the other end, Damien Martyn. "Pup" Clarke was disconsolate, and admitted later that for four overs he had been battling against growing frustration at being contained. This was the best bowling he had ever faced, but "I play my way, and I'll go on playing my way." Did he especially enjoy batting with Martyn? "Yeah, we have a lot of things in common." Such as? "Our cars, our motor-bikes . . .!"

Everyone was wondering: was it over for England? Gilchrist was surely bound to be a problem? Well, England probably thought that of Vic Trumper in 1905, but his scores in that series were 13 (retired hurt), 31, 8 and 0, 11 and 30, 4 and 28. "Gilly" seems a certainty to better that.

The final three-quarters of an hour belonged to England. In the over after Clarke's dismissal, Martyn was leg-before to Harmison, the batsman airborne as the ball came through slightly low. His 65 was another vital contribution, remembered not for any particular stroke but for an even serenity, an innings of massive significance.

For the second time in the match Flintoff got rid of Gilchrist (10), who edged a drive into his wicket, and from what became the final ball of the day Harmison bounced one at Warne (2), who could do no more than steer it to gully. Australia finished 279 for seven, a comfortable 314 ahead, and Katich had only the tail to work with.

Kevin Pietersen faced the media that evening and looked straight into their collective eye. Optimistically he thought the match was pretty even now, and reminded the gathering that England had done pretty well in recent years when chasing big targets. That dropped catch? (Some ghoul was bound to throw it at him.) "That's all part of cricket," said KP without so much as a blink. "I've dropped lots of catches in my career." It came as a surprise to hear him confess that he had been "a bit nervous" before his first Test innings. The pitch, he thought, looked a lot better now, and it was how they dealt with McGrath and Lee with the new ball that would be all-important. His own switch to all-out attack earlier in the day? "It's what you call thinking on your feet!"

THIRD DAY. Saturday, July 23, 2005

Australia were still batting when the bails were lifted for lunch, and the lead was past 400. There had been rain spots on the pavement in Baker Street, but although the light was eerie the overcast sky held back almost all of its watery contents.

With 10 runs added Lee set off for a run after taking one on the glove from Harmison, only for Giles's daring throw from cover to break the stumps at the bowler's end. Had he missed there would have been four overthrows. But England's thoughts must now have been moving towards the likelihood or otherwise of life-saving assistance from the weather.

Gillespie batted stubbornly, intelligently, and Katich still made survival paramount, which had to be interpreted as a compliment to England. Just before Jones knocked Gillespie's off stump out, the batsman had edged him, only to see the other Jones, Geraint the wicketkeeper, lurch to his right and unaccountably extend one glove only for the catch. It went down, and with it went more of the support remaining for this keeper-batsman's claim to a Test place while there were supposedly so many others more highly-skilled around the counties.

The cost was not great, as was the case with five other England drops in the match. It was Pietersen's off Clarke which would never be forgotten. Nor would the Australians let Hoggard soon forget the ball that he let run between his boots for a boundary. Some of his mild public remarks had been noted: he thought McGrath and others were now on the downside of their careers.

Katich took a calm single to reach 50 after 136 minutes' batting, another invaluable contribution from somebody who would have played much more Test cricket had he not been born in Australia. At lunch the score was 372 for nine, Katich 66 and the man who just loves batting, Glenn McGrath, 10 not out.

With McGrath starting to look like Stan McCabe, something must have been distracting England's fieldsmen, for Flintoff dropped him from a straightforward chance at slip, and Geraint Jones missed him again, diving forward. It was Katich who went, caught at third man for 67, leaving Australia 419 ahead and comfortable.

England set out on a bleak journey that surely had only one ending. When Strauss drove Lee through the covers, the full house cheered raucously – apart, that is, from the Australian Prime Minister and the several carpets of yellow caps signifying Australian tour groups in the open stands. McGrath steamed in again. But this time there was to be no early collapse. A pig of a ball rose at Strauss's ribs. Trescothick was equally calm, letting the ball fly, occasionally thick-edging. Strauss hooked gamely and successfully, and just before tea Trescothick was extremely lucky to survive an lbw shout from Warne. When a decision made by Aleem Dar proves to have been wrong it causes widespread surprise, such is this umpire's reputation.

At tea England was 65 without loss, and speculation was growing. After tea some of Warne's appeals were so long and loud and insistent that he must have run the risk of a Code of Conduct penalty – not that he is averse to risk-taking. But it was Brett Lee who broke through. With the total 80, Strauss (37) pulled out of a hook shot but left his bat up, periscope fashion. The ball spooned out towards cover and the bowler hurtled across and held the ball close to the grass as he dived.

Law 32/3c states *inter alia*: "A catch shall be considered to have been fairly made if: The ball does not touch the ground, even though the hand holding it does so in effecting the catch." It looked here very much as if Lee inadvertently touched the turf with the ball as he hit the ground, before turning his clasped hands upwards. Something similar happened during England's dismissal of West Indies for 54 here at Lord's in 2000. Brian Lara edged high and wide of Dominic Cork who took a flying catch and crashed to earth. He broke his fall with the downward-facing hand clutching the ball, which, of course, hit the turf. In either of these cases it would have taken a very alert and courageous umpire to have disqualified the catch.

It seemed that Trescothick (44) was handling Warne without undue trouble. The Somerset batsman was later to make an interesting remark: England's batsmen were now playing the ball and not the player. In past series they had certainly been overawed by the likes of Warne and McGrath, but it seems now that the coach, with the important input of the team psychologist, has done a good job. However, a ball is still a ball, and Warne spun one in, Trescothick pushed at it, and Hayden held the slip catch. Another collapse was thus launched.

Bell, having skipped out confidently to drive Warne for two, was lbw to a slider which held its course against the slope. And after Pietersen had signed on with a robust square-cut for four to his second ball, the capital wicket of Vaughan fell. Lee bowled him with a very fast leg-cutter up the slope, and the captain's dreadful match, bowled both times for next to nothing, was over. Being one of the few players not contributing a newspaper column might be seen as an unnecessary abstinence on his part.

Vaughan was honest and direct as usual that evening: England's *bowling* had been good; it was difficult to explain the dropped catches; if the Australians were targeting Giles they did fairly well;

Brett Lee plunges England into deeper trouble in the fourth innings by bowling England captain Michael Vaughan for another single-innings score.

the man who came in for Thorpe [Pietersen] did fairly well; and "I batted No.3 and made 3 and 4, and that's not good enough."

Umpire Dar crossed to point. Why? No sun was blinding him at square leg and no leg-side fieldsman was interfering with his view. Was he re-examining Brett Lee's action? Under the new humanitarian system, nobody will be called for throwing *during* a match. It remained to be seen whether Mr Dar was about to lodge a report on the bowler, whose early elbow problem seemed to have been sorted out some time ago.

England's batsmen needed to continue to treat every ball on its merits, and when Flintoff saw Warne drop one a fraction short he stood up and cut at it. He got only the finest edge and Gilchrist held it: 119 for five, last man 3. Freddie's effort with the bat in this Test had been even more dismal than his skipper's: key factors both.

Warne, occasionally showing off with leg-breaks that spun a metre, had taken 3 for 10 to push Australia close to victory. But no more wickets fell that evening. Pietersen, supported by Geraint Jones, held firm, always looking for a chance to score, driving Lee with purity and slogging to midwicket against Warne. Lee released a bail-high full-toss which crashed into Pietersen's pad-flap, perilously near his box, knocking him over. The batsman thought little of that particular delivery and even less of the (close) leg-before appeal that went with it. In Lee's next over Pietersen was doubly ready for anything short. His pull for six into the Tavern Stand was the shot of the match.

KP's self-belief was so evident in every movement. He is intelligent enough to know that victory was really out of the question – well, dull fellows like me thought so – but he thrives on being centre stage, and with his talent, why shouldn't he?

Rain began to fall around half-past-five, just as Jones played a dainty leg-glance for four off the still-wicketless Gillespie, and the final shot from Pietersen's armoury this day was a four off Warne, swept away between two boundary riders by the Warner Stand. England stuffed, barring two days of incessant rain, at 156 for five, Pietersen 42, Jones 6; Australia relieved, exultant.

England's star at Lord's was debutant Kevin Pietersen, who twice passed 50. This shot of the match off Lee sent the ball into the Tavern Stand.

FOURTH DAY. Sunday, July 24, 2005

There seemed every chance that not a ball would be bowled on this Sunday. Rain was pelting down and spectators – and journalists – settled to streams of chatter, post-mortem and speculation over a cup or glass of something. Lord's now had a first-class underground drainage system (Denis Compton's ashes as well as those of Bill Edrich, and possibly Plum Warner, too, went out unceremoniously with the old turf when it was dug up). There would be no lasting puddles on that velvet outfield now, and the hovercraft-driven covers were fully effective. It was just a question of patiently waiting for the rain to relent and then for some light mopping-up.

The hold-up was still extensive. Not until 3.45pm could play resume. The remaining allocation for the day was 42 overs. Immediately English hopes crashed as Geraint Jones pulled tamely to mid-on. There was scathing comment over this dismissal, not altogether warranted. Hardly any modern batsman could be expected to block or leave the ball all through the length of the day's play. The soundest advice usually is to play naturally. It was McGrath who bowled the long-hop, and it ought to have been hit for four through midwicket. Jones slightly miscued and was subsequently lampooned and strung up.

Giles was out in the same over, pushing tamely to gully. The rain returned. But only for 10 minutes, and McGrath soon picked up his third wicket of the day, trapping Hoggard with a wicked breakback to complete the batsman's "pair". Pietersen reached a 68-ball fifty, and was about to become the first England player to top-score in both innings on debut since fellow South Africa-born batsman Tony Greig in 1972. (Since 1972 only Andrew Strauss had made twin half-centuries for England on Test debut: 112 and 83 against New Zealand here at Lord's 14 months ago.) Fascinatingly, not only were/are Greig and Pietersen both 25 years of age at the time, and tall chappies too, but there are clear similarities in personality. Put succinctly, neither is a shy man.

Harmison now went scoreless, leg-before to Warne, who was poised to acquire the final wicket for a five-for which would place his name at last on the Lord's dressing-room honours board. Pietersen showed what he thought of that prospect by lofting him into the Grandstand; then a two and an off-driven four with the fielders in close. Simon Jones was left to face McGrath.

Warne did feature in the last dismissal of the match, but not as a bowler. Jones edged and Warne comfortably held the catch at first slip. "I was expecting that last catch to go down!" joked Ponting afterwards.

So the last five batsmen had gone without contributing a single run for England this day. Five wickets had gone for 24 runs, an incredible slide to defeat by 239 runs, and for the first time for

51 Tests (since Trent Bridge in 2001, when Australia bowled them out for 185 and 162) England had been dismissed for under 200 in each innings. There were 14 single-figure scores in a calamitous performance that propelled all pre-match optimism into the bin.

Glenn McGrath, Man of the Match, took four of the five wickets, to finish with nine in the match, and Matthew Hoggard's vivid imagery in his *Times* column is worth repeating: "McGrath . . . is only about four inches tall when you watch him on the TV. Take my word for it, he's a lot bigger coming in from the pavilion end at Lord's."

"Hoggy" (the English one) reminded his readers that England were now good at learning from defeat, as when they reversed a dismal loss at Cape Town a few months earlier with an outstanding victory at Johannesburg in the next Test. We'll see.

The run of 10 consecutive home Test victories since September 2003 was now sealed off, and the impressive record of 15 victories home and away – almost all big ones too – in England's past 19 Tests in that time, three of them drawn, with only the Cape Town match lost, had been badly dented. That great surge had taken them to the No.2 ranking in the world.

There could be no warm afterglow for England now that Australia's giant stature had been reconfirmed. Ashley Giles was stung by former Zimbabwe batsman Dave Houghton's statement that England were playing with 10 men as long as Giles was in the team. Houghton, now director of cricket of a pathetically un-successful Derbyshire, must have forgotten the Warwickshire man's contributions over past seasons and tours – if he ever knew. The affable but now distressed Giles went so far as to claim that some of the former England players now pontificating in the media did not really want England to win the Ashes. This is not only a feasible proposition but affords wondrous possibilities for further analysis. The unflappable Marcus Trescothick tendered a morsel of wisdom via his own column: players should avoid media beat-ups: "you only feed the fire".

Meanwhile, in retrospect, Simon Jones's duck might have had something to do with an upsetting scandal story that burst around his head that morning. A "pack of lies" was how he described a newspaper tale which had caused his girlfriend to leave him.

As for the captain of Australia, he had a conspicuously relieved air about him after the match. Was England's spirit broken? Ponting wouldn't go that far, though he reckoned that Vaughan didn't like facing McGrath. McGrath, with his two fair-haired little children at his knee, dismissed the spurious "too old" allegations as "all fun and games before a series starts", but he felt that Vaughan had "got a bit of work to do".

Vaughan got to work straightaway, netting assiduously with coach Duncan Fletcher over the next few days and then hitting a century for Yorkshire at Headingley in a limited-overs match against Kent, who, needless to say, had nobody anywhere near the class of McGrath in their bowling ranks.

As for that dependable oracle Shane Keith Warne, he had proclaimed, quite remarkably really, in his column on the opening morning of this Lord's Test match: "I hope that when we go to The Oval in September for the fifth Test the series is still alive. That way the public, who have waited for a competitive Ashes battle for so long, will have got what I think they really want."

Nice to agree with him on such a major issue, but his sentiments would surely have found little concurrence among his team-mates – from some of whom, incidentally, we were hearing that Warne had been distanced as a result of his off-the-field behaviour. It was the mark of the ultimate professional that from the moment he began that sinister walk in to bowl late on Thursday afternoon, he seemed as good as ever.

FIRST TEST MATCH
Lord's, July 21, 22, 23, 24, 2005

AUSTRALIA		mins	balls	4s			mins	balls	4s
J.L.Langer	c Harmison b Flintoff	40	77	44	5	run out (Pietersen)	6	24	15	1
M.L.Hayden	b Hoggard	12	38	25	2	b Flintoff	34	65	54	5
*R.T.Ponting	c Strauss b Harmison	9	28	18	1	c sub (J.C.Hildreth) b Hoggard	42	100	65	3
D.R.Martyn	c G.O.Jones b S.P.Jones	2	13	4	–	lbw b Harmison	65	215	138	8
M.J.Clarke	lbw b S.P.Jones	11	35	22	2	b Hoggard	91	151	106	15
S.M.Katich	c G.O.Jones b Harmison	27	107	67	5	c S.P.Jones b Harmison	67	177	113	8
#A.C.Gilchrist	c G.O.Jones b Flintoff	26	30	19	6	b Flintoff	10	26	14	1
S.K.Warne	b Harmison	28	40	29	5	c Giles b Harmison	2	13	7	–
B.Lee	c G.O.Jones b Harmison	3	13	8	–	run out (Giles)	8	16	16	1
J.N.Gillespie	lbw b Harmison	1	19	11	–	b S.P.Jones	13	72	52	3
G.D.McGrath	not out	10	9	6	2	not out	20	44	32	3
Extras	b 5, lb 4, w 1, nb 11	21				b 10, lb 8, nb 8	26			
Total	(40.2 overs, 209 mins)	190				(100.4 overs, 457 mins)	384			

Fall: 1/35 2/55 3/66 4/66 5/87 6/126
    7/175 8/178 9/178

1/18 2/54 3/100 4/255 5/255 6/274
7/279 8/289 9/341

BOWLING: Harmison 11.2-0-43-5, Hoggard 8-0-40-1 (2nb), Flintoff 11-2-50-2 (9nb), S.P.Jones 10-0-48-2 (1w)
SECOND INNINGS: Harmison 27.4-6-54-3, Hoggard 16-1-56-2 (2nb), Flintoff 27-4-123-2 (5nb),
S.P.Jones 18-1-69-1 (1nb), Giles 11-1-56-0, Bell 1-0-8-0

ENGLAND		mins	balls	4s			mins	balls	4s
M.E.Trescothick	c Langer b McGrath	4	24	17	1	c Hayden b Warne	44	128	103	8
A.J.Strauss	c Warne b McGrath	2	28	21	2	c & b Lee	37	115	67	6
*M.P.Vaughan	b McGrath	3	29	20	–	b Lee	4	47	26	1
I.R.Bell	b McGrath	6	34	25	1	lbw b Warne	8	18	15	–
K.P.Pietersen	c Martyn b Warne	57	148	89	8*	not out	64	120	79	6*
A.Flintoff	b McGrath	0	8	4	–	c Gilchrist b Warne	3	14	11	–
#G.O.Jones	c Gilchrist b Lee	30	85	56	6	c Gillespie b McGrath	6	57	21	1
A.F.Giles	c Gilchrist b Lee	11	14	13	2	c Hayden b McGrath	0	2	2	–
M.J.Hoggard	c Hayden b Warne	0	18	16	–	lbw b McGrath	0	18	15	–
S.J.Harmison	c Martyn b Lee	11	35	19	1	lbw b Warne	0	3	1	–
S.P.Jones	not out	20	24	14	3	c Warne b McGrath	0	12	6	–
Extras	b 1, lb 5, nb 5	11				b 6, lb 5, nb 3	14			
Total	(48.1 overs, 227 mins)	155				(58.1 overs, 268 mins)	180			

    * plus 2 sixes   *plus 2 sixes

Fall: 1/10 2/11 3/18 4/19 5/21 6/79
    7/92 8/101 9/122

1/80 2/96 3/104 4/112 5/119 6/158
7/158 8/164 9/167

BOWLING: McGrath 18-5-53-5, Lee 15.1-5-47-3, Gillespie 8-1-30-0, Warne 7-2-19-2
SECOND INNINGS: McGrath 17.1-2-29-4, Lee 15-3-58-2, Gillespie 6-0-18-0, Warne 20-2-64-4

Toss won by Australia
Test debut: K.P.Pietersen
Match award: G.D.McGrath

Umpires: Aleem Dar (Pak) & R.E.Koertzen (SAf)
Replay umpire: M.R.Benson (Eng)
Match referee: R.S.Madugalle (SL)

AUSTRALIA WON BY 239 RUNS

5

Second Test

Reflection, entirely without malice, on the possibility that it might soon be Australia's turn to suffer major injury problems (refer back, if you will, to pages 23–24) became a dramatic reality at Edgbaston on Thursday, August 4. At a quarter past nine, 75 minutes before the start of the second Test, Glenn McGrath, the most effective pace bowler in the world, was loosening up by tossing a rugby ball around with Brad Haddin. Accidentally he trod on a stray cricket ball. Errol Alcott rushed to his aid and knew straightaway that the injury was serious. McGrath was wheeled away in a motorised buggy with a grade two lateral ligament tear in his right ankle. Michael Kasprowicz was drafted into the side and the Ashes odds shifted somewhat.

Only two days earlier it had seemed that England were the camp suffering unexpected and damaging injury woes. Michael Vaughan was struck on the right arm by a bouncer from Chris Tremlett in the nets. His agony was apparent as he fell, writhing from the pain. It was a surprise the following day when, after ice treatment and other specialist attention, he was declared fit. Paul Collingwood had already been called into England's squad to give an extra option, but was now sent away. If Vaughan had been ruled out, somebody like Robert Key would have had to embark on a helter-skelter motorway journey.

The Australians had one first-class match between Lord's and Edgbaston, and that was against Worcestershire, who had been negotiating with McGrath for a new spell of employment. Rain prevented all but one over on the opening day, and golf clubs were beginning to seem more natural accessories than cricket bats. However, the tourists enjoyed a run spree on the Sunday. Hayden waded in with 79 before mistiming a pull, some of the bowling coming from Zimbabwe spinner Ray Price, off whom he had made the run that brought him the world Test record in Perth 22 months before. Australian Matt Mason claimed both openers after they had had a good net with 110 for the first wicket. Gillespie, who so enjoys batting, got himself a half-century and helped Haddin restore a fading innings.

Gillespie took a couple of wickets, including that of Graeme Hick, but the figures went to Kasprowicz, priming him – if only he had known it – for an emergency recall to the Test side. Shaun Tait, meanwhile, did nothing much wrong, dismissing both openers and conceding no more than four runs an over in his 13 overs. Clarke and Ponting opened the second innings and carved out warm-up fifties apiece before the short trip to Birmingham, where Australia planned to go two-up in the Ashes series.

WORCESTER, July 30, 31, August 1, 2005
AUSTRALIANS 406 for 9 dec (J.L.Langer 54, M.L.Hayden 79, B.J.Haddin 94, J.N.Gillespie 53*) and 161 for 2 (M.J.Clarke 59, R.T.Ponting 59*); WORCESTERSHIRE 187 (S.C.Moore 69; M.S.Kasprowicz 5 for 67). *MATCH DRAWN.*

❊❊❊

FIRST DAY. Thursday, August 4, 2005
It was only by the grace of God that the Edgbaston Test match was spared from cancellation after an astonishing natural disaster. Seven days before the Test was scheduled to begin, a freak tornado roared in from nowhere to rip through nearby suburbs – Kings Heath,

Sparkbrook, Balsall Heath – tearing off roofs, smashing garden sheds. Injuries were few, but streets were left resembling bomb-sites, and over at the cricket ground Steve Rouse, the head groundsman, had his work cut out after several inches of rain inter-rupted his preparation for the big match. If the tornado had whooshed a kilometre off its course there would have been no Test match. Severe damage to the pavilion, the Eric Hollies Stand and much else could not have been made safe in time.

England remained unchanged from the Lord's Test, a rare thing, and Australia had only the one enforced change. The pitch, like so many others, defied accurate behavioural prediction, but the sky was overcast, so that when Ricky Ponting won the toss again he put England in. Among the adjectives employed were "aggressive", "crazy", "complacent", "defensive" and – from Mike Gatting – "arrogant". Did the Aussie skipper fear another Harmison onslaught as at Lord's? Was he trying to demonstrate that McGrath's absence didn't worry him? Was he still reeling from McGrath's injury and incapable of clear thought? If England were 70 for six at lunch Ponting would be a bold hero.

England actually went to lunch at 132 for the loss of Strauss, after 27 overs. Vaughan and others had drawn strength after Lord's by reminding themselves that since 2002–03 England had lost six Test matches and had bounced back immediately each time to win the next one. This resilience now seemed to be a vital part of their culture, the result of positive thinking rarely evident in England teams of recent years.

The Australians, all bedecked in those wonderful baggy green caps (some of them now looking rather worn – the caps, that is), watched askance as Trescothick cover-drove Lee for three fours in the third over on a pitch that showed a certain amount of life but which, after the rude interruption by Nature a week earlier, did groundsman Rouse proud.

There was a sharp chance in the fourth over when Strauss, on 4, edged Gillespie. Warne threw himself down to his left, completing a body flip, but just failed to nail the catch. The only other let-off in the opening session came when Trescothick was caught by Hayden at gully, only for the no-ball shout to deny the deflated Gillespie. After an hour England were romping along at 56 without loss, and Warne came on to bowl from the City end. Strauss skipped down the pitch and lofted him for four. The ball came back soaked, so they broke for drinks.

Weak sunlight spread across the ground as Strauss seemed to target Warne, driving and pulling fours in one over before his partner lofted him for six. Runs flowed. Kasprowicz went around the wicket to the left-handers and Strauss cover-drove him for two more fours to bring up the century in 101 minutes. The booming chants of "Ing-er-land!" arose from the lads on the terraces. It was the sixth three-figure opening stand by Trescothick and Strauss since they came together 15 months earlier. Dare England say they now have a Langer/Hayden of their own?

Marcus Trescothick, moving frustratingly close to his first Test century against Australia, sweeps during his stoical 90 in England's first innings.

Trescothick banged Warne to midwicket for another four, and England's first-wicket record against Australia at Edgbaston was superseded: the unbroken 105 posted by Jack Hobbs and C.B.Fry in 1909, when England won by 10 wickets (only to lose the next two Tests and the series). Soon afterwards the stand was broken when Strauss (48) was bowled by one from Warne which spun and gripped and came in a very long way.

Did England then play for lunch? Not a bit of it. While his captain admired from the other end, Trescothick took 18 off Lee's final over, flicking him for four and six over the vacant gully area, then driving two more fours to go to lunch 77 not out, aggressive England 132 on the board, Ponting looking doleful.

With 32 added, and Vaughan seemingly at ease, Trescothick (90) reverted to his pokey self, nicking Kasprowicz to the keeper. So, having made a pair of centuries here in last year's Test against West Indies, he still had no Test hundred against Australia. Even that similarly rotund left-hander from the 1930s, Maurice Leyland, was never calmer than "Tres". If this dismissal hurt, he never showed it.

Ian Bell came in, probably aware of the desperate set of statistics which had been circulating, showing that Warwickshire batsmen have never done much in Tests on this their home ground. Dennis Amiss's prolific period had been rudely halted by Dennis Lillee in Australia in 1974–75, and then further stultified a few weeks later here at Edgbaston with scores of 4 and 5 (the match in which Graham Gooch began his great Test career with 0 and 0). Indeed, in Ashes Tests here the only local player who had reached double figures was that perennial No.11, Bob Willis, who managed 13 against Kim Hughes's 1981 Australians. That was the match in which Australia were marching to victory when Ian Botham snatched five wickets for one run to bring England a stunning 29-run triumph. Folk of nervous dispositions were not going to welcome anything that exciting this time round.

Poor Bell (6) played half-forward and touched Kasprowicz to Gilchrist, his Test average finally dipping below 100. He was replaced by Pietersen, whose Test average after his one match was still in three figures. A fairly long delay was orchestrated, but his nerves are strong, and he turned his first ball to the boundary. How much longer could England maintain this murderous run rate? After 35 overs it was a dizzy 5.23 per over.

No thought was given to consolidation. Short ball from Gillespie; no attempt by Vaughan (24) to hook downwards; deliberately he got under it, eyeing the shortish boundary; up it went, with Lee waiting near the rope. He held it as he fell and rolled. At 187 for four England might now, after all, be contained for a moderate score.

During the 17 overs left before tea, thoughts returned to that cheeky text message sent by Flintoff to Pietersen some weeks earlier. Would this pair indeed "cause some damage", and if so, when? Now was as convenient a time as any.

Pietersen just cleared a fieldsman with a drive, then Warne bellowed a petulant appeal for a short-leg catch off the batsman's pad. Off back foot and front the pair sought runs every ball, Flintoff punching one from Warne over long-on and into the terraces then slamming Gillespie through the covers. Pietersen displayed extraordinary flexibility in hitting the same bowler from outside off to the leg boundary, a brisk manoeuvring of the wrist joints surely never excelled by any Oriental. Warne looked pained again when Flintoff smashed another six over wide long-on. Then KP hit a ringing square-cut off Gillespie, followed by a vigorous pull. In nine overs their 50 stand arrived.

Brett Lee was brought back and a Flintoff hook fell only just short of Kasprowicz. Unaffected, Flintoff took a third six with a half-hook, and sought further thrills with a sharp single which just beat Langer's throw from cover. Now came his fourth six, an off-drive off Warne, followed by a checked drive that might otherwise have carried to the cover fieldsman. Lee moved some balls sharply, but there was little sign of caution from Flintoff. He must have read all the books on the buccaneering Botham's exploits in 1981 and taken inspiration.

Between Tests, the players of both sides had done their best to unwind and relax. Hayden and family had enjoyed the peace and beauty of the Cotswolds (the team stayed in Tewkesbury after a couple of days in London), Flintoff and family had gone down to Devon, Strauss freshened up in the Lake District after golf with Trescothick at The Belfry, Gilchrist and family had crossed over to France to visit EuroDisney. Australia's keeper-batsman must now have been wondering if Disneyland had come to Edgbaston: Brer Bear on the rampage, with the Seven Dwarfs as fieldsmen.

"Freddie's" fifty came in a minute under the hour, off 48 balls, with a punch through cover off Warne. Next over, off Lee, he registered his fifth six with a hook, then thick-edged a four. The sizzling century stand came in only 66 minutes off 97 balls, and Flintoff needed one more six to equal Botham's Ashes record of six in an innings. Warne went around the wicket, with a fine leg halfway, a backward square on the line, a forward short leg, midwicket and mid-on. Tea came with England 289 for four, Pietersen 40, Flintoff 68.

Third ball after tea relief came to Australia. Flintoff, without addition, was caught behind, giving Gillespie his 250th Test wicket in his 68th Test. It was mighty cheering for a man who had seemed so out of touch during the tour. Another new England record against Australia at Edgbaston had been set: 103 for the fifth wicket. In came Geraint Jones, a fashion prop with his three-quarter-length flared sleeves. Unluckily he got a rare kicker from Kasprowicz which he could only edge to the keeper.

Were the Australians through now? Ashley Giles saw to it that they weren't. Tucking his emotions away after the recent media-borne insults, the big chap, ungainly but effective, cut his second ball for four, edged another to raise the 300, and punched Gillespie and Kasprowicz for further fours. Pietersen, unusually patient, now indulged himself in an over from Lee, employing an amazing pull-drive to reach his fifty and taking two further fours off the over. Across the 835 Tests played by England (including this one; this was Australia's 358th) only Herbert Sutcliffe, Paul Gibb, Tony Greig and, oddly enough, two players in this match, Andrew Strauss and Ian Bell, had ever begun their careers with three half-centuries.

Warne was now close to apoplexy. Two leg-before shouts were turned down by umpire Billy Bowden, and the bowler's frustration was so great that his captain had to soothe him, aided by a few words from the umpire. In Warne's next over he struck Giles almost on the full as the tall man stretched forward to sweep, and Bowden granted the shrieked appeal. Giles's 23 had not only sustained England's growth but was the best score ever by a Warwickshire batsman here against Australia.

It was time now for Pietersen to move into overdrive. He coshed Lee for six over midwicket. Then, trying for a repeat, he holed out for 71, giving Lee a wicket at last: 1 for 96 in his 14th over.

Hoggart, an occasional *Times* columnist, took a neat three to midwicket off Warne, another *Times* columnist, and when Harmison swept him for two the bowler's 100 came up, thunderously cheered from both sides of the ground. Warne graciously doffed his sunhat. He was less responsive when the Barmy Army began chanting, "Where's yer missus gone?"

Harmison, once so useless with the bat, has worked on it, and now a ball from Lee went sailing into the crowd on the pull, the six followed by a four in this spectacular day of boundary hits. By the end, 54 fours and 10 sixes had been struck, and England's score was their highest in a day against Australia since 1938, when 210 of Wally Hammond's 240 runs, Eddie Paynter's 99, and 50 of Les Ames's 83 took them to 409 for five at Lord's (after Ernie McCormick had begun the day by slicing the top off the innings at 31 for three). Only a fortnight earlier, England had been 422 for four by the close of the opening day at Trent Bridge, with Charlie Barnett extending a 98 not out at lunch to 126, young Len Hutton making 100 on Ashes debut, and Paynter and 20-year-old Denis Compton (he was also on Ashes debut) well on the way to their eventual scores of 216 not out and 102. Nor was the bowling weak. The fiery McCormick played in this Test too, as did Fleetwood-Smith, a tricky left-arm spinner, and Bill O'Reilly, who, as is well documented, was regarded by Don Bradman as the finest bowler he ever saw. After this, of course, came Stan McCabe's epic

232, which was to save Australia's bacon even though they had to follow on.

So this performance by England in 2005, measured against history, was very special, and there can be no doubt that everybody present will from time to time bore others with their impressions of the day's play as long as they shall live. Inclined as I often am to yearn for a Time Capsule to take me back to certain cricket matches long gone, I could never derive more pleasure and absorption than this Edgbaston Test has offered.

Harmison sailed down the pitch and hit Warne back above his lengthy locks, but was then foxed by a slider which tapped his off stump. Oddly enough, two bowlers (Warne and Gillespie) had hundreds beside their names, something enjoyed by no batsman midst this profusion of runs. Simon Jones even hammered a six over extra cover off Gillespie. Warne had Hoggard lbw sweeping, and it was all over for 407 just before half-past-five. Australia's openers came out – to disgraceful boos from a section of the crowd – but the light had deteriorated, and this brought a tidy end to the day's play.

Among the flood of facts and figures at the start of the day was the assertion that in the past 13 Edgbaston Tests only one had been won by the team which batted first, even though the last two Tests had seen 500 on the board. This – if he had seen it – was a crumb of comfort for Captain Ponting.

Michael Kasprowicz, the first of several players to speak to the media that evening, said it had been a pretty amazing day. "I turned up not expecting to play!" Yes, there had been some fantastic stroke play; but there's plenty of belief in this Australian side.

The double act of Flintoff and Pietersen began with "Freddie's" expression of relief: "I hadn't been keeping my side of the bargain," he said in reference to their springtime promise to cause mayhem together.

Then Glenn McGrath entered, on crutches, by his side Errol Alcott, who has seen so much injury and heartache in his long term as Australian cricket's medico and players' comfort bunny. The bowler said he reckoned he was out of the match even before he hit the ground. "Someone get Hooter!" he had bellowed. (Alcott's nickname came from his early days with the team when he pretended to be so ignorant of cricket that he asked when – as in Australian Rules Football – the full-time hooter/siren would sound.) "I know Glenn's got resilience," said Hooter. "He's good to work with." It might be two matches, maybe longer. "I just know I'm ruled out of this match!" murmured McGrath, grinning bravely.

※※※

SECOND DAY. Friday, August 5, 2005

The loud playing of *Jerusalem*, England's anthem, backed by a huge roar as the team took the field, might have proved just a tiny bit intimidating for the world's greatest opening pair, Justin Langer and Matthew Hayden, as they walked to the middle on a dull morning. The nocturnal rain had ceased, but the air of anticipation was actually quite oppressive.

Some of the big names had expressed disappointment that England had been bowled out the day before. They – including, not surprisingly, Geoff Boycott – felt that a measure of caution might have seen England making 500. The innocent spectator who believed he had witnessed as entertaining a day's play as you could ever reasonably expect must have been puzzled by this solemn yet pragmatic interpretation.

At Lord's, Harmison's second ball had struck Langer on the elbow. Here, his third ball clanged his helmet, leaving the batsman dazed. Distasteful cheers went up, the kind more usually associated with football crowds.

From the pavilion end, Hoggard rolled in. His first ball was a half-volley, Hayden drove lazily and gave a head-high catch to short cover. It was the first golden duck in his 120 Test innings, his first duck of any kind since May 2002, and reward for England for the unconventional field placement.

The next ball nearly did for Ponting, but there was just enough air between willow and ball to spare him. He tapped a single and won four overthrows. Such is life. The runs were soon stacking up: Ponting pulled Harmison sweetly for four; the fifty was posted in the ninth over. While Langer played doggo, his skipper was ever ready to let go with that classy straight-drive. When the timing is right, that frontwards sway of the right hip comes after the ball has been struck. Giles came on. He has never really bothered Ponting. The batsman swept. The ball bounced a bit. Leg gully held the gentle catch: 88 for two.

Martyn had happy memories of Edgbaston with that Ashes debut century four years ago. He made 20 now in his unfussy way, and the luncheon interval was about to be taken when he strolled a single, accelerating as he saw Vaughan move to swoop on the ball wide of mid-on. The England captain is nowhere near the best fieldsman in this side, but he now did something worthy of the immortal Colin Bland: he picked up cleanly, twisted more than 180 degrees and broke the wicket with a dead-eye throw on the turn. Australia 118 for three at lunch (Langer 27), and slightly contrite.

With Langer simply determined never to get out, Clarke brought his stylish batting to bear on the second session. A pull off Harmison and an extra-cover drive off Hoggard were beautiful things, a slash off Giles over the slip fielder less so. Langer chiselled out another fifty (94 balls, 173 minutes), and when drinks were taken, Australia could feel that 178 for three might yet be turned into something comparable to their opponents' 407.

But after Langer had almost played the ball into his stumps, his partner had no answer to a slightly faster ball from Giles. Clarke played neither forward nor back and Geraint Jones accepted a good catch off a thickish edge. The young Australian's 40 had spanned just on an hour and a half and his disappointment at not going further was plain to see.

While the sun shone, the Barmy Army groups went from chant to chant, slinging in the provocative *God Save* Your *Queen* as a change from *You All Live in a Convict Colony* (to the tune of *Yellow Submarine*), interspersed with the ditty specially devised for Australia's captain by a certain Bernie Silvester:

Ponting's special friend
Is a man called Glenn McGrath
You'll see them holding hands
At the Sydney Mardi Gras

Giles had a man out on the boundary square on the off side. I wondered what old Wilfred Rhodes, the master slow left-armer, would have thought about that. He believed that a slow bowler should never be cut. But Giles's strategy comes with the modern fast-scoring game and ensures he will not be milked expensively in that sector. That helps secure his peace of mind. He now actually spun one hard and the ball turned and shot past both Langer and keeper Jones for four byes. And soon he found the edge of Katich's bat and the wicketkeeper's cheer was restored. Katich had made only 4, and Australia, while having avoided the follow-on, were half out for 208. Danger man Gilchrist came in for his 100th Test innings.

His second ball went burning through the covers for four, and after Langer had edged a rare boundary the pair paid a lot of attention to tapping small blemishes on the pitch. After tea (219 for five) Langer met the challenge of Flintoff's first-ball bouncer with a hook for four, after which Geraint Jones had a ragged over to Giles's bowling. There was a near-stumping of Langer and then four byes. Gilchrist, meanwhile, was batting on off stump when Flintoff went around the wicket, and he hit him through mid-on. It was time for Simon Jones, master of reverse swing, to come back.

The Welshman had been generating as much attention off the field as on. Having posed naked for *Cosmopolitan* magazine in the interests of a prostate and testicular cancer charity, and endured a romantic upheaval scripted by a tabloid newspaper, he had been reported in another as having been seen drinking and smoking at midnight after a Lord's Taverners game on the weekend between these two Test matches. The spirits of Denis Compton and Keith Miller probably hovered over him.

Today, although he had a concern when umpire Koertzen issued an official warning for running down the pitch, he earned his money with two wickets, the first of them the anchorman Langer. Jones fired in a yorker, the batsman fell into his stroke, and he was leg-before for 82 after well over four hours of vigilance. He freely admitted that evening that he had "hardly enhanced my reputation as an elegant stroke player", but batting out there was hard work. Australia, he said, were looking for a challenge, and this was a challenge. He expected Shane Warne to play a "huge role" in the next England innings.

Australia, four wickets left, were still 146 behind. Warne came in, to boorish booing.

He charged at Giles, then hit him through the covers. Jones then beat him with three consecutive balls before being cover-driven to the rope. Warne was on a mission and it wasn't defensive. Down the pitch he went again, but Giles slipped the ball past his flailing bat and hit the stumps, making the batsman look rather silly. Had he hoped to save his side with a swift fifty? That was more Gilchrist's style. Others needed to stay with the world's most destructive batsman if the deficit was to be dealt with.

Lee stayed only a short time before another lovely fast outswinger from Jones found the edge and went waist-high to Flintoff at second slip. Gillespie risked being timed out, but finally made it to the middle, to hang on with Gilchrist for nearly half an hour before Flintoff trapped him in front. The mighty Lancastrian did the same to Kasprowicz next ball, leaving Gilchrist stranded on 49, and Australia, 308 all out, 99 behind on first innings. It was the first time in 22 Tests that they had trailed England, another reminder of Australia's long-term superiority. England now had about half an hour to bat.

Like a left-handed Colin Cowdrey – rounded of shape if without quite having his smooth touch – Trescothick stroked Lee's first ball through the covers, repeated the shot and pulled him in his next over, and cut Kasprowicz for another four when he replaced Gillespie for the sixth over. The positive play of the first innings was to be repeated.

The ball was tossed to Warne. There was the usual dramatic

delay. Then he shuffled in to spin one at Strauss, just as he had that first time in Ashes Tests against Gatting at Old Trafford 12 years ago. Warne is the sole survivor from that match still playing Test cricket. This ball, while not having quite the aerodynamics of the Gatting ball, pitched wide and turned almost a metre. Left-hander Strauss thrust his front leg across, bat raised high. The ball spun *across* him, *in front* of him, and clicked his leg stump.

Suddenly the perspective of the match altered. England might be 124 ahead, but if The Magician could go on bowling these near-unplayables tomorrow, the world champions could end up chasing only 200 or so, and knocking them off for the loss of only a wicket or two. One ball had spoiled English cricket-lovers' day, and possibly their night's sleep as well.

THIRD DAY. Saturday, August 6, 2005

If there was a sleepless night for anyone, it was soon justified. Brett Lee brought Australia right back into contention with three quick wickets. Under a sky now overcast once more, the blond smiler from Wollongong benefited from one of Trescothick's endemic waves of the bat. Vaughan (1) was then mortified to hear his wicket smashed yet again after he played half-forward then back. His off stump was unplugged, the third time in four innings in this series that he had been bowled for 4 or less. This was now England's greatest anxiety.

Hearts were in mouths when nightwatchman Hoggard (1) then steered Lee low into Hayden's large hands at gully. And when Pietersen survived a roar of appeal for a catch as he tried to glance his first ball off his ribs, the excitement meter was rocking on its fixings.

Pietersen's response was to land Warne over the line at mid-wicket, putting another delivery in the same over onto the terraces. When Warne bowled a glorious curver that dipped and spun away, Bell played it down to slip with soft wristwork. Here was an enormous opportunity for the local chap to show his worth. At last he reached double figures with a four nudged off Lee, followed by a pull for three, then four to midwicket when Warne overpitched. Then came a flukish dismissal.

Warne bowled, Pietersen (20) swept, edged up onto his body, from where it rebounded again and then fell earthwards. The ever-alert Adam Gilchrist suddenly caught sight of the darting ball and thrust out his left glove to hold it. When Bell (21) played forward and edged in Warne's next over, Australia were screaming back into this match: England 75 for six, only 174 ahead. This was not the cleverest day for me to have left my blood-pressure tablet back at the hotel.

The Big Fella was in, Freddie Flintoff, star of both completed innings to date. Could he imprint his name once and for all on this vital match? He seldom has to wait long for his first boundary. Off Gillespie he tucked a ball effortlessly wide of long-on for four. There was a moment of fear for English fans when Flintoff cut vigorously at Warne and drew up in pain. His bat had gone through to strike his left shoulder, paralysing him for a time. There were some worried faces as he received attention. "I thought my arm was going to drop off or something," he said later. It was uncomfortable for half-an-hour afterwards.

Australia forwent a chance when Geraint Jones popped one back past Gillespie, who was shocked by it and failed to get his hands in position. It was not to be an expensive miss. At lunch, England were 95 for six, 194 ahead.

Warne, spinning briskly and applying all his wiles, presented no problems to Flintoff. But Jones was lost when a ball from Lee got up from a length and flew off the edge to second slip.

Flintoff was not going to nick and nudge England to a solid lead. He looked always for the boundary hit. Two came off Lee from the bat-edge, one wide of slips, one down the leg side. When Clarke dived flat by the third-man rope to save three runs, I scribbled "Brilliant! – what if it's a close finish?!"

Giles hung in grittily for three-quarters of an hour, helping another 30 runs onto the board before edging one which pitched perfectly from Warne, who was bowling around the wicket. Next ball, Harmison jabbed forward and was held by Ponting at silly point. Warne had his five-for and duly held the ball up in response to the applause. Now he was looking at a second hat-trick against England, 10 years after the first. There was a long, unnerving delay before Simon Jones was permitted to face up. Surprisingly, it was a wasted ball, wide and low.

Flintoff had reached 38 and looked like being stranded. There was only one thing for it, and Kasprowicz was the unlucky bowler. The field was spread out, but Freddie launched into it: a six over midwicket, then another two balls later, taking him to his fifty off 63 balls. When Jones got the strike he had a big swing and eluded Ponting's leap wide at slip. Twenty runs came from that over. Yes, what if it is a tight finish?

There was such tension. Jones reached forward, dabbed defensively at Warne, and as the crowd let its breath out, the batsmen met for a reassuring little punching of gloves. All nine fieldsmen were on the extremity of the sunlit field as Lee took over from Kasprowicz. Jones drove him for four. In his next over, straining to end the mockery, Lee pitched well up to Flintoff, who, like Botham against Craig McDermott 20 years before, drove the ball into the upper reaches of the pavilion. On this ground, the pavilion isn't so very far away. But this man was bowling around 90 mph. A slashed four to third man was followed by another hoist into the pavilion, Flintoff's 54th six in Tests, and Lee hardly knew where to look or what to say. When umpire Bowden refused an lbw shout against Jones which looked to be plumb, Lee kicked the ground in frustration at the end of another expensive over.

The fifty partnership came in a mere 34 minutes and yet again the balance had been tilted. As in that memorable Test at Sydney 50 years ago, tenth-wicket stands were to be a decisive factor. Then, last man Brian Statham had put on 43 with Johnny Wardle in England's first innings and 46 with Bob Appleyard in the second in a low-scoring contest eventually won by England by 38 runs. Apart from rain and lousy umpiring decisions, is there anything in cricket more irritating than a tenth-wicket resistance?

Andrew "Freddie" Flintoff, never happier than when hitting sixes, lofts one of his nine in the match into the pavilion off Brett Lee.

At 73 Flintoff's tour de force ended with a swipe at Warne from down the track, giving the Victorian his 10th wicket of the match for the third time against England and the 599th wicket of his Test career. Manchester, it seemed, would be the setting for the world's first 600th Test wicket. The cheers now, though, were mainly for Flintoff who had smashed nine of his side's 16 sixes in the match. It wasn't the largest ground in the world, certainly, but most of those hits would have been six on most other Test grounds.

As tea was gratefully sipped, the new set of figures to study were Australia's target – 282 – and the time available – 45 overs plus two full days. There was also the odds. Not often have so many runs been made to win a Test, and at Edgbaston, in its 40 previous Test matches, although there have been many high-scoring matches, no team has scored that many to win. It would be safe to say that England's dressing-room was currently a more placid place than Australia's.

Steve Harmison and Matthew Hoggard looked strangely unthreatening in their early overs, and Giles came on for the eighth over, soon followed by Flintoff from the pavilion end. The atmosphere changed instantly. Langer, having progressed without flurry to 28 alongside Hayden, played half-forward to the fast and furious Flintoff, only for the ball to crash into forearm thence stumps. Ponting survived a roared lbw appeal first ball, only to succumb to his fourth ball when Flintoff's outswing did the trick: 48 for two.

Soon Flintoff tried a yorker on Hayden who managed to clamp down on it. The bowler grinned. At the other end, however, Hayden (31) played away from his body at Jones, and Trescothick took off to his left at slip to grab a smart two-handed catch: 82 for three. The bowler was later fined a fifth of his £5000 match fee for showing Hayden which way to go for the pavilion.

Martyn had been picking up a boundary or two with his easy style, and when Harmison returned cover-drove him for four, with Clarke easing him past Hoggard at mid-on for another. With the hundred now up, Giles came back, and Martyn clipped him off the back foot for another pleasant four. The match was in the balance.

A loose shot by Martyn (28) returned the initiative to England. He drove almost straight to Bell at short midwicket: 107 for four, 175 still required.

Katich was soon away, playing his first ball through point for four and, a couple of balls later, late-cutting for another. The game continued to move fast. Giles, still not gaining or (presumably) seeking much turn, saw Clarke place him wide of mid-on then through the covers, and when Hoggard bowled to him the field was scattered. Flintoff was called back into the attack, always a move to attract attention.

But it was Giles who dealt Australia a double blow. Katich (16) edged to Trescothick, standing close at slip, the ball rebounding favourably off his arm. Gillespie, we later heard, was to go in ahead of Gilchrist, but he wasn't padded up in time. Such is fate. In his next over Giles persuaded Gilchrist (1) to step out and hit. He didn't

Simon Katich unfortunate to be caught on the rebound by Trescothick at slip after Giles found the edge of his bat.

middle it properly and a catch floated out to mid-on. Normally that man would have been back on the rope. It was a clever piece of cricket. Flintoff not only held the catch, he drop-kicked the ball into space. Australia's most dangerous player was gone for next to nothing and England could scarcely believe their luck.

When Flintoff won an lbw appeal against Gillespie (0) next over, Australia were in disarray at 137 for seven. Warne entered, to the usual booing, and we wondered if the extra half-hour (eight overs) was being claimed. The umpires conferred and England duly had their extension of play in order to finish Australia off. Warne's response was to sweep Giles twice for six.

Flintoff tried a yorker on Clarke, but it was repelled. Harmison came back at the City end with three overs remaining. Excitement bubbled. The bowler nearly ran Warne out in his follow-through. Then came four leg-byes. Flintoff again, and Warne flayed him through the covers. A couple of wild over-pitched balls and there were words between Clarke and Flintoff, umpire Bowden cooling it down.

With Clarke (especially) and Warne batting so confidently and Lee and Kasprowicz to come, Australia, needing 107 more, were not out of the reckoning yet. If these two survived, tomorrow could be sensational.

Then came not just a decisive blow, but as clever a piece of bowling as Harmison has ever mustered. With three balls remaining he let go a slower ball off the middle finger, and at a mere 65 mph it was well directed. Too late, Michael Clarke (30) saw what had happened. His bat failed to keep it out. It hit the off stump and England had as good as won. Or so they thought.

Thus ended a day which stretched over eight hours from start to finish and left everybody exhausted. The nation had stayed tuned as it had in 1981. Cricket was the biggest attraction. The footballers can sweat in the sun, but Birmingham, city of tornadoes, is where the greatest action is to be found.

Vital wicket for England on the third evening at Edgbaston: Michael Clarke deceived by Steve Harmison's slower ball.

FOURTH DAY. Sunday, August 7, 2005

Would it take two balls or two overs? The people rolled up (having paid a lot for their tickets), just as they did (free) at the MCG in December 1982, when, with only one Australian wicket intact, Allan Border and No.11 batsman Jeff Thomson, having added 37 the evening before, sought a further 37 for the most amazing victory in Test history. They made 33 of them before Thommo edged Ian Botham to Chris Tavare, who missed the catch but knocked the ball up, enabling Geoff Miller (an England selector 22 years later) to run behind him and secure it. England won by three runs, the joint-closest finish in an Ashes Test. I was watching the Test in Australia and just before that final ball, Channel 9's ill-timed and tedious commercial was spruiking for a brand of spanner. By the time they returned to the cricket the fatal ball had done its work, and all you could see was a close-up of Botham's crazed features as he sprinted from the field. It was some time before they replayed that ball, and I vowed that if the car broke down on the way back to Sydney from Queensland, I would certainly not seek to buy one of those wretched spanners. I'd rather use my teeth.

In 1902, at Old Trafford, Jack Saunders, the Australian left-armer with a suspicious action, bowled England's last man, Fred Tate, when four were needed. England won the next Test, at The Oval, by one wicket.

But exciting conclusions are not the strict preserve of the old days.

The narrowest possible result – outside Test cricket's two ties – came at Adelaide in January 1993, when Craig McDermott either did or did not get a touch to a short ball from Courtney Walsh as he turned away from it, with Australia one run short of levelling the scores. The image of Border, up in the players' gallery, hurling the ball to the floor in anguish, remains vivid. This was Justin Langer's maiden Test match. He was hit on the head – of course – and scored a valiant half-century – of course.

❋ ❋ ❋

None of these precedents was being widely contemplated at the ingenuous opening of this unforgettable day. England were surely destined to win by either 100 or so runs, or maybe 50. The ball that mattered had been Harmison's the evening before. Had he survived, Michael Clarke might have got most of these runs off his own bat. The series was surely about to be levelled just when it mattered.

The most runs ever acquired by the ninth and 10th wickets combined to win an Ashes Test is 73. That was also at Melbourne. In January 1908, needing exactly the same total as Australia now did – 282 – England were 243 when last man Arthur Fielder joined Sydney Barnes at the wickets. Wicketkeeper Joe Humphries had contributed 16 to a ninth-wicket stand of 34. Now 39 were still needed. By steady, correct batting Barnes and Fielder did the job. Only at the end was there any sense of panic. With the scores level, 19-year-old Gerry Hazlitt threw wildly from short cover when a simple return would have brought Test cricket's first tie. Soon to become a teacher at King's School, Parramatta, Hazlitt died seven years later from heart failure. It is not thought that this pulsating Test finish affected his health. He had a congenital heart condition.

In that Test match the legendary Jack Hobbs made his debut. Of the frantic finish, the England manager, Major Philip Trevor, later wrote: "The English victory was very generously received, and by none more generously than by the beaten eleven." No doubt the Australian skipper, M.A.Noble, would have seen to it that, after the climax, his men did the sporting thing midst so much shattering disappointment. One thing probably helped soften the blow. The previous Test, another thriller at Sydney, had been won by Australia by two wickets, Tibby Cotter and none other than Hazlitt having made a hectic 56 together for the ninth wicket to clinch the match. A golden age indeed, just about fit to rank with this early 21st Century golden age of our own.

❊ ❊ ❊

With the reader's indulgence, the final session of this second Test of the 2005 series is best recorded through a change of tense and in a kind of shorthand which reflects the nerve-shredding nature of this memorable morning. My handwritten notes are not easy to read.

It's sunny, thank goodness. Brett Lee takes Clarke's place. Harmison finishes his overnight over and Lee takes a two off the first ball. Flintoff no-balled three times in an over. Poor show. Warne, Bradman-style, steps to leg to cut Harmison. Successful at second attempt. Four runs. Then steps across stumps and gets runs to square leg. Clever. Lee is lucky as ball flies from bat shoulder over gully for a single. Two to square leg by Warne, and a massive 88 are still needed.

Lee turns Harmison through midwicket for four. These batsmen have no hang-ups, nothing to lose. Same cannot be said of the bowlers. Warne back-cuts Flintoff for four, Australia now past 200. Assumption of an England victory develops faint wobble. Warne across his stumps again, Harmison sees him, nearly decapitates him: blind fend gets him four more runs over the slips. Single to cover next ball. Lee off-drives a sweet four. Runs flowing. English smiles a little forced.

Ball simply not moving sideways. Flintoff surely the man? Warne pulls him for a single, Lee off-drives for three. Ball crashes into Warne's pad and he limps a leg-bye – disallowed by Bowden: no stroke. After 35 minutes Giles replaces Harmison at 220 for eight. Maiden to Lee, though the last ball lobs towards mid-on from a front edge.

Flintoff to Warne: he's bowled! No he's not. The stumps are in disarray, but the ball squeaked *past* the leg stump. Replays then show that the batsman, performing a little jig as he moved to the off, side-kicked the off stump with his right shoe. Warne's out. Nine down, last man 42, an astronomical 62 still needed by Australia for the greatest win of all time.

Michael Kasprowicz is not a mug with the bat. Single first ball. Lee shaken by blow to the arm from the very fast Flintoff. No-ball placed to third-man boundary as English heads shake with frustration. Breakthrough! Lee caught by Geraint Jones. No. It was off his thigh. Giles beats Kasprowicz, who's then very nearly lbw to Flintoff: leg-bye. Lee brazenly cuts over slips. Pietersen's throw flies over the keeper for an extra run.

Lee cuts for another precious single. Vaughan places himself at leg gully. According to plan, Kasprowicz glances, but the ball flies squarer, all the way to the rope. Flintoff tries fast yorker. Kasprowicz digs it out like a prize potato. Lee takes four through mid-on off Giles and the requirement shrinks to 42. A single, then Kasprowicz lofts and edges fours: 13 off the over; 29 added in a crazy quarter of an hour; suddenly it's only 33 to win.

I reflect on a conversation I had last summer with a Polish pilot who flew in the Battle of Britain. Unusually for me, I switched the subject to cricket: "Actually, Ludwik, there's an Australian cricketer with a Polish name – *Kas*-prowicz." "Ah," he said, "You mean Kas-*PRO*-wicz!" And that's how I've thought of him ever since.

KasPROwicz keeps his end up. Flintoff again: single to Lee to raise 250, Kasper two to long leg. Drinks bring to an end a riveting 63 minutes of play in which 77 runs have been made and only Warne has gone – by his own hand, so to speak. Two nations are spellbound. Most at home in Britain and in early night-time Australia will be pouring stiff drinks.

On it goes. Giles back, Lee untroubled singles either side of Kasprowicz's sweep for one. Harmison back. This is surely it. Lee another single, Kasper a two airborne through square leg. A nervous full-toss zooms down leg side for four byes. England seem to be cracking. Twenty to win.

Flintoff for Giles. Short one hurts Lee's left hand. Hold-up. Lucky it didn't spoon to gully or, worse still, break a bone. Errol Alcott runs out, calm yet anxious at the end of this game as he had been just before the start. To lose McGrath and Lee would almost certainly be to lose the Ashes.

Couple of non-productive balls then single to fine leg: 19 needed. Lee inside-edges four off Harmison, then plays and misses. First one team then the other seems about to clinch it. Lee edges to gully: it doesn't carry. Then beaten again. At the other end, Flintoff bowls to Kasprowicz, who steers it in a high arc towards third man. Simon Jones sights it, moves in, sees it dropping on him, dives, and spills the catch. Will his name go into the book as The Man Who Lost a Test Match?

England are slipping: Flintoff's wild no-ball eludes wicketkeeper and speeds to the line for five priceless runs to Australia. Total of 40 extras in this innings is deplorable. Only nine runs needed now.

Lee is so impressive. Strong off-drive could have gone for four, but its direction is not quite right. It's fielded. He then manages a single, as does Kasprowicz. Seven wanted. Lee takes another single. One shot could be enough now. Kasprowicz beaten by Flintoff but survives.

Harmison again. Another single by Lee to mid-on. Leg-side ball fizzes through to Jones. Yorker dug out by Kasprowicz. So much Australian character on display. England's fieriest bowlers are found wanting. Flintoff bangs in another bouncer which Lee ducks. Two more follow, keeper Jones stretching elastically to take the last one and saving his country. Lee comes close to edging, then scrambles a run off the last ball, dropping his bat as he races off. Four silly little runs now for victory.

Harmison nearly gives it to Australia. He flings down a ripe full-toss outside off and Lee pounds it to the far reaches. Five metres to the right and victory was Australia's. Instead, the fielder on the boundary takes swift delivery and returns the ball instantly to the keeper.

Exposed again, Kasprowicz plays defensively at the second ball. Everybody playing, watching, televiewing, or, worse still, listening to radio, with the imagination running riot, is in a cold sweat. Harmison bounds in again and sends down a pig of a delivery. The batsman is helpless. He falls towards the off, trying to parry the rising ball, and a split-second later Geraint Jones plunges forward to take the catch.

England have won by two runs, the narrowest margin ever in an Ashes Test match. Pandemonium. Even the unflappable Michael

Vaughan forgets himself now, running around madly with eyes to the Heavens and arms open wide. There is hugging and screaming and thunderous applause as thousands of human lungs release. Geraint Jones, having thrust the ball in the direction of the Australian fans who had been taunting him, is persuaded to give it to umpire Bowden. This seems wrong, and shortly afterwards it was returned to the player who loaned it for the summer to the museum at Edgbaston.

And in the midst of all this, Freddie Flintoff demonstrates the knightly courtesy of comforting words to the shattered Brett Lee, down on his haunches. Kasprowicz too pauses for a while, before going to shake the hands of his opponents. These very tender post-combat moments bring a sudden tear to my Anglo-Australian eyes.

Peerless climax. Three runs short of victory, Australia lose their last man, Michael Kasprowicz, taken down the leg side by Geraint Jones off Harmison.

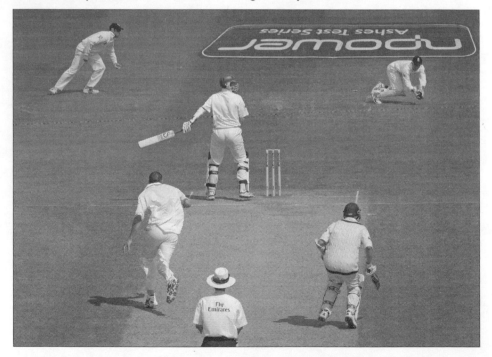

Within the minute it was discovered in the television replay room that there might have been a technical doubt about that last dismissal. The ultra-slow replay revealed that Kasprowicz's bottom hand seemed to have separated from the bat handle as the ball brushed the glove. The ball may also have touched the bat, but all this was uncertain. Strictly speaking, had that glove not been touching the bat at the moment of impact the batsman should not have been given out. But umpire Bowden simply had no way of knowing. Had total video scrutiny been in use, Australia would probably have won this Edgbaston Test.

Something similar occurred at Headingley in 1987 when Chris Broad was given out caught behind against Pakistan. The side-on view showed clearly that the glove which was struck by the ball had come away from the bat-handle as Broad jumped. That evening we impudently asked umpire David Shepherd (he is jovial enough to deal with such an enquiry) if he knew that the hand had to be in contact with the bat. "Of course I do," he said. He simply hadn't realised that the hand in this instance was not in contact.

In a related sense it was not dissimilar to that Lee caught-and-bowled at Lord's. Things so often look different under a microscope.

* * *

Cricket was on everyone's lips now. Countless new fans were being drawn to the game, just as in 1981, the Year of Botham. And somebody cleverly described this sensational Test match as "Testy/20" cricket.

There were a thousand quotes and utterances: Kasprowicz understandably nominated that last ball as the most "vivid" ever, one which he would replay in his mind as long as he lived. "It just got big quick and I didn't see too much of it." Lee generously said, "As much as we're hurting right now mentally and physically [he had indeed taken a pounding], it's good for cricket . . . We knew we had to take a few on the body. I'd do it, plus tax, again to make sure we give everything we can to make Australia win." Thus did Brett Lee express the spirit of Villers-Bretonneux.

Allan Border, shattered yet again, said he thought this was going to be the "payback" for that three-run defeat at Melbourne, Christmas 1982, while Matt Hayden, in his column, described the Australian dressing-room in those drastic last stages of the match: Gillespie and Katich marking off the runs five at a time, MacGill demanding silence, Gilchrist pretending to read a magazine, Ponting, Langer and Hayden simply sitting and wishing and willing runs to come.

Harmison admitted that out on the field there had been panic in the English ranks. Vaughan gave credit to Australia in this "epic" game and to Flintoff: England would go to Old Trafford now with momentum. Giles, who said he felt physically sick in the closing stages of the match, admitted that the England boys had stopped expecting and started praying when Australia needed fewer than 10 to steal victory. Flintoff, the npower Man of the Match, complimented Lee, who, he said, "bowled his arse out!" It was a great advert for Test cricket.

Too right it was. Perhaps those fools running around in the heat in football shirts during the cricket season would now kindly wait their turn, until winter comes.

Can England now, Flintoff was asked, go on to win the Ashes? "We've got to!" he said, with that disarming chuckle. Would this reversal have a psychological effect on the Aussies? "I'm not clever enough to get into psychology. We have won a Test match and we are happy. I don't know about them." Like his cricket, Fred's mental processes benefit from keeping it simple.

Edgbaston was again the scene of heartache for Australia: bowled out for 36 in 1902, undone by the dubious decision (Wayne Phillips given out caught via Allan Lamb's boot) which precipitated defeat in 1985; now this.

While the players of both sides shared a few drinks together in the dressing-rooms, the scores and narrative of the most exciting Test match of all 308 played so far between England and Australia were entered with shaking hand upon the holy tablet of Ashes history.

SECOND TEST MATCH
Edgbaston, August 4, 5, 6, 7, 2005

ENGLAND		mins	balls	4s		mins	balls	4s
M.E.Trescothick	c Gilchrist b Kasprowicz	90	143	102 15#	c Gilchrist b Lee	21	51	38 4
A.J.Strauss	b Warne	48	113	76 10	b Warne	6	28	12 1
*M.P.Vaughan	c Lee b Gillespie	24	54	41 3	[4] b Lee	1	2	2 –
I.R.Bell	c Gilchrist b Kasprowicz	6	2	3 1	[5] c Gilchrist b Warne	21	69	43 2
K.P.Pietersen	c Katich b Lee	71	132	76 10x	[6] c Gilchrist b Warne	20	50	35 –#
A.Flintoff	c Gilchrist b Gillespie	68	74	62 6+	[7] b Warne	73	133	86 6z
#G.O.Jones	c Gilchrist b Kasprowicz	1	14	15 –	[8] c Ponting b Lee	9	33	19 1
A.F.Giles	lbw b Warne	23	34	30 4	[9] c Hayden b Warne	8	44	36 –
M.J.Hoggard	lbw b Warne	16	62	49 2	[3] c Hayden b Lee	1	35	27 –
S.J.Harmison	b Warne	17	16	11 2x	c Ponting b Warne	0	2	1 –
S.P.Jones	not out	19	39	24 1x	not out	12	42	23 3
Extras	lb 9, w 1, nb 14	24			lb 1, nb 9	10		
Total	(79.2 overs, 356 mins)	407			(52.1 overs, 249 mins)	182		

plus 2 sixes   x plus 1 six   + plus 5 sixes   z plus 4 sixes

Fall: 1/112 2/164 3/170 4/187 5/290   1/25 2/27 3/29 4/31 5/72
6/293 7/342 8/348 9/375   6/75 7/101 8/131 9/131

BOWLING: Lee 17-1-111-1 (3nb, 1w), Gillespie 22-3-91-2 (3nb), Kasprowicz 15-3-80-3 (8nb), Warne 25.2-4-116-4
SECOND INNINGS: Lee 18-1-82-4 (5nb), Gillespie 8-0-24-0 (1nb), Kasprowicz 3-0-29-0 (3nb), Warne 23.1-7-46-6

AUSTRALIA		mins	balls	4s		mins	balls	4s
J.L.Langer	lbw b S.P.Jones	82	276	154 7	b Flintoff	28	54	47 4
M.L.Hayden	c Strauss b Hoggard	0	5	1 –	c Trescothick b S.P.Jones	31	106	64 4
*R.T.Ponting	c Vaughan b Giles	61	87	76 12a	c G.O.Jones b Flintoff	0	4	5 –
D.R.Martyn	run out (Vaughan)	20	23	18 4	c Bell b Hoggard	28	64	36 5
M.J.Clarke	c G.O.Jones b Giles	40	85	68 7	b Harmison	30	101	57 4
S.M.Katich	c G.O.Jones b Flintoff	4	22	18 1	c Trescothick b Giles	16	27	21 3
#A.C.Gilchrist	not out	49	120	69 4	c Flintoff b Giles	1	8	4 –
S.K.Warne	b Giles	8	14	14 2	[9] hit wkt b Flintoff	42	79	59 4#
B.Lee	c Flintoff b S.P.Jones	6	14	10 1	[10] not out	43	99	75 5
J.N.Gillespie	lbw b Flintoff	7	36	37 1	[8] lbw b Flintoff	0	4	2 –
M.S.Kasprowicz	lbw b Flintoff	0	1	1 –	c G.O.Jones b Harmison	20	60	31 3
Extras	b 13, lb 7, w 1, nb 10	31			b 13, lb 8, w 1, nb 18	40		
Total	(76 overs, 346 mins)	308			(64.3 overs, 307 mins)	279		

a plus 1 five   # plus 2 sixes

Fall: 1/0 2/88 3/118 4/194 5/208   1/47 2/48 3/82 4/107 5/134
6/262 7/273 8/282 9/308   6/136 7/137 8/175 9/220

BOWLING: Harmison 11-1-48-0 (2nb), Hoggard 8-0-41-1 (4nb), S.P.Jones 16-2-69-2 (1nb, 1w),
Flintoff 15-1-52-3 (3nb), Giles 26-2-78-3
SECOND INNINGS: Harmison 17.3-3-62-2 (1nb, 1w), Hoggard 5-0-26-1, Giles 15-3-68-2, Flintoff 22-3-79-4 (13nb),
S.P.Jones 5-1-23-1

Toss won by Australia   Umpires: B.F.Bowden (NZ) & R.E.Koertzen (SAf)
Test debut: none   Replay umpire: J.W.Lloyds (Eng)
Match award: A.Flintoff   Match referee: R.S.Madugalle (SL)

ENGLAND WON BY 2 RUNS

6

Third Test

Tucked in among the heaps of words inspired by the Edgbaston cliffhanger was a column by a media doctor who plausibly claimed that when a match boils up into such a frenetic climax, spectators can be in greater peril than the players. "If any biochemist in the crowd had been able to collect the blood of the players," wrote Dr Thomas Stuttaford in *The Times*, "an analysis would have shown that the cricketers' adrenal glands had deluged their brains and other organs with noradrenalin, their cortisol levels would have been monstrously raised and there would have been enough testosterone circulating to enable each of them to rival Don Juan." Or Shane Warne, perhaps?

The cricketers are accustomed to these strains, wrote the good doctor. Their hearts and arteries are young and elastic and they are trained to withstand these biochemical changes. Conversely, spectators have no immediate means of relief from the excitement. "Instead, their hearts and blood vessels, often still and inelastic, have to take the strain. Sometimes the blood pressure rises so quickly that a plaque of fat is dislodged or ruptures and the television viewer has a heart attack."

Enough to turn anybody off watching the remainder of this 2005 Ashes series.

For a time it seemed that Brett Lee might be reduced to the status of spectator for the third Test. He spent two nights in a Birmingham hospital enjoying the attention of the nurses, it was said, while anxiously eyeing his swollen left knee. The problem stemmed from a graze sustained while fielding in the Lord's Test, and "Bing" was now on an intravenous drip. With Jason Gillespie nursing a slight knee injury the Australian camp set about protecting its options. Mick Lewis, currently playing for Durham, and Shane Harwood (St Annes in the Northern League) were called in as net bowlers and Stuart Clark, the tall New South Wales fast bowler (playing for Middlesex) and Shane Watson (Hampshire) were on standby.

And out of this bleak scene emerged a startling picture: not only was Lee cleared to play, but Glenn McGrath had been sighted at the nets bowling without any apparent discomfort. Clad in a plaster boot until four days before the next Test, and tended almost around the clock by Errol Alcott, McGrath was about to "do a Steve Waugh (The Oval, 2001)" and return to the battle days if not weeks before he had been expected to be fit again. For his part, John Bull might now have been whispering into the Kangaroo's ear: "We wouldn't be happy, you know, about beating an Australian team that was depleted."

FIRST DAY. Thursday, August 11, 2005

"He was such a brave little kid," said Michael Vaughan, "and I thought to myself, what on earth have I got to be worried about?" He was referring to the tiny six-year-old England team mascot who went to the middle with the captain for the ceremony of the toss. Connor Shaw had had three heart transplants and the skipper was right. Against the background of life's harsh realities we sometimes get too intense about sport. Notwithstanding, we were about to get very, very intense again.

Without question it was Vaughan's day. He not only won an important toss – the pitch was "rock solid" said the groundsman – but he also at last got among the runs. England, most unusually, were fielding the same XI for the third time. Australia reverted to their Lord's XI (McGrath back for Kasprowicz; Stuart MacGill rather surprisingly not coming in for Gillespie), and "Punter" Ponting's failed call of "heads" denied McGrath an extra day or two of further recovery.

It was sunny, with light cloud cover over Manchester, as England quickly demonstrated that luck seemed to be with them now. Trescothick, facing McGrath from the Stretford end, gloved the second ball of the match. It flew not to the keeper and not to the slips but high over the lot of them for four. It was not the first time the Somerset left-hander had had a close shave. Nor is it easy sometimes to determine whether he has been beaten or has just withdrawn his bat. He is a calm character.

The ball was bouncing steeply, and Lee, from the Brian Statham end (previously known as the Warwick Road end), was whipping them down at over 90 mph. But more bad luck came Australia's way when Michael Clarke stiffened after fielding a ball and left the field with a damaged back muscle. Brad Hodge came on as substitute, to remain on the field for as long as Australia were bowling.

To Australia's bad luck was now added some bad cricket. Trescothick (13) edged McGrath, and Gilchrist went for it one-handed, just as Geraint Jones had done at Lord's in missing Gillespie. For all the high-quality cricket in this series, the art of wicketkeeping was being ill-served.

Andrew Strauss now came to grief against Lee. He was struck on the neck as he tried to hook. Two balls later he ducked another scary bouncer of blistering pace, before then being completely deceived by a slightly slower ball which sent his off stump clattering. It was a masterly piece of bowling, leaving England 26 for one, and bringing Lee his 150th Test wicket (40 Tests) after that long, frustrating "sabbatical".

Vaughan ("what on earth have I got to be worried about") surveyed the field and spotted two men out for the hook. He took a single to fine leg, and with his vice-captain he handled the bounce calmly while noting that there was little sideways movement. McGrath was manageable, and had the outfield not been so slow there would have been more than 93 runs on the board come lunch.

Vaughan played a wristy on-drive through the gap when Lee replaced McGrath at the Stretford end, and when Trescothick cover-drove him smoothly, he made the next jag back, the batsman responding with a reflex jerk off his ample waistline. Having ducked some bouncers, "Tres" threw his bat at Lee's wider, fuller delivery for four more runs.

Vaughan was clearly in the form that had lightened English gloom during the 2002-03 Ashes series, and Gillespie was the one to suffer most: a back-foot cover-drive, a cavalier square cut, and, to another ordinary ball, a powerful push to the cover boundary. We wondered why Ponting ignored Warne in this first session.

McGrath was made to look average. Trescothick's defensive push sent the ball to the straight boundary. A thick edge got him four more to third man. When McGrath went around the wicket, Trescothick pulled him for three. Soon another chance of a wicket came. Vaughan (41) edged McGrath, and Gilchrist snatched right-handed at full stretch when the ball would probably have finished in the hands of Warne as he leapt up from first slip. It didn't seem to matter after the next ball plucked Vaughan's off stump out of the ground. Then umpire Bucknor's extended right arm was spotted. It was a no-ball. Vaughan took three runs now to third man, and McGrath strode away, head shaking involuntarily.

Soon he was back in the hunt, slipping in a couple of clever slower balls which Vaughan chopped out. Another cut back sharply. England could take no liberties. The century partnership was posted, and at 1.50 pm Warne came on at last at the same (Warwick Road) end as in 1993 for that famous maiden Ashes delivery to Michael Gatting. Michael Vaughan played forward with studied caution.

The England captain showed once more his intrinsic class. He is a pedigree. A back cut off McGrath flew across the quickening outfield, and was followed by a four through the covers hit off the back foot on the up. Australia's options were narrow. Lee returned for McGrath (0 for 61 off 13) but his full-length attempts at reverse swing didn't compare with the stuff Simon Jones and Flintoff regularly serve up. The Ashes looked like being decided by the bowlers: Australia are using four, of whom one is not firing; England have five, all of whom have been doing their bit.

After drinks (151 for one after 38 overs, Trescothick 58, Vaughan 69) Lee let rip with a ball measured at 96 mph. It was still not fast enough. His menu listed only two choices: yorkers or bouncers. Something further was needed for any three-card trick.

A new England second-wicket record against Australia on this ground came when the 124 by Bill Edrich and Cyril Washbrook against Bradman's 1948 side was surpassed, and then England's overall second-wicket record here was erased, the 134 by Arthur Fagg and (mostly) Wally Hammond against India in 1936.

Shane Warne remained Australia's best bet, and sure enough, after Vaughan had steered him off the back foot through the covers, only to be beaten by a beauty next ball, it was Trescothick (McGrath's 500th victim at Lord's) who became "Hollywood's" 600th Test wicket. It came not from any prestidigitation. The batsman merely swept at a leg-break (off-break to him) which was not pitched quite far enough up, touched the ball in his follow-through, and saw it run up Gilchrist's chest before the keeper bagged the catch.

Warne, playing in his 126th Test match, had gone where no bowler would ever go, according to old thinking. Where might it end? What was any single Test wicket worth when a man can acquire 600 of them? How startled everybody was in 1964 when Fred Trueman, at The Oval, became the first to take 300. Nobody, surely, could ever have imagined that somebody (as yet unborn) would one day double that bag, in the process reviving the near-dead revered art of leg-spin, and apparently still with the power and appetite to go on adding. Warne's first 200 wickets had come from 42 Tests, the next from 50, and this last 200 from a mere 34.

It was a moment of deep emotion for him. He held the ball aloft then kissed the white bracelet he wore, a gift from his eight-year-old daughter Brooke when they recently parted. Soon the ball would be going to Lord's, on loan to the MCC Museum, and Lancashire CCC would present him with a commemorative silver salver. The

Shane Warne's 600th Test wicket: Trescothick caught by Adam Gilchrist on the opening day at Old Trafford.

cricketer will surely treasure this, and can doubtless be trusted to disown tennis player Andre Agassi's recent quip when asked wherever else could such a beautiful watch be found as the one just presented to him: "Tomorrow – on eBay!"

As Warne spun one to Bell that kicked shoulder-high, Gilchrist's constant encouragement in his Donald Duck voice was becoming tiresome, as it was probably intended to. No less wearying was the unending Barmy Army chant on the terraces.

The run rate almost froze for some time, though Bell remained serene and studious against Warne. He profited from a Katich full-toss before enjoying a let-off from that bowler when 10. The return catch squeezed out of his outstretched left hand. At tea England were comfortable at 195 for two, Vaughan 93, freckle-faced Bell 14.

Vaughan went to 99 from a Warne full-toss dispatched to mid-wicket, but there was high risk in playing at anything pitching outside leg, so he padded away, again and again. The chance came off McGrath: a three to midwicket brought Vaughan his fourth century in eight Tests against Australia, his 15th overall. He had been in for just over 200 minutes. Ten of his fours had come through the off side. At last he was out of the series trough. Few had expected the first century by either side to have been so long in coming.

A third Australian blunder followed. Bell popped a ball back high to McGrath's right, and the bowler grassed it. His next ball was lobbed just short of mid-off. At the other end it was stalemate as Warne, around the wicket, pitched into the fresh rough. The breeze was fairly stiff. The sun shone. This was England v Australia, one-all and everything to fight for, the ultimate that cricket has to offer.

Poor Gillespie had another try. The shorter run and the loss of zip inconceivably have transformed him into a run-provider. Vaughan

England captain Michael Vaughan strokes more runs during his classic century in the third Test.

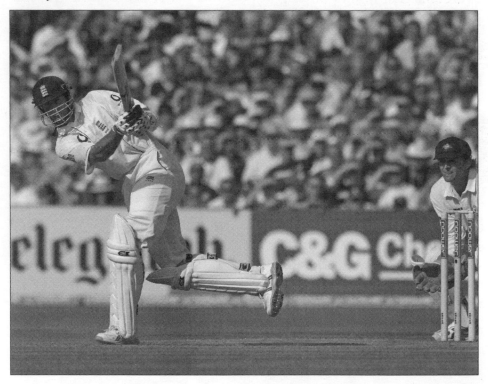

pulled him for six then placed him to the third-man rope. In his next over the captain punched him through mid-off and turned him through square leg. Bell meanwhile had been as watchful as a cat against Warne. He had practised against that "Merlyn" machine, but now the "machine" glared at him, growled at him, and sent down the occasional ball foreign to "Merlyn". Bell handled the straight-on slider well.

England's 250 came just before the drinks break, Bell getting a lucky four from an inside-edge off Gillespie. Then came more trauma for Australia.

On 141, Vaughan cut Warne fast to Hayden at slip, thigh-high, and the chance was lost. The batsman celebrated at Gillespie's expense. A straight-drive was classical, beautiful, and it was followed by a clip through mid-on to reach 150, then a pull to the boundary.

If Vaughan has a weakness – now that he seems to have overcome that hesitation to play forward – it is his running. Katich just missed with a throw from gully which would have had him. When Katich bowled, Vaughan clipped him over mid-on, feathered a back-cut, and swept him in a miniature masterclass. Partner Bell, on 29, might have fallen to a Hayden catch off Warne's bowling had the slips fielder not been back on his heels.

The 300 lay ahead, with England's sights on a fairly enormous first innings, when Vaughan's concentration slipped. Anti-climax: he banged a Katich full-toss to deep mid-on. The stand was worth 127. It was not a great sight for the Australians to see Kevin Pietersen coming in to join Bell.

The new batsman immediately tried to impose himself, taking risks. The sixth fifty of the innings was the fastest yet (55 balls), and with survival from mis-hits now habitual, Pietersen took on his mate Warne again with slashes and hoicks to leg, while Bell front-edged. Warne issued a stern warning to Pietersen about backing up. KP was learning with every hour of his nascent Test career.

Bell came into his own as the shadows lengthened, a measured straight-drive off Warne and four through the covers off a Katich full-toss taking him to 49. His patient fifty came from his 135th ball, and was rewarded by a keen hug from his partner.

Australia took the new ball 13 minutes before the scheduled close, and it accounted for Pietersen (21), who launched into a cavalier pull which substitute Brad Hodge held near the rope. Hoggard came in as nightwatchman ahead of Flintoff, jabbed a four through Langer at gully, and survived a Lee bouncer before losing his off stump to the final ball. Two late wickets heartened Australia appreciably. Bell had made an important 59 not out, and Lee – where would Australia be without him? – had taken 3 for 58 off his 19 overs.

England 341 for five: not a happy day for Australia. Symbolically, television news showed snow over southern Australia. There had even been a light fall on the Macpherson Range in south-east Queensland.

Among the evening utterances, Vaughan described how he had gone out to "play on instinct", with every intention of enjoying himself (since when were players meant to *enjoy* Test matches?), and he said he was "deli'ed for Ian Bell".

Miracle man McGrath felt he might have had too long a spell to start with, and was feeling the ankle a bit. Warne was, of course, exultant at his 600th Test wicket, but restrained enough to state that "I don't like using cliches". It would be encouraging if this was to be the players' new creed.

SECOND DAY. Friday, August 12, 2005

Circulating dark clouds continued to be a threat. This flourishing Ashes series needs to be spared damaging weather interruption.

Another key consideration, one remarked upon repeatedly, is the luck factor. In the first few minutes, McGrath bowled one through Bell, Lee did the same to Flintoff, and just when Australians must have been bewailing their bad luck, fortune swung their way. Bell, on his overnight 59, hooked at an off-side short ball from Lee and was given out caught. Umpire Bucknor, for some reason, looked across at his square-leg colleague before giving his verdict, a verdict with which the snickometer disagreed. It picked up no contact between bat and ball: 346 for six.

Lee greeted Geraint Jones with a red-hot bouncer. Then an edged four brought up 350. More boundaries came: a muscular cut by Flintoff off McGrath, a stretching back cut, abstinence from the hook. Jones steered Lee to the fertile expanse at third man. Rain began to fall as Warne measured his short run-up. Moisture threatened to inflict verdigris on his ear studs. They left the field for 20 minutes.

When play was resumed Brett Lee was concerned about the footholds. Jones drove a full-toss down the ground. The next was an overhead wide. The Briton with the mild Australian accent skipped out to Warne and lofted him for four, and the visitors were looking scrappy again: Martyn misfielded, and Lee's bowling was all over the place. Jones raised the 400 midst something of a run-flood. Flintoff and Jones have had some profitable partnerships in their short England association, three into three figures already.

Some of the baggy green caps look so faded they could have been pre-war issue. One, tilted nonchalantly on Langer's head, nudged a degree or two further as he slipped trying to stop a four. The ball, along with Australia's spirits, got wet in the gutter. A throw by Hayden from gully would have sent non-striker Jones packing just before lunch. Gillespie again looked harmless. Flintoff pulled him straight for four. England's strength grew. Then the twist.

On the fringe of a fifty in his 50th Test, Flintoff had a bash at Warne, got too far under it, and was caught at deep mid-on. It was the bowler's 150th England wicket, just over two-thirds of them having come in England. A run later, Jones got a touch to one which Gillespie managed to cut back at him and was bowled for 42. An even morning it became after all, with England 434 for eight.

Warne fixed up the tail, as leggies so often do. Giles fell to a conventional slips catch and Simon Jones's swipe simply missed one which turned in: 444 all out, and McGrath left to contemplate his worst-ever figures in Tests: 0 for 86.

Australia's sturdy openers were soon chalking up their 5000th run in tandem (average 53.77), a proud figure overshadowed by their current dearth of runs. It was 27 innings since Hayden had reached 70 in a Test. Nor was Vaughan sitting back and waiting for a mistake. His field placings were unconventional, fluid and brainy. Hayden knew they had done their homework and were after him, with Vaughan himself staring at him from halfway down the pitch on the off side. Sweepers were out to limit the cost of edges or big shots (mostly off Hoggard). But still the fifty came off 77 balls.

Simon Philip Jones replaced Hoggard at the Stretford end, Ashley Giles on at the other after Harmison and Flintoff had been tried. Success followed. Langer (31) moved forward and offered, and Giles's Warwickshire team-mate Bell shot out a hand to take a slick forward short-leg catch. Ponting came in, and at tea, with the brooding clouds still keeping their distance, Australia were 73 for one.

The third session was calamitous for them. First ball after the interval, Australia's captain pushed hard-handed at the shaven-headed Jones and spooned to gully. The Glamorgan bowler had subtly overtaken Harmison and Hoggard to become England's main weapon with Flintoff, reverse-swinging as well as the great Pakistani Waqar Younis ever did. Soon Jones was bowling an accidental beamer somewhere in Hayden's direction (they were said to be the best of pals after the tension of that incident in the one-day international at Edgbaston six weeks ago), and while the other Jones's wicketkeeping again lapsed into untidiness, Giles slipped in with a wicket.

Hayden (34) played back to him. The ball would have hit middle stump. But there was debate as to whether the point of contact was outside the line. Maybe it was, by a few millimetres. A great many worse decisions have been delivered. In came Katich to survive an appeal for caught behind first ball and to edge his second, from down the pitch, for four.

Flintoff replaced Jones after Martyn had taken 11 runs from shots to all parts, and just before the drinks break Katich somehow survived an lbw appeal against Giles. It mattered little. First ball afterwards Flintoff from around the wicket brought the ball in after several had cut away and removed his off stump, with Katich (17) holding the bat high, as if saving a baby from a pit-bull terrier. A quarter-hour later, with Trescothick directing proceedings in Vaughan's temporary absence, Australia's fifth wicket fell, the upshot of some fascinating geometry.

Giles, bowling over the wicket to Martyn (20), curved the ball slightly and pitched it on what we used to call the blind spot, from which it turned just enough to elude the careful forward defensive, striking the outside of the off stump. Fifteen millimetres' deviation either way would not have been good enough. It brought to mind Hedley Verity's story of how he sat on a river bank on the rest day (blissful memory) of a Sydney Test match, pondering hard on how to defeat Don Bradman on a wearing pitch in his final innings of the Bodyline series. From over the wicket, the Yorkshireman, having left a tempting gap in the field, aimed at a worn patch of only a foot by three inches (30cm by 7.5cm). It was like hitting the bullseye at a rifle range from 200 metres from a standing position and with ordinary sights. After two boundary shots The Don was bowled off that little patch for 71: precision stuff.

The alarm bells were ringing again for Australia, and Michael Clarke had hastily been summoned to the ground from the team hotel three miles away, the taxi nosing through peak-hour traffic. Meanwhile, Warne came in at No.7, oozing aggression. Only hasty reaction prevented a Flintoff bouncer from rearranging his facial features, and when something was muttered by the slipsmen the batsman walked over. It looked as though the comments were repeated in case he hadn't quite heard the first time.

It was in this over that English groans reached their highest pitch to date, for Gilchrist (12), thus-far-tamed danger man, was missed not once but twice. Bell flung himself to the right at gully and put down a two-handed catch, and a push to cover found Pietersen diving to his right but grassing the ball. Gilchrist, six runs later, hoisted the ball just over Harmison's upstretched hand, and England's frustration was visible, even though Australia – still

300 runs behind – seemed set to be exposed to the follow-on for the first time since Karachi 17 years and 190 Tests ago. Was this to be Gilchrist's great escape, setting up one of his barnstorming centuries or double-centuries?

Harmison, who had bowled only three overs to date, returned to see a defiant Warne thump him over mid-off before being beaten on the slash and twice on the waft. Australia were hitting rather than grinding their way out of trouble. More punishment for Harmison who was a pale copy of the man who had terrorised West Indies last year.

The stand reached 53 before Jones, S.P. ran the first ball of his new spell away from Gilchrist (30), who touched it low to Jones, G.O:

The Jones boys celebrate Gilchrist's dismissal – Simon the bowler, Geraint the wicketkeeper.

186 for six. Clarke walked in, slightly stiffly, with Hayden as his runner, and instantly revealed his discomfort, losing his balance as he played forward. Faith in the umpires was further tested when Steve Bucknor, having earlier in the innings failed to signal four boundary no-balls from a wild Jones full-toss (an amendment was issued overnight), now wrongly signalled a wide instead of a no-ball when Jones bounced one too many over Clarke's head. Perhaps the Jamaican was preoccupied with Jones's follow-through which was taking him close to the forbidden area.

It was no great surprise when Clarke was seduced by Jones's slower ball, outside off, and drove loosely to mid-off, where Flintoff plucked the ball out of the air.

And so, with three wickets left, Australia needed 44 to avoid the follow-on. Warne's defiant straight six off Giles showed that all wasn't lost, and at the close of this long and tiring final session Australia were 214 for seven. It would not be the worst news for Vaughan if Australia were to get a further 31 runs and spare him the tricky follow-on decision.

THIRD DAY. Saturday, August 13, 2005

The superstitious would say "Told you so" when the 13th brought with it widespread rain over the region. It was the halfway point of the series, halfway through the middle Test match, and maybe we all appreciated a breather. Precisely a year ago, on Friday the 13th, there was no play here at all in the England v West Indies Test, though it failed to halt England's progress to a 4–0 whitewash.

During the long waiting period, while the rainwater was squeegeed off as fast as it fell, there was time for reflection and speculation. John Buchanan, Australia's coach, was in candid mood, telling viewers that "we haven't responded to England's bowling plan as well as we would have liked", while insisting that he was finding it all "quite enervating and exciting at the moment". Pressed on the apparent decline in Australia's performance, he loyally remarked that he didn't think it was anything to do with ageing.

Many will have taken note of the nail-biting draw achieved by England's women at Hove in the first of their two Test matches against the mighty Australians. Arran Brindle, a 23-year-old from Lancashire, reached a century off the final ball of the match to force a draw with her side seven wickets down. Belinda Clark, Australia's illustrious captain, registered two ducks, and star fast bowler Cathryn Fitzpatrick was stoutly resisted. After her 81 in the first one-dayer, Ms Brindle's reaction had a familiar ring about it: "We can win this series. We've shown our team has got a lot of fight and we know we can knock Australia off their pedestal." With the England (male) Under-19s on their way to a clean sweep in the one-day series against Sri Lanka, it was shaping to be a summer to remember.

This rain-spoilt Saturday was not a complete loss. When play began at 4 o'clock, with 38 overs to be bowled, the bowlers had at least had some time to put their feet up. How amusing it would be if we now had a repetition of that fiasco in the fifth Test at Sydney in 1954-55, when Ray Lindwall and Ian Johnson, last men in, got into a run-out tangle when only a single was needed to avert the follow-on. It was the final afternoon of a rain-ruined Test, but it allowed England to pour further humiliation on Australia by having them 87 for six by the end.

Shane Warne rode his luck, oozing confidence, as if he had not a care in the world either on or off the field. Australia's plight had been highlighted by a table showing that extras were third-highest contributor to their runs so far in this series. Warne now at least pushed Mr Extras (his sobriquet in the other hemisphere being Mr Sundries) back into fourth place. He clobbered his fifty off 70 balls, and when Flintoff delivered a hostile over, Warne weathered it, and then smashed Giles back so hard that the ball, after flicking the bails, came close to braining umpire Bowden. The next spun some distance, stranding Warne well down the pitch, but Jones could not hold the ball as it jumped above his right shoulder. It was cause for dismay, but the Englishmen, trained to a tee, all smiled, even the suffering bowler. Predictably, Warne slogged the next few balls, a sweet blow to the long-off boundary erasing the follow-on option.

Warne again was proving a major irritation. Clever use of his feet cancelled the danger of the spun ball in the rough, while at the same time his own boots were coarsening the ground further (legitimately), a calculated risk since Australia would bat last.

Another downpour closed a very handy 35-minute session for Australia, but the dark skies gradually lifted and six more overs were to be bowled on a lovely sunny evening. Who knows what hidden force in Warne's mind was now driving him on to extra effort and determination, the bad boy knowing that his "exiled" family might be watching him from the other side of the world, his heroic feats perhaps diminishing his sins in the eyes of the appalled?

While Flintoff had Warne jumping about and parrying, Gillespie looked as if he would never get out. Geraint Jones's horror stretch was furthered when four byes whistled over his upstretched glove and, next ball, Warne got a snick off Flintoff waist-high to the keeper, who dropped it. His reaction suggested that the glare of the low sun had been a factor, even though he wore sunglasses. With umpire Bucknor calling a seven-ball over, this shortened day's play was not without its absurdities.

Australia finished 264 for seven, Warne 78, the defiant Gillespie 7 (54 balls). The deficit was still 180, and there were two days left. Spectators were to get half their entrance fee refunded because of the time lost, and the universal prayer was for a restoration of blue skies. This contest was too mesmerising to be spoiled.

FOURTH DAY. Sunday, August 14, 2005

Flintoff's glaring weakness – a proliferation of no-balls – was on show early on this Sabbath. Harmison was guilty also at the other (Statham) end. It is so unprofessional.

Nineteen runs came in the first half-hour before Simon Jones replaced Flintoff. Warne hit the first ball through the covers to go to 90, and the next one high to deep forward square leg, straight into Giles's hands. It was exactly the way he had got out for 99 in that

Perth Test. Fluke or good field placement? The eighth-wicket stand – 86 – was the best of the innings, and poor Warne extended his lead at the top of that poignant table which shows most runs without a Test century. His tally of 2688 placed him well ahead of Sri Lanka's Chaminda Vaas (2162).

Jones's delight was curbed by Bucknor's warning for running down the pitch, but he still made the ball all but talk. He bounced Lee, who twisted away with that broad grin. But not for long. Jones bagged his first five-for against Australia when Trescothick dived to his left at slip and held a high-class catch.

Barnacle Gillespie's last partner was McGrath, who had batted only 122 times in his 111 Tests, but was a more confident competitor now after his 61 against New Zealand at Brisbane last November. There, with Gillespie (54 not out), he had put on 114 for the 10th wicket. But their stand today was worth only nine. After being pulled for a six, Jones did for Gillespie with the new ball, though the lbw seemed slightly high. Gillespie may have lost his bowling, but his obduracy with the bat was some compensation: 26 off 111 balls in 144 minutes.

As for Simon Jones, his standing continued to rise. This 6 for 53 was the best analysis for England against Australia at Old Trafford since Jim Laker's incredible 9 for 37 and 10 for 53 in 1956, and it was also the best by any Glamorgan bowler in Test cricket. The previous holder of that honour? I.J.(Jeff) Jones, 6 for 116 against Australia at Adelaide in 1965–66. One happens to be father of the other.

What might England make of this situation? Leading by 142 with the best part of two days remaining, they could only rue the amended shape this contest had taken on after such heavy loss to rain. Victory was a burning ambition, quick runs the first item on the prescription.

The start was dampened by a bloody blow to Strauss's head. Lee, as only he can, found a way through the attempted hook. When the batsman removed his helmet it looked as if Mike Tyson had got at him. Blood trickled from the left ear-lobe and there was a hold-up for repairs. A suspicion occurred that Strauss and his erstwhile Middlesex team-mate Justin Langer might be vying for some clandestine prize for most blows to the skull.

There is something about Strauss that reminds me of that cheerful England left-hander of long ago, Peter Richardson, a centurymaker in Laker's Old Trafford massacre. He held the record for the slowest England Test century, and nowadays modestly describes himself as a "pseudo Test batsman". In the 1956 series he was caught by the wicketkeeper in all eight of his innings, but still averaged 45. Like Strauss, he smiles a lot, a winning quality.

McGrath and Lee needed the closest scrutiny. Trescothick's square-drive brought up his 5000 Test runs. Fifteen England batsmen have passed this way before. The Somerset man has it in his power to overtake them all. Only Hobbs, Hutton, Hammond and Barrington had got there in fewer than Trescothick's 64 Tests.

Strauss edged Lee waist-high between the frozen figures of Warne and Ponting, and the next ball was delivered with a loud roar of frustration and aggression. It was a no-ball, and soon the unflappable Strauss was guiding another delivery down to the third-man rope. Warne came on six minutes before lunch, and although he spun it miles, the bails were lifted with England 26 for none.

They took the initiative in the afternoon. They needed to. Both left-handers cut Lee freely, and Trescothick steered him over slips to take the overall lead to 200. Warne returned, and after Trescothick had pulled him through mid-on came an lbw appeal of grotesque, prolonged proportions.

It was McGrath who broke through: Trescothick (41) played a ball down and set off for a run, noticing too late that the ball was bobbing back onto the off stump.

While clouds the colour of England's helmets lurked in the distance, Old Trafford was still sunlit as Vaughan stroked Warne through midwicket and Strauss succeeded in his main mission, which was to show that he could handle the leg-spinner. Vaughan, though, nearly fell to Warne by pushing too soon, substitute fields-man Hodge diving forward at mid-off but disclaiming any catch. A slash off McGrath went down to Gillespie at third man . . . and over the boundary line. Heads slumped, especially the fielder's.

At 97 the second wicket fell when Vaughan zestfully pulled Lee almost for six, only for Hodge to sprint a short distance, hold the catch, and slide along on his knees.

Next, more English luck. Bell (4) was hit in the stomach by a ball from Lee which went through to hit the off stump without removing the bail. Survival was fragile as Warne beat the young-ster with a perfect leg-break and then almost bowled him as he swept. Strauss righted matters by pulling Lee for six. Still Lee bounced them, and an uncontrolled hook by Bell plopped onto open grass at midwicket, and Strauss sent a no-ball spiralling just short of Gillespie at long leg. When the poor chap fumbled it few seemed surprised.

With a sweep to the midwicket rope off Warne, Andrew Strauss collected his first fifty of the series. Down the pitch he went to hit a full-toss to midwicket. Brett Lee patted him on the helmet as they left the field for tea, England 128 for two, 270 ahead, four sessions remaining.

While Bell remained pegged down, Strauss hit a carefree square-cut, back to his 2004 form at last. Langer's fumble on the cover boundary brought further groans, including one from the offender. When Gillespie had a bowl he finally managed some pronounced movement – only for umpire Bowden to warn him for running down the pitch. His indignity was complete when he tumbled over in delivering a no-ball.

At the other end, Warne continued to carry the flag, letting loose some faster roundarm stuff which spun vast distances. But his frustration was evident. Bell advanced, missed, and was let off by Gilchrist, the thinnest of edges also passing Hayden at slip. When McGrath took over from Gillespie, Bell emerged from his bunker to take two fours in an over that cost 13. When Warne put his arm around Ponting's shoulder during a conference, an over-zealous dramatist's interpretation might have seen the captain as shedding a tear or two.

By drinks, Strauss had moved to 81, Bell 38, and the latter immediately switched into top gear by lofting McGrath's slower ball for
six. Warne and his skipper were booed for taking time over field
adjustments, but the century stand still came up in 104 minutes. Bell
(45) was then missed again, a long way down to Warne's around-
the-wicket spin, almost as Warne himself had been when Jones let
him off. Gilchrist was crestfallen.

They had over 1100 Test wickets between them, but McGrath
and Warne were now being treated like apprentices. It could
be done. Strauss went to 95 with a pull off Warne into the crowd,
and when McGrath dropped short, away went the pull shot, and
Andrew Strauss had his first hundred against Australia and his
sixth in 17 Tests. Only Herbert Sutcliffe (7) had bettered this for
England, with Hammond and Peter Parfitt also on six. Strauss
smiled sweetly as he removed his helmet, revealing that white
plaster on his lacerated left ear.

The prolific Andrew Strauss
adds Australia to his century
board: his sixth hundred against
four different countries in only
15 months of Test cricket.

He was out shortly afterwards, held at turf level by Martyn from another pull, and there was another nice touch as Lee shook his hand as he left the arena. Next ball Pietersen was out too, losing his balance as McGrath fired a yorker into his boot. The hat-trick ball found Flintoff standing well out of his crease, and he played the lifter down from in front of his face.

At 225 for four, England were near the 400 lead considered a minimum for declaration. The whole day had been about setting up a finale, a job complicated by the time lost on Saturday, testing a captain's nerve and intelligence. Few doubted Michael Vaughan's ability to get his calculations right.

Four leg-side byes, Warne to Bell, made for a messy addition to the unhappy wicketkeeping account, though this hardly mattered with the declaration imminent. Flintoff, head up, lost his middle stump to McGrath. Geraint Jones, the babyface, brought up the 400 lead with a pull. Bell threw his wicket away at long-off, giving McGrath his fifth wicket, after which Jones hit McGrath for a six either side of a top-edged four. Off they came at 5.40pm, Australia needing 423 to win in 50 minutes this evening and a maximum of 98 overs tomorrow.

By the close the target had been reduced to 399. Few believed it gettable. Giles and Vaughan had done most of the bowling as the light closed in. There was frustration for some when the Hawkeye device on television showed that a flighted ball from Vaughan, padded away by Langer, would have hit middle and off, but umpire Bucknor disallowed the appeal. Langer 14, Hayden 5 off these 10 overs; Australia 24 without loss. Weather forecast good. It cannot, surely, be another Edgbaston.

FIFTH DAY. Monday, August 15, 2005

Players and non-players, we all braced ourselves. Countless thousands had descended on Old Trafford (£10 admission, £5 for juniors) in the hope of seeing the action, some queuing from two hours after midnight. The ground quickly filled to its 23,000 capacity, so thousands of dejected souls were sent home, with

Greater Manchester Police doing their best to prevent hordes of further travellers from far and wide heading in vain by train, tram and car to the ground. David Beckham and Wayne Rooney were suddenly insignificant to the local lads. This had better be good.

Steve Harmison started it off from the Statham end, from where the breeze blew. Then Hoggard came in from the Stretford and stunned everyone, probably including himself, by getting a wicket with his first ball of the day. Langer played half-forward, bat angled, and edged to the keeper. The one fellow who might have batted all day was gone immediately. What next?

Hoggard, for once bringing the ball back, troubled Ponting several times, but after half-an-hour Giles was on, probably to bowl most of the day. Flintoff took over from Hoggard and one of his specialties, a no-ball, was pulled for six by Ponting, who then was hit on the glove by Giles with ominous lift. Great bowlers, we are often told, don't bowl full-tosses. Giles did, and Ponting helped himself to four: 71 for one. The awesome target could be got at 65 runs an hour.

Matthew Hayden was getting his runs mainly through the slips, until, after a lengthy drinks break, he survived a convincing lbw cry and tonked Giles for six. A sweep sent the ball spinning back past the off stump, and the left-hander was getting into all kinds of contortions. Ponting, too, escaped a big lbw shout, and English hands were repeatedly on heads.

I had a vision of early Flintoff c.1998, all puppy fat, gormless grin, aspiration and hope and failure. Now, having reverted to over the wicket, formidable of physique (just like Hayden), the world's premier all-rounder raced in, left hand covering the grip on the ball. It caused Hayden to wonder where he was, and the leg stump was clipped. It was his fourth 30-odd in five Test innings. Australia 96 for two; England rampant again.

Another might have fallen there and then. Martyn was out of his crease when Bell intercepted at short leg. His back-flick was just wide of the target. Ponting, as at Edgbaston, topped a sweep off Giles, but it fell safely. Simon Jones came on, but for once failed to take a wicket with his opening delivery. Instead, having cut over point for four, Martyn played another cut, missed, and although there was no appeal, the snickometer detected a touch. Luck for Australia – soon to be cancelled out.

There were further thrills before the lunch break, and Harmison hit Martyn between the shoulder blades, but Australia survived, to be 121 for two, 302 still required. If these two – Ponting and Martyn – were still together at tea, a full-scale Australian charge was a certainty in the final session.

Harmison had no third man for Martyn – possibly a tempter – but bowled too wide at Ponting, until he eventually had to play one in front of his face. The captain moved past Greg Chappell's aggregate of 7110 Test runs, then, slicing at the ball, edged Jones for four. But now he lost Martyn.

It was another sad dismissal. Umpire Bucknor failed to hear the snick before the ball bumped the pad, and the Australian was on his way for 19. What did people who are so forgiving of human error and who believe these mistakes "even themselves out" think about this one? Ricky Ponting wasn't very philosophical. He engaged in some animated conversation with the umpire as the dejected Martyn tramped off.

Simon Katich never looked at ease. Beaten by Jones, he then nervously stretched forward at a widish ball, and after Ponting had reached a 103-ball fifty, the left-hander managed a couple of fours, though Flintoff kept passing him. Giles came back and Ponting helped himself to a pair of pulled fours. When he hit another off the back foot through the covers, fieldsmen dropped back. This was not to be Ashley Giles's best performance of the summer.

However, he did cling to an excellent catch at third slip when Katich (12) mis-hit at Flintoff, who then greeted his bunny, Adam Gilchrist, with a superb yorker first ball and an away-cutter with the next. A mad single would have resulted in a run-out if Vaughan's throw has been straighter, and not only were the Barmy Army in strong voice with their mesmeric chants, a bugler was in fine tune, playing *Men of Harlech* whenever Simon Jones was in action.

Vaughan brought in an extra gully fielder, and in the 58th over Flintoff forced Gilchrist (4 in 36 minutes) to edge high to Bell, that new man. In the 88 balls Flintoff had directed to Gilchrist in this series he had taken his wicket three times for 61 runs.

Australia were 182 for five, Ponting 79, Clarke in with no need of a runner. There was still an outside chance, but the sight of the abbreviation AUST'A on the electronic scoreboard prompted the reflection that several times already in this series this team had shaped up more like Australia A.

But they now perked up. Michael Clarke's class shone again, and this was developing into one of Ponting's finest innings. There have been so many in recent times, apart from his rather fallow 2004, and yet his hundreds have usually come when Australia were on top, a familiar position against all comers for some years now. Vaughan had a bowl, but Clarke took fours through cover and mid-off before being beaten by a wider ball. Against Flintoff, who was due a rest, he fended just wide of short leg. There was a rare captains' duel when Vaughan floated a few down at Ponting, and when Hoggard returned Clarke was ready for that juicy leg-stump half-volley. Back came Giles, but like Warne in England's second innings, instead of a handful of wickets he was denied any.

At tea Australia were 216 for five, Ponting 91, Clarke 20, 42 overs remaining, 207 runs required. If wickets could be held safe this target might yet be reached, even if Test history showed nothing quite to match it. (West Indies' astonishing 418 for seven against Australia at Antigua in May 2003 was the new high for targets reached.) If there was to be an outright result here, England were still favourites.

But they needed to hold their catches; and in the first over after tea Giles put down a return low to his right from Clarke (20). Every ball produced excitement. Clarke drove the next for four, and the following ball beat the upper edge as he launched into a cut.

Ponting's century came with a cover-driven four off Harmison. It was his 23rd, and fifth against England, completing a rare double in an Ashes Test, for his opposing captain had also just made three

A captain's innings if ever there was one: Ricky Ponting takes a deep breath after reaching his match-saving century.

figures. Ponting's restrained reaction showed that his preoccupation was on survival, maybe with victory lurking in the depths of his mind.

The five overs since tea had brought 33 runs. Vaughan rotated his bowling, exhorting his men vocally and with vigorous clapping. Pietersen joined in.

As at Edgbaston the crucial breakthrough came with Clarke's dismissal. Jones engineered it. Australia simply weren't reading his swing variations, and embarrassingly Clarke (39) raised his bat and saw the ball swerve back a long way to hit off stump.

Gillespie came in ahead of Warne to supply some stonewalling. Jones's pleasure was dampened by a warning about running down the pitch.

On this dramatic, sunny evening England had 32 overs left in which to get four wickets. Within minutes that became three wickets. Gillespie played half-forward and was leg-before to Hoggard, who, in between no-balls, now beat Warne's outside edge.

After the drinks break England took the new ball, and had the match almost won at 271 for seven, 27.4 overs remaining.

But Harmison was surprisingly harmless, Jones let a full-toss slip, and Flintoff had problems with the footholds. Ponting and Warne conferred frequently, irritating their opponents and perhaps bent on showing that the rumours of a rift between them were outrageous. Flintoff gave Warne in particular a torrid time. The 300 came up, the last fifty (112 balls) being equal-slowest with the first fifty of the innings. Still the batsmen were absolutely resolute. No temptation could buy their wickets.

Then the chance came. Warne, on 30, played Jones uppishly to midwicket and Pietersen dived to his right. But the catch went down. That made five misses and no catches for him in the series. Perhaps that flamboyant exterior conceals a hand-hardening tension.

More welcome drinks were taken, and with 15 overs left Australia were 314 for seven. Jones came on at the Stretford end and Ponting twice glanced him for four. When Warne slashed Hoggard through the covers Pietersen crashed into the boundary boards and limped back onto the battlefield. When Ponting carved Jones over gully, 89 were needed off 75 balls, and still nothing could be taken for granted.

Flintoff returned and beat Warne – twice. There was no familiarity between adversaries now. Ponting had been in for just over six hours when his 150 came up, and Jones was still working on him: two outswingers followed by an inswinger, none easily detectable from the hand.

Then Warne went for 34 and the gate was open again. It was a brilliant dismissal. Strauss at second slip mishandled the chance and the ball bounced off his knee. Geraint Jones's acrobatic dive saved the situation, and Flintoff celebrated with a bit of break-dancing before lifting the unsuspecting Hoggard over his shoulder.

For the new man, Lee, there were slips and short legs galore. He was beaten by his first ball, and again. England seemed about to clinch it.

It was a thrill a minute. Lee was covered in grey dust after diving in to save his skin. Then an edge fell just short of gully. Ponting, clinging to the strike, was beaten again by Flintoff. Jones, coming in to bowl to Lee, suddenly pulled up with cramp. And that was where England lost some momentum. Off he went and Harmison eagerly took over. He hit Lee's arm-guard, and then had him patently lbw – except that umpire Bowden turned down the appeal.

England now had a wonderful opportunity. Lee was a long way from home when substitute fieldsman Stephen Peters, a Worcester-shire batsman, threw from cover. He missed. So Harmison tried a rocket of a yorker, and Lee repelled it.

Six overs left. Flintoff beat the weary Ponting, but he survived. Five overs left. Ponting placed a four to midwicket off Harmison, just before an lbw shout: too high. The Durham man loped in for the last ball of the over. It was on the body and Australia's heroic captain persuaded it down the leg side. Off the glove, he was caught by Jones for 156, and again it seemed all over: Australia 354 for nine and 24 balls remaining.

Ricky Ponting was stunned. He had fixed his mind on being there at the end, and after hours of cast-iron resolve and high-tech batsmanship he had been evicted. The thought of all this being in vain was too much for him to take in. He wandered off as McGrath came in, feeling much as Kasprowicz did as No.11 at Edgbaston.

There were seven in the slips cordon as Flintoff thundered in and beat Lee with a leg-cutter. Another shaved the bat's edge, and another. Whoever tried to estimate the influence of luck on a cricket match? A four through the covers left McGrath to face at the other end. Harmison was the bowler. Here's how the over went: a leg-side bouncer; a yorker dug out; and the next; a push to mid-on; a full-toss glanced for four; through to the keeper. "Pigeon" had survived the shotguns.

Penultimate scheduled over: Flintoff to Lee: he played a good ball; then another; an inswinger sparked a huge lbw appeal; a wider, harmless ball; Lee calmly played one aimed at his off stick; he tried to tap a single off the last, but to his and his team's chagrin the ball ran all the way to the boundary. Thus, for the final over McGrath had to face Harmison, the bouncing fast bowler who snatched last-gasp victory for England at Edgbaston.

Stuart MacGill ran onto the field with a message: a suggestion/instruction to McGrath to stand well out of his crease. This he did. Harmison wasted the first ball down the leg side. The next kept rather low and went through McGrath's tentative prod. When wicketkeeper Jones threw the ball back from his prone position on the ground to the helmeted Hoggard at short leg, who in turn tossed it back to the bowler, batsman McGrath just stood there, some way out of his crease.

It was suggested afterwards that if only Hoggard had broken the wicket England would have won the match there and then. Was this omission a supreme gesture of sportsmanship or negligence or rank naivety? McGrath later said he reckoned the ball was dead, but one can think of many an opponent who would not have hesitated to go for the run-out. And you can never tell with some of these umpires. Warne mischievously wrote later: "McGrath and Hoggard – see the common factor? Both fast bowlers."

One thing was certain: when W.G.Grace, in the famous Ashes match at The Oval in 1882, ran out Sammy Jones, the young Australian, when he was attending to divots on the pitch after taking a run, Anglo-Australian relations were harmed for years to follow.

McGrath managed a single to midwicket. Lee waited for Harmison's next offering. The bowler was found wanting: down the leg side sailed the over-pitched ball. Two balls to come. Lee was at liberty to let the next go outside off.

One left for perhaps the most sensational finish since – well, Edgbaston maybe. And the best that Harmison could muster was a full-toss, which Lee turned away to the vacant boundary. He beamed that smile. Edgbaston had been avenged . . . sort of.

English chins dropped and the ground fell almost silent. Vaughan, though, immediately signalled for a team huddle, and as the Australian last-wicket pair raced into the ecstatic fist-pumping embrace of their team-mates, the England captain's voice could be heard, reassuring his crestfallen players that they had been on top throughout this Test match, and, as he told a wider audience later, "We can take a huge amount out of this game. We have dominated four days against the No.1 team in the world. Three weeks ago we were being written off. Now we are at 1-1 in the series and more than matching Australia." His suppression of disappointment was exemplary: "I think we won every session. There are a heck of a lot of positives to take."

As for Ricky Ponting, he admitted that "it doesn't feel like a win but it feels like we've worked very hard and snuck [sneaked] away with a draw. It was a long, hard, tough day of Test cricket." His late dismissal seemed to have thrown it all away? "I had my little tantrum in the dressing-room . . . I thought the game had slipped away. It was hard enough for me facing Flintoff and Harmison, and I didn't have much faith in our last pair."

Brett Lee, champion of the rearguard action, might have been scripted by C.J.Dennis as he claimed that "the difference between today and Edgbaston was that there I was talking a lot with Kasper to keep us pumped up. Today, Glenn didn't want to know. He just kept ignoring me and walking away."

Brains and organs "deluged with noradrenalin", cortisone levels "monstrously raised", the players prepare to vacate the field at the end of one of the most nerve-shattering Test matches of all time.

The Australian wives and girlfriends were not completely captivated by the tension of the closing stages of this Test classic. From their seats near the pavilion they were overheard discussing airline schedules and facilities, and when the final 15 overs began they decided against prolonging their day at the cricket. Soon they would be flying home, and their men would be left to wrestle without them through what remained of this astonishing Ashes series.

THIRD TEST MATCH
Old Trafford, Manchester, August 11, 12, 13, 14, 15, 2005

ENGLAND		mins	balls	4s		mins	balls	4s
M.E.Trescothick	c Gilchrist b Warne	63	196	117	9	b McGrath	41	71	56	6
A.J.Strauss	b Lee	6	43	28	–	c Martyn b McGrath	106	246	158	9+
*M.P.Vaughan	c McGrath b Katich	166	277	215	21#	c sub (B.J.Hodge) b Lee	14	45	37	2
I.R.Bell	c Gilchrist b Lee	59	205	155	8	c Katich b McGrath	65	165	103	5#
K.P.Pietersen	c sub (B.J.Hodge) b Lee	21	50	28	1	lbw b McGrath	0	3	1	–
M.J.Hoggard	b Lee	4	13	10	1				
A.Flintoff	c Langer b Warne	46	93	67	7	[6] b McGrath	4	20	18	–
#G.O.Jones	b Gillespie	42	86	51	6	[7] not out	27	15	12	2+
A.F.Giles	c Hayden b Warne	0	11	6	–	[8] not out	0	4	0	–
S.J.Harmison	not out	10	13	11	1				
S.P.Jones	b Warne	0	7	4	–				
Extras	b 4, lb 5, w 3, nb 15	27				b 5, lb 3, w 1, nb 14	23		
	(113.2 overs, 503 mins)	444				(61.5 overs, 6 wkts dec	280		
						288 mins)			

plus 1 six   + plus 2 sixes

Fall: 1/26 2/163 3/290 4/333 5/341 6/346   1/64 2/97 3/224 4/225 5/248 6/264
      7/433 8/434 9/438

BOWLING: McGrath 25-6-86-0 (4nb), Lee 27-6-100-4 (5nb, 2w), Gillespie 19-2-114-1 (2nb, 1w), Warne 33.2-5-99-4 (2nb), Katich 9-1-36-1
SECOND INNINGS: McGrath 20.5-1-115-5 (6nb, 1w), Lee 12-0-60-1 (4nb), Warne 25-3-74-0, Gillespie 4-0-23-0 (4nb)

AUSTRALIA		mins	balls	4s		mins	balls	4s
J.L.Langer	c Bell b Giles	31	76	50	4	c G.O.Jones b Hoggard	14	42	41	3
M.L.Hayden	lbw b Giles	34	112	71	5	b Flintoff	36	123	91	5#
*R.T.Ponting	c Bell b S.P.Jones	7	20	12	1	c G.O.Jones b Harmison	156	391	275	16#
D.R.Martyn	b Giles	20	71	41	2	lbw b Harmison	19	53	36	3
S.M.Katich	b Flintoff	17	39	28	2	c Giles b Flintoff	12	30	23	2
#A.C.Gilchrist	c G.O.Jones b S.P.Jones	30	74	49	4	c Bell b Flintoff	4	36	30	–
S.K.Warne	c Giles b S.P.Jones	90	183	122	11#	[9] c G.O.Jones b Flintoff	34	99	69	5
M.J.Clarke	c Flintoff b S.P.Jones	7	19	18	–	[7] b S.P.Jones	39	73	63	7
J.N.Gillespie	lbw b S.P.Jones	26	144	111	1#	[8] lbw b Hoggard	0	8	5	–
B.Lee	c Trescothick b S.P.Jones	1	17	16	–	not out	18	44	25	4
G.D.McGrath	not out	1	20	4	–	not out	5	17	9	1
Extras	b 8, lb 7, w 8, nb 15	38				b 5, lb 8, w 2, nb 19	34		
	(84.5 overs, 393 mins)	302				(108 overs, 474 mins) 9 wkts	371		

plus 1 six

Fall: 1/58 2/73 3/86 4/119 5/133 6/186   1/25 2/96 3/129 4/165 5/182 6/263
      7/201 8/287 9/293   7/264 8/340 9/354

BOWLING: Harmison 10-0-47-0 (2nb, 1w), Hoggard 6-2-22-0, Flintoff 20-1-65-1 (8nb), S.P.Jones 17.5-5-53-6 (1nb, 2w), Giles 31-4-100-3 (1w)
SECOND INNINGS: Harmison 22-4-67-2 (4nb, 1w), Hoggard 13-0-49-2 (6nb), Giles 26-4-93-0, Vaughan 5-0-21-0, Flintoff 25-6-71-4 (9nb, 1w), S.P.Jones 17-3-57-1

Toss won by England   Umpires: B.F.Bowden (NZ) & S.A.Bucknor (WI)
Test debut: none   Replay umpire: N.J.Llong
Match award: R.T.Ponting   Match referee: R.S.Madugalle (SL)

MATCH DRAWN

7

Fourth Test

Unaware of my confused allegiance, a number of people who recognise that Ashes cricket is my lifeblood have been innocently enquiring whether the Edgbaston result upset me and whether the Old Trafford draw had brought consolation. They were not to know of my current preference for an England victory. But what concerned me now, after these two heart-stoppers, was whether it might be at all possible to develop immunity to such high stress levels. We were about to find out.

The Australians had two fixtures – if they can be termed as such – between the third and fourth Tests. The one-dayer against Scotland, scheduled for Edinburgh on August 18, was washed out, to crushing disappointment locally. Two days later, in a two-day match against Northants, Matthew Hayden, having freshened up with some fishing in cool Scottish rivers, far from his Queensland waters, made a heartening century on what was once his own county pitch. Michael Clarke also reached three figures in a match in which both teams fielded 12 men, and Justin Langer captained the Australians for the first time. It was here that Jason Gillespie, deflated from both loss of form and recurrent jeering from the crowds, learned of his omission from the Test team. Another worthy international career seemed to have closed.

This allowed a new name dramatically to enter the slot. Shaun

Tait, the 22-year-old from Nairne, in the Adelaide hills, announced himself like Jeff Thomson 30-odd years ago, with blood on the pitch. The unfortunate was Northants batsman Tim Roberts, whose left eyebrow gushed blood after a fast one from Tait exploded between helmet-grille and peak. This was not the only outpouring of red corpuscles, for Glenn McGrath struck the 6ft 6ins (2 metres) Ben Phillips, who had to go off for stitches to his right eyebrow. "I was a little bit worried," Tait reflected later, "because I'd never actually seen that much blood on a cricket field before."

And yet all this time it was to be Australia who were to sustain the serious on-going injury problems, for trouble was brewing in McGrath's right elbow.

NORTHAMPTON, August 20, 21, 2005
AUSTRALIANS 374 for 6 dec (M.L.Hayden 136, M.J.Clarke 121) and 226 for 2 (S.M.Katich 63, J.L.Langer 86*, D.R.Martyn 43*); NORTHAMPTONSHIRE 169 (B.J.Phillips 37*, G.D.McGrath 3 for 24). *MATCH DRAWN.*

***

A fascinating behind-the-scenes manoeuvre had been going on concerning Australia's forgotten man, Stuart MacGill. The highly talented leg-spinner had scarcely played since the tour began, so permission was sought for him to have a couple of matches with Somerset. In years gone by permission would generously have been granted. But England played tough now (not tough enough for some, who continued to look despairingly at the numerous Aussies occupying top places in the county averages). Somerset would not be engaging MacGill, thus denying themselves almost-certain Championship points but vitally – and reasonably – serving the nation's cause.

There seems no end to the statistical findings in this age of the computer. The Cricinfo website found that England's batting rate of 4.01 runs per over in the series so far put them ahead of Australia for the first time since 1986–87, which, not surprisingly, was the last time England won an Ashes series. Perhaps more significantly, England had taken wickets at a strike rate of 49.66 balls, the best by any side against Australia since *1912*. Australia's 2005 bowling rate is even better (45.38), but they have been "leaking" runs at the aforementioned rate of 4.01. Lies, damned lies, and stats?

Without question England had impressed much more than Australia since the Lord's debacle. If there is such a thing as a tidal movement in a Test series, it was flowing England's way now. At Trent Bridge, although the green and juicy outfield would reduce the likelihood of reverse swing (both sides of the ball would stay shiny longer), head groundsman Steve Birks declared that there shouldn't be anything in the pitch "for that spinner of theirs . . . the less help he gets the better". Shane Warne fired back: "He should keep his mouth shut and get on with his job." Whatever happened to Edwardian reticence?

So all was set for the 150th Test match between these countries to be staged in England since the first in 1880. The 100th Test of all between them was also played at Trent Bridge, and if the current England players were to have glanced at the scores of that 1921 match they would have been fired up further for revenge, if such were possible. The bombardment by Jack Gregory and Ted McDonald, eight wickets apiece, had polished England off by the second afternoon.

The 100th England-Australia Test in England was the Headingley Test of 1972, when Derek Underwood exploited a pitch which the Australians regarded as sub-standard. The Ashes were retained, but this odour of suspicion helped fire Australia up in the next series, when Lillee and Thomson awaited England on a suspect track at the Gabba. And so it goes on.

It might have seemed that even local taxi-drivers were doing their bit to help when Brad Haddin, the Australians' reserve wicket-keeper, sustained damage to his knee when struck by the vehicle at the hotel. The injury which really counted, however, was McGrath's dodgy elbow. As at Edgbaston, he was ruled out. There was inflammation inside the joint, a problem often found in ageing fast men. He could have bowled an opening spell but would almost certainly have been ineffective later. So Kasprowicz and young Tait were in.

FIRST DAY. Thursday, August 25, 2005

That luck factor again: Vaughan won the toss. The pitch was the colour of the pale-brown autumn fields and the sun shone brightly. Unchanged yet again, England batted, perhaps buoyed by what Geoff Boycott had written that morning: "However much psychological claptrap the Australians may come out with, the fact is that Ricky Ponting's team has been outplayed."

Lee from the Radcliffe Road end, Kasprowicz from the pavilion end, due care and attention by Trescothick and Strauss, and a big total seemed on the cards. Trescothick wore a black armband in memory of a little boy who had sat with the cricketer during the Twenty/20 international in June and had just died of leukaemia, a rare reminder of a world beyond the boundary.

There was no Australian breakthrough, but people leaned forward when Shaun Tait came on as first change to sling his first ball down in Test cricket. And sling is the word. His action seems similar to Tibby Cotter's, and it might have served as inspiration to the giant South Australian had he been aware that Cotter bowled out four good England players in the Trent Bridge Test of 100 years ago. Not that Tait was short of motivation: "Our guys have copped a few. It does make me want to get out there and help them a bit." Fast bowlers "Bull" Alexander and Laurie Nash had similar thoughts when Australia's batsmen were taking a battering from Jardine's Bodyline squad in '32–33.

England's openers batted intelligently, taking no risks, with Trescothick back-cutting Tait for four, then driving square as if he knew the bowler would make the adjustment.

The frequency of no-balls continued to surprise. Professional cricketers looking for that furthest front boot placement continue to let themselves and their side down.

It was a comfortable 74 without loss when Warne came on. Trescothick larruped him for six to the pavilion. Soon his fifty came, from only 77 balls, his seventh against Australia. Maybe he would convert this one into a maiden century.

Strauss, his running mate, fed on a rare fat half-volley from Warne. Then he swept, edged onto his boot and lobbed a catch to slip. He stayed, unsure – like umpire Bucknor – as to what had actually happened. There was referral, and up went the judicial finger. England 105 for one.

Michael Vaughan seemed in fine fettle. He slammed Warne's first ball through the covers off the back foot, played a lovely off-drive off Lee, then cut for four, and England lunched on 129 for one – though not before some further Australian anguish. Brett Lee bowled Trescothick off the inside edge, only to hear umpire Aleem Dar's call of "no-ball". The next delivery was also a no-ball, which the burly Somerset man pulled dismissively for four.

Rain from the north-west caused an hour's play to be lost after lunch, and after a further 20 balls another squall swept the ground. It was almost 4 o'clock before resumption, and Tait then earned his maiden Test wicket, hitting Trescothick's stumps via the pad with a slower ball of near-yorker length. A handy little obscurity emerged: that Trescothick (65) had passed Trevor Bailey's record total of runs against Australia (875) without a century.

Soon Tait captured his second wicket and the balance was restored. Ian Bell (3) was defeated by a beauty which cut away after drawing him forward, giving Adam Gilchrist his 300th wicketkeeping dismissal in Tests, a mark only crossed previously by Rod Marsh and Ian Healy of Australia and Mark Boucher of South Africa.

The field was sunlit one moment, in cloud-shade the next, as it was to be throughout. Kevin Pietersen, incurably hyperactive, seemed keen to raise 500 in a day. His missed drive at Tait was followed by a four to midwicket and a shot through the covers which could have come from a hockey player bullying off. KP was, as ever, living dangerously, and soon enough, on 14, he hit one back waist-high to Kasprowicz – who spilt the chance.

With the total 174 for three, Pietersen (30) offered another chance to deep gully. Hayden got both hands to it as he fell, only to lose it. Australia used to hold almost everything offered or even half-offered. As light rain fell, watched bemusedly by his captain, Pietersen uppercut Lee to the empty third-man region, then slashed and missed a shoulder-high delivery. England continued to pursue their policy of all-out aggression. KP slashed a three to third man. Vaughan, almost contemptuously, tried the same, and missed. Then the tall, slim captain played a classical drive through the covers which brought out the sun again and would have settled him easily into the company of the Golden Age luminaries of a century ago. This writer reflected that here was his favourite ground in England, favourite weather, favourite contest, favourite time of day. It would surely be revisited in memory.

Kasprowicz trundled some more and Pietersen played the exaggerated forward defensive that so annoys opponents, and Vaughan glanced Lee just out of reach of Gilchrist's left glove. It was time for the unexpected. With the grass still slightly slippery and Warne's back still a little stiff, Ponting gave himself a bowl. The four wickets he had taken in his 91 Tests were all good ones. He began with a rusty wide before non-striker Vaughan, over-keen to get at Ponting, bolted when there was no real prospect of a run, and just made it to safety.

Vaughan ducked very quickly when Lee dropped short, just as his ancestor Johnny Tydesley had done against Cotter on this ground in 1905. Now he had Ponting in his sights. A ball seamed away and lifted, Vaughan (58) was drawn into the trap, and captain had overthrown captain, a comparative rarity in modern Ashes cricket. Gilchrist jubilantly gloved the thin edge.

Flintoff's third ball was almost his last and nearly gave Ponting a delicious double coup. The burly Lancastrian played it onto his boot. Pietersen on-drove Tait for four, and there was then the unusual sight of McGrath and Gillespie coming onto the field as drink waiters, not to bowl lethally in tandem. As more heavy clouds drifted over, and 5½ hours since he had last bowled, Warne returned. The light was offered to the batsmen, and off they went at 6.07 pm, England 229 for four off 60 overs, Pietersen 33 (113 minutes), Flintoff 8, Australia having donated 22 no-balls and a wide.

SECOND DAY. Friday, August 26, 2005

A riotous day followed, launched first ball by a four to long leg by Pietersen off Lee. No question of playing himself in again: Pietersen cut exquisitely between point and deep point. It brought massive relief to Australia when this dangerous customer was beaten by pace and edged a full-length ball from Lee: 241 for five.

The match was now poised: further breakthrough or resistance? Geraint Jones began unsteadily while Flintoff flung his club of a bat at an off-side ball and got four through the emptiness at third man. He went after Warne, too, crashing him through the covers and lofting him. Jones timed Lee sweetly through extra, and when Kasprowicz replaced Lee there was a tangible lessening of tension. The sixth-wicket stand reached a half-century in 46 minutes.

Warne naturally needed watching very carefully and Jones seemed uncertain, playing him by reflex. Flintoff had no such inhibitions, going to his fifty with a sweep for six. Warne's 10 overs so far today had cost 29 runs when the new ball was taken. Tait bowled with it and Jones welcomed it with a cover-driven four. Flintoff drove Lee to the pavilion, focussing then on Tait who was beefily pulled and off-driven for fours. Flintoff was in top gear, without a care in the world. When a pulled four came next, bowler Tait received a motherly hug and much counselling from some of his team-mates.

The hundred stand (Flintoff 64 of them) came off 126 balls, and at lunch England were riding high at 344 for five, a position that might have been weakened with the first ball of the afternoon when Lee believed he had found Jones's edge. Umpire Bucknor would have none of it, and the bowler had a long way to walk back to his mark from his exultant followthrough into the slips cordon.

Flintoff enjoyed Kasprowicz's bowling. Wherever the bowler directed the ball, Fred was ready for him. Three fours in an over ran

England to their highest partnership of the series, and wicketkeeper Gilchrist began to sense, as he told questioners later, that "everything starts to feel like it's going against us".

Geraint Jones's clean strokeplay took him to his first Test fifty against Australia off 93 balls, and after 14 overs with the new ball had produced 73 runs, Warne returned. Flintoff raised the 400, and after Jones had stroked a Hammond-like cover-drive through Ponting's defensive field, Flintoff, on 99, faced Warne, a dramatic cameo. Australia's hard man operated around the wicket and the brawny batsman flashed at the first ball, was hit on the boot by a full-toss, and had to endure patiently until he managed a single to leg to bring a much-savoured maiden century against Australia, his fifth in Tests. In for just over three hours, he had struck 14 fours and a six and realised the abundant promise retarded for so long. In India nearly four years ago Flintoff's failures had reduced him to dressing-room tears. There followed some weight-reduction, good management, marriage to Rachael, and fatherhood, and now his countless admirers were sharing this likable fellow's joy.

Soon after Langer had let a four through on the line, Flintoff was out, leg-before to Tait. It was no bad thing as his bowling would soon be needed, and no man has unlimited stocks of energy. His batting average was now 33.36 against a bowling average slightly below that (32.63), which rendered him at last an all-rounder with a credit balance, with his catching skill a bonus.

The partnership of 177 was the biggest of England's seven century stands in the series so far. Australia had registered only one in return.

Eyes were now on Geraint Jones in expectation of a hundred by him. Elegant strokeplay took him to 85, but he then fluffed a drive at Kasprowicz who held the return with palpable relief: 450 for seven.

Giles, well forward, was given out lbw to Warne while sweeping, Harmison had a wild woof and was stumped, and the delayed tea was taken after a merry last-wicket stand of 23 by Hoggard and Simon Jones, who once played Lee into his rigidly-rooted stumps

Freddie Flintoff and
Geraint Jones, the
giant and his mate,
who set up England's
big first-innings total
at Trent Bridge.

only for the bails to remain unshaken. England had a sturdy 477, a figure for any superstitious fool to savour, for the big stand of the innings was 177 and England won the Ashes back in 1977.

There were 34 overs to be bowled this evening, and it was time enough for Australia to be sent reeling again. Five wickets toppled for 99. Hayden, who had done well if he had dodged the mass of newspaper space devoted to his dreadful form in the Tests, was plumb lbw to Hoggard for 7 in the 10th over. Desperate events then overtook Australia. Next over, Simon Jones won an lbw appeal against Ponting (1) and, in the over following, Hoggard claimed Martyn (1) with another lbw shout. Unfortunately, in both instances the batsmen got inside edges just before the ball struck the pad. More strength was thus fed into the argument that decisions at this level must be scrutinised by the third umpire. Yet again, while millions were privy to the truth, it was absurdly denied to the only person who mattered, the adjudicating umpire in the field. It would be so simple – and just – for the third umpire to correct such errors.

Disappointingly, a couple of boundary strokes were barely acknowledged by the full house before Langer (27) glove-padded and Bell dashed in to hold a diving catch: 58 for four, and three wickets to the toiling, swinging Hoggard. It could have been even worse, for Katich pushed the ball low to Bell before he had scored, but the chance was too sharp.

For the day's final over, after Clarke and Katich had begun to retrieve Australia's stark situation, Harmison was called in, and after Clarke had edged the first ball over slips, he nipped the third back to win an impeccable lbw decision from umpire Bucknor. Australia were half out and still 378 runs in arrears as the Englishmen skipped back to the pavilion like excited schoolboys.

Freddie Flintoff again was there to meet the Press. "We're doing all right, aren't we?" he chortled disarmingly, following with the caution: "We're not daft. We know what the Australians can do. We can't get ahead of ourselves." How was he bearing up to the mental and physical workload? "After Old Trafford I was tired, but I got away from the Ashes for a while. In France they're not too worried about the Ashes!"

Adam Gilchrist bravely faced the questioners, modestly attributing his 300 dismissals to the on-going quality of Australia's bowling. He acknowledged that England had been playing with greater consistency, but "we're not bad cricketers; we still believe we're champs." It is always a risk to ask cricketers for public utterances about umpiring decisions, but Gilchrist's response was reasonable: "Marto" was "extremely frustrated" about his. (He had got a bad one in his previous Test innings as well.)

THIRD DAY. Saturday, August 27, 2005

How would Australia mark the 97th anniversary of Don Bradman's birth? Not, as it turned out, with any conspicuous performance. In fact, for the first time in 191 Test matches since Karachi 1988, they were forced to follow on.

There was an early vision of something spectacular from Gilchrist, who lashed Flintoff through the covers before mauling Hoggard with a four and six to midwicket in a memorable over containing two no-balls and two fours from Katich: 22 off. They tried to get after Flintoff as well, Katich whacking fours over point and through cover, and when Vaughan persisted with Hoggard his next over cost 10. Jones replaced him.

His second ball was cut by Katich (45) low into Strauss's hands, and the next turned Warne round, the ball finding the shoulder of a disorientated bat. Suddenly it was 157 for seven and Lee was in to prevent the hat-trick. He played carefully forward, something he was seldom allowed to do thereafter. Master of the nasty rising ball, he was now at the opposite end of the shooting gallery.

A suspicion was starting to take hold that, at the seventh time of asking in this rubber, Gilchrist might produce one of his explosive match-turning specialties. But Flintoff locked him up again by switching to around the wicket, with the smart Fletcher/Vaughan restrictive field setting, and when something came along slightly off-line the batsman tried to clip it away. It flew well wide of the slips, and few – least of all the batsman – could believe what happened next. Andrew Strauss launched himself into space, reached out with both hands, extended the left as the ball screamed past, and clung to a catch which many said had never been bettered. How could it ever have been?

It was a pitiful 175 for nine when Jones bowled Kasprowicz, bringing him 3 for 1 in 14 balls, but a last-wicket resistance of 43 lifted Australia slightly, Brett Lee disdainfully launching two sixes off Harmison (one of them into the street) and one off Jones, top-edging several other balls, protecting Tait with the field well spread, and winning the battle within the battle. At last he was caught near the third-man rope, so very close to a deserved half-century. But he had not done quite enough. Australia, 218, were 259 behind and Vaughan sent them in again. At lunch they were 14 without loss second time round.

As brilliant a catch as any ever seen: Andrew Strauss brings off a stunner to end Adam Gilchrist's innings for 27.

Questions were floating in the air. Who could explain why Harmison had been so ineffective since the opening Test at Lord's? What had happened to render the globally-dominant Hayden-Langer act suddenly so fragile? They were now vulnerable and ordinary, struggling to survive. Hayden admittedly was now making Hoggard look ordinary again, until the Queenslander sliced Flintoff to gully: 50 for one.

A spillage soon followed, Langer, on 37, edging Flintoff to second slip, where Strauss failed to hold a chest-high catch. The batsman was looking more his old self otherwise, cover-driving Flintoff after Ponting had pulled Harmison for six. The bowler then had Langer fending hurriedly, very hurriedly, in front of his face.

Just before tea, for the 28th over, Ashley Giles came on for the first time in the match, and when they trooped off, Langer was 54, his captain 28, and at 115 for one a solid rearguard had been established. Among the crowd, in the media, and in homes all around Britain there was much premature celebration going on, and relishing of a victory as yet to be achieved. There seemed insufficient awareness of the fact that, like Hydra, Australia take a lot of killing.

The stormiest session of the series was about to unfurl. In the third over Langer (61) was taken off glove and pad, as in the first innings, this time off Giles, the bowler's Warwickshire team-mate Bell diving with brilliant reflex action. Ponting and Martyn then held firm in bright sunlight . . . until Martyn dabbed a ball to cover and trotted off for a single. His skipper had to accelerate as he saw the fieldsman swooping on the ball, and as Ponting threw himself at the crease the stumps were shattered. While the umpire's referral was being considered the facts began to fall into place: the fieldsman was Gary Pratt, a 23-year-old Durham player who had not been picked for any County Championship match this summer, but who had been utilised by England coach Duncan Fletcher in six previous Test matches – for reasons which hardly needed spelling out. Had Pratt instead of Stephen Peters been on duty at Old Trafford his throw might have won the match for England.

While the decision was awaited here at Trent Bridge it became apparent that something irregular was going on. Ricky Ponting was talking animatedly with the umpire and shouting across at the Englishmen. When he was signalled out he stomped off, and as he mounted the pavilion steps he was seen to address some remarks to the England balcony, where coach Fletcher noticed, as he later remarked, that the Australia captain was "mumbling something towards us".

Ponting's anguish arose from a long-running problem. During the tour he had felt that England had for some time been abusing the spirit of the game, if not the letter of it, by employing substitute fieldsmen when not strictly necessary. Fast bowlers in particular were the beneficiaries, leaving the field ostensibly to relieve themselves either after a bowling spell or just prior. These absences were

Trigger to trouble: Ricky Ponting is beaten by a sharp pick-up and throw from Gary Pratt, a dismissal that infuriated him because the fieldsman was a substitute, a matter which had been a recurrent grievance to Australia.

viewed with acute suspicion. Were they benefiting from unfair physical treatment and preparation?

I was reminded of the English objections to Dennis Lillee's frequent disappearances with soaked shirt stuck to his back after bowling spells during the 1981 tour. The explanation then was that he was keen to avoid catching pneumonia.

Where Ponting misjudged the situation – an expensive misjudgment, for he was later fined 75% of his match fee – was in failing to see that this particular substitution was entirely legitimate, for Simon Jones was off the field with a serious ankle problem. Pratt's presence in no way could be interpreted as an abuse of the system.

The captain issued an apology for his outburst immediately – and then provocatively repeated his objection to England's actions during a radio interview to a Melbourne station the following day.

As the matter circulated, it was commented more than once that if Australia were so concerned about the spirit of the game, how come some of their bowlers indulged in such grotesquely prolonged and intimidatory appeals?

Tensions were rising, and tomorrow there would be yet another matter for the match referee's serious consideration.

Fast bowler Jones's ankle injury had not been thought serious to begin with, but talk of scans and absence for the remainder of this match caused anxiety. The trouble was a bone spur in the right ankle, an anterior impingement. It could be a struggle to get him right for the final Test 12 days hence.

It would not have pacified Ponting had he noticed that England now had a second substitute in the field, Trevor Penney, the 37-year-old Zimbabwean on Warwickshire's staff, as good an outfielder as any in the land.

Ponting's departure for 48 was soon followed by Martyn (13) when Flintoff found the edge: Australia now 161 for four, still 98 behind.

But Katich and Clarke saw through the last 20 overs of the day, despite some challenging close-in field placements and probing bowling. England did have one chance to separate them, but Geraint Jones fumbled a stumping off Giles when Clarke was 35 and well down the track. Might the recent anonymous, abusive letter to Jones have caused a milli-second of distraction to flash across his brain?

For 88 minutes Katich (24) and Clarke (39) held on until poor light ended play at 6.12pm, Australia 222 for four, still 37 in arrears.

Some English jubilation sounded from Worcester this day after news that the England women's cricket team, led by Clare Connor, had retrieved their own Ashes trophy from Australia at long last by winning the second of their two Tests (the first was drawn) in front of only 100 spectators. If the Border-Taylor-Waugh grip on the Ashes seemed endless at 16 years, how must the women have felt with Australia's possession extending through 42 years back to 1963? Michael Vaughan sent his congratulations before the girls transferred their thoughts to winning the one-day series. They had recently beaten Australia in the shorter game for the first time since 1993, the winning margin at Stratford-upon-Avon being the same as Vaughan's recently at Edgbaston: two rotten little runs. The omens continued to flow.

FOURTH DAY. Sunday, August 28, 2005

There were the usual gasps at near misses, but Clarke and Katich fought on through the first hour of a sunny day, Clarke reaching his elegant fifty off 134 balls, and England wishing that Simon Jones was still with them. Harmison took the new ball and when drinks were taken only 26 runs had been squeezed from 17 overs. This was more like the Australian obduracy of old.

The first boundary did not come until 76 minutes had elapsed, and that was an edge by Clarke. The scores were levelled overall, and then the century stand was posted (191 minutes), only the second of the series by the visitors. The most infuriating way for this resistance to have been broken would have been a run-out, and the bolting Katich was lucky that Flintoff just missed the stumps. The long-awaited wicket came at the other end instead.

Hoggard released one of those mesmerising outswingers and Clarke (56) couldn't resist this one: 261 for five, and Gilchrist instantly down to business, crunching two fours before lunch. As Dr W.G.Grace once shrewdly put it, there is no such thing as a crisis, only the next ball. Players and spectators might have benefited from relying on this philosophy more during this astonishing series.

After lunch Gilchrist (11) soon went, lbw to a seam bowler for the first time in his Test career (105 innings). The strands of the rope bridge of Australia's innings were snapping one after the other.

Simon Katich reached a well-earned fifty after 229 minutes of acute concentration, good Tavare/Mackay stuff, while Warne brought his extroversion and aggressive defiance to the battle. He took several boundaries off Flintoff, who scratched his head.

Out of the blue Harmison took a wicket, though it was not strictly out. Katich was dispatched when a ball pitching outside leg and probably going over the stumps was deemed fatal by umpire Aleem Dar. On his way back to the pavilion the doubting batsman dallied to watch the replay on the big screen, and his jaw dropped. Thereafter he let off his fury, turning some of it onto the spectators airing their views in the pavilion seats. Another batsman, driven over the edge, was about to be fined, half his match fee in this instance. The match was taking on a disturbing trend with these inaccurate verdicts.

Geraint Jones erred again when he leapt to his right to catch Lee before he had scored. The ball fell from his glove. Trescothick at slip might have held the catch. Things were getting frantic again. Warne smashed Giles for six, edged the next, hit a four, was nearly bowled, should have been given out lbw, then Lee might also have been run out, except that Jones knocked a bail off before the ball arrived. It was a period of black comedy.

An edged four by Lee off Harmison preceded another six by Warne off Giles, who then had him stumped for a 45 which had taken only 42 balls and had given Australia the first vision of some kind of target to set England. Simon Jones was missed.

Kasprowicz dealt a few useful blows before Flintoff replaced Giles, a strike high to midwicket seeing Pietersen unbelievably missing his sixth catch of the series (out of six offered). It was not costly. Kasprowicz edged Harmison, and in the excitement umpire Dar called over a ball early and had to reconvene. Flintoff leapt like a giant salmon when Tait edged, and then hit Lee's leg stump without shaking the bails off. An edge or two later it was all over as Tait exposed his stumps to Harmison, and Australia had somehow got to their highest score of the series: 387. England's target was 129, and there cannot have been anybody with brains who considered this a foregone conclusion.

Lee charged in from the Radcliffe Road end and almost bowled Strauss in the opening over. Kasprowicz at the other end was far less dangerous, and after four overs Trescothick had belted 24 of England's 27 runs, mostly off Kasper. The batsmen wanted to get it over with. Warne came on for the sixth over and that was the end of any liberties. From around the wicket he spun his first ball into Trescothick's pad via the bat's edge and Ponting grabbed the rebound. The first ball of the spinner's next over drifted to leg and pitched in the rough, Vaughan (0) tried to drive it towards mid-wicket, and Hayden caught him at slip. It was a major misjudgment, and the first time that Warne had dismissed the England captain this series: 36 for two.

With much dramatic utterance coming from the thespians grouped around the bat, Strauss struck some honest blows, but with the total 57, still not halfway to the target, he turned Warne blindly round the corner where Clarke took the catch so low down that the batsman asked for confirmation from the umpires.

At the other end, without addition, Bell (3) utilised the stroke which is not his best, the hook, and spooned a catch off Lee who was roaring in as if possessed: 57 for four. A sensation looked to be on the cards even though the tough guys, Flintoff and Pietersen,

England's panic rises on the final afternoon as captain Vaughan, playing to leg out of the rough, edges Warne to Hayden at slip.

were together. There were top-edges and inside-edges, but precious runs were fossicked, and there was an unearthly sound about the roars that greeted a genuine four through the covers by Flintoff off the demonstrative, ever-threatening Warne. Pietersen took a highly daring two from a glance down to Kasprowicz. Ponting continued to adjust the field. What could a captain do?

The all-revealing animated television replay showed that an lbw shout by Warne against Flintoff was totally justified, but there is no justice: the batsman lofted the next ball to the boundary. As a stiff breeze rippled shirt-sleeves Pietersen smacked a Tait full-toss to midwicket to bring the hundred up, and after calling for a drink spooned a crude dab off Warne into no-man's land beyond the bowler. England were getting there.

Then Lee returned, and his first ball was a sizzling outswinger. Pietersen (23) attempted to drive and touched it to Gilchrist. Flintoff was joined by his first-innings accomplice Geraint Jones, with 26 still needed, and drinks were brought on.

Lee's no-ball was gratefully received, but Jones's flash at a 96 mph streak made no contact. If anything, Warne had become the soft option in this awkward situation.

Feet as wide apart as any batsman in history, Flintoff (26) waited for more of Lee. It was a shattering ball. It was extremely fast, on a length, and snapped back to hit the off stump. The batsman's jaw simply dropped. Six down now, 18 still needed, England on the Devil's number, 111, as Ashley Giles strode in, a solid, reassuring figure, though surely doomed when some bright spark blurted out that Warne had got him out four times already in this series while conceding a mere eight runs. Greeted with predictable banter, he dealt with his first ball, a yorker, a wasteful no-ball. Then he took a two to midwicket.

After another long discussion between Warne and Ponting, Giles took a single to midwicket off a full-toss. So Warne was not immune to tension either. With 13 needed, Jones (3) decided to break this tension. Some said it was panic. It was more a worthy attempt to seize the initiative. He danced out to Warne, drove without quite middling it, and was horrified to see the ball swirling out to deep mid-off: 116 for seven.

Matthew Hoggard plodded to the centre. "Coom on, let's you and me get it done," he said to Giles, smiling. His partner decided to fill him in on a reality or two: "It's reversing at about 95 mph!" There was only Harmison and the injured Simon Jones to follow. ("I was crapping my pants as I waited to bat," Jones later delicately recalled, "but Harmy was worse than me because he was next in.") "Hoggy" himself had been sheltering in the physio's room, while the captain had not known quite where to sit, such were the comings and goings of the batsmen. Millions were sharing the torment.

Hoggard drove Lee for a two before a bellow for lbw was correctly turned down. England then welcomed another no-ball donation. Giles drove Warne for two wide of mid-off: 121 for seven. If another wicket were to fall now . . . .

Lee to Hoggard: a fierce bouncer calmly avoided; another outside off; a thick edge to Ponting at gully; then a poor ball, on the full, drilled by Hoggard to the cover boundary, a shot his partner claimed never to have seen from him before. There was a mental flashback to Edgbaston: Lee himself had been given a similar ball, but had hit it for only a single when it would have been the winning four had it gone a few metres wider. Hoggard took a two to square leg off the last ball. Two runs now required.

Warne, his quadruple nemesis, crept in to bowl to Giles. It was a full-toss and the batsman hit it against Katich at short leg. No run. Giles next was a whisker away from being bowled between bat and pad. Warne again. The ball came down on the leg stump, the batsman reached forward and calmly and surely placed it to mid-wicket and bolted. England had won by three wickets to go ahead 2–1 in this most stupendous of all Ashes series, Channel 4's audience having just reached a record 8.4 million.

Taking stock of the situation as the blood pressure subsided: England could not lose the series now. They could win the Ashes merely by drawing at The Oval. And the weather forecast indicated extensive rain interruption there from Atlantic troughs.

As the players of both teams drank merrily together for several hours in the Trent Bridge dressing-room, the superstitious reflected on the fact that the winning partnership here had amounted to 13.

Local heroes: lower-order batsmen Ashley Giles and Matthew Hoggard leave the arena after taking England to victory at Trent Bridge with a 13-run stand which was really worth a fortune.

FOURTH TEST MATCH
Trent Bridge, Nottingham, August 25, 26, 27, 28, 2005

ENGLAND		mins	ball	4s			mins	balls	4s
M.E.Trescothick	b Tait	65	138	11	8+	c Ponting b Warne	27	24	22	4
A.J.Strauss	c Hayden b Warne	35	99	64	4	c Clarke b Warne	23	68	37	3
*M.P.Vaughan	c Gilchrist b Ponting	58	145	99	9	c Hayden b Warne	0	8	6	–
I.R.Bell	c Gilchrist b Tait	3	13	5	–	c Kasprowicz b Lee	3	38	20	–
K.P.Pietersen	c Gilchrist b Lee	45	131	108	6	c Gilchrist b Lee	23	51	34	3
A.Flintoff	lbw b Tait	102	201	132	14+	b Lee	26	63	34	3
#G.O.Jones	c & b Kasprowicz	85	205	149	8	c Kasprowicz b Warne	3	25	13	–
A.F.Giles	lbw b Warne	15	45	35	3	not out	7	30	17	–
M.J.Hoggard	c Gilchrist b Warne	10	46	28	1	not out	8	20	13	1
S.J.Harmison	st Gilchrist b Warne	2	9	6	–					
S.P.Jones	not out	15	32	27	3					
Extras	b1, lb15, w1, nb25	42				lb 4, nb 5	9			
	(123.1 overs, 537mins)	477				(31.5 overs, 167mins)7 wkts	129			

+ plus 1 six

Fall: 1/105 2/137 3/146 4/213 5/241 6/418   1/32 2/36 3/57 4/57 5/103 6/111
     7/450 8/450 9/454   7/116

BOWLING: Lee 32-2-131-1 (8nb), Kasprowicz 32-3-122-1 (13nb), Tait 24-4-97-3 (4nb), Warne 29.1-4-102-4, Ponting 6-2-9-1 (1w)
SECOND INNINGS: Lee 12-0-51-3 (5nb), Kasprowicz 2-0-19-0, Warne 13.5-2-31-4, Tait 4-0-24-0

AUSTRALIA		mins	balls	4s			mins	balls	4s
J.L.Langer	c Bell b Hoggard	27	95	59	5	c Bell b Giles	61	149	112	8
M.L.Hayden	lbw b Hoggard	7	41	27	1	c Giles b Flintoff	26	57	41	4
*R.T.Ponting	lbw b S.P.Jones	1	6	6	–	run out (sub: G.J.Pratt)	48	137	89	3+
D.R.Martyn	lbw b Hoggard	1	4	3	–	c G.O.Jones b Flintoff	13	56	30	1
M.J.Clarke	lbw b Harmison	36	93	53	5	c G.O.Jones b Hoggard	56	209	170	6
S.M.Katich	c Strauss b S.P.Jones	45	91	66	7	lbw b Harmison	59	262	183	4
#A.C.Gilchrist	c Strauss b Flintoff	27	58	36	3+	lbw b Hoggard	11	20	11	2
S.K.Warne	c Bell b S.P.Jones	0	2	1	–	st G.O.Jones b Giles	45	68	42	5x
B.Lee	c Bell b S.P.Jones	47	51	44	5y	not out	26	77	39	3
M.S.Kasprowicz	b S.P.Jones	5	8	7	1	c G.O.Jones b Harmison	19	30	26	1
S.W.Tait	not out	3	27	9	–	b Harmison	4	20	16	1
Extras	lb 2, w 1, nb 16	19				b 1, lb 4, nb 14	19			
	(49.1 overs, 242 mins)	218				(124 overs, 548 mins)	387			

+ plus 1 six   x plus 2 sixes   y plus 3 sixes

Fall: 1/20 2/21 3/22 4/58 5/99 6/157   1/50 2/129 3/155 4/161 5/261 6/277
     7/157 8/163 9/175   7/314 8/342 9/373

BOWLING: Harmison 9-1-48-1 (3nb), Hoggard 15-3-70-3 (4nb), S.P.Jones 14.1-4-44-5 (1nb), Flintoff 11-1-54-1 (8nb, 1w)
SECOND INNINGS: Hoggard 27-7-72-2 (1nb), S.P.Jones 4-0-15-0, Harmison 30-5-93-3 (1nb), Flintoff 29-4-83-2 (9nb), Giles 28-3-107-2, Bell 6-2-12-0 (3nb)

Toss won by England	Umpires: Aleem Dar (Pak) & S.A.Bucknor (WI)
Test debut: S.W.Tait	Replay umpire: M.R.Benson (Eng)
Match award: A.Flintoff	Match referee: R.S.Madugalle (SL)

ENGLAND WON BY 3 WICKETS

8

Fifth Test

It's the waiting that hurts. While there were those who wanted the ominous weather forecast to be fulfilled and for rain to pour plentifully over London SE11 between September 8 and 12, others wanted England to win, and win more empathically than at Edgbaston and Trent Bridge – along the lines of the final Test of the 2002–03 series, when a Warne-less and McGrath-less Australia went under by the huge margin of 225 runs. The host nation thus separated into two schools of thought as this unique summer of cricket reached boiling point. Either way England would take back the Ashes. What the two groups had in common was a choking excitement never before experienced.

Aware of the escape clause which a draw offered to England, everyone knew that playing an unnecessarily defensive game in this final battle could lead to trouble. Simon Jones was the chief worry. After long sessions in a sealed hyperbaric oxygen chamber to hasten his recovery from the ankle injury, two days before the Match of a Lifetime a major blow befell England's hopes when Jones was declared unfit to play. At least this time the fast bowler – who meant as much to his side as McGrath meant to his – was not forced to listen to the oik who shrieked "You weak Pommie bastard!" as he was stretchered off the Gabba after his horrifying knee injury in November 2002. What must have stung Jones was the term "Pommie". He is a "Taffy".

Chris Tremlett spoiled his chance of a Test debut at The Oval with a mediocre performance for Hampshire in their victory over Warwickshire in the tense C&G Trophy final at Lord's on September 3 (an undistinguished match for Kevin Pietersen for the winners and Ashley Giles for the losers, though Ian Bell batted well for 54 until leg cramps thwarted him). England called up two others into the squad: Paul Collingwood, with heaps of runs behind him for Durham, and James Anderson, the blunted prodigy who had recently regained his pace and swing with Lancashire.

Australia, via various interviews and quotes, and in the face of some crushing reactions in the media back home, were trying to convince everybody that all the pressure was on England. Ought it to be accepted now that England are indeed the better team? Matthew Hoggard, for one, thought so. He wrote after Old Trafford that "to hear the Australians celebrating a *draw* so loudly in their dressing-room . . . was an indication of the way the balance has shifted."

So how might a composite team look now, chosen on performances in the first four Tests? Perhaps Trescothick, Strauss and Vaughan would be the top three, followed by Ponting and Clarke; Flintoff at six, of course; Warne, Lee, Simon Jones and McGrath to bowl; nothing to choose between the wicketkeepers, so we'll settle for Geraint Gilchrist: evens!

❊ ❊ ❊

The peculiar tour itinerary threw up a two-day (and therefore non-first-class) match against Essex before the fifth Test, and to their embarrassment the Australians were kept in the field throughout the 105 overs bowled on the Saturday while the county pounded out 502 runs. A double-century came from tall 20-year-old left-hander Alastair Cook, a former England Under-19 captain, who had received his Young Cricketer of the Year award at the Cricket Writers Club's annual dinner in London the night before. Ravi Bopara, also 20 and also English-born, delighted with a century.

They had a stand of 270. Just as well prolific batsman Andy Flower had taken the match off.

The Australians of 1948 had famously scored a record 721 on the opening day of their match against Essex (at Southend). Their 2005 successors might have fancied a crack at that – if they ever knew about it, that is. Bill Brown, Don Bradman, Sam Loxton and Ron Saggers made centuries on that memorable mid-May day 57 years ago, when the run rate was 5.59 per over. Essex's bowlers in 1948 sent down 129 overs, conscientious endeavour no longer to be found, the current county "attack" settling for only 95 overs, off which 561 runs were blasted at 5.91, a rate even higher than in 1948.

Calmed down after the blown gasket at Trent Bridge, Ricky Ponting briefly took the field as twelfth man, and after firing a return over the bails he turned to the onlookers and quipped, "Not bad for a sub!"

CHELMSFORD, September 3, 4, 2005
ESSEX 502 for 4 dec (W.I.Jefferson 64, A.N.Cook 214, R.S.Bopara 135, J.S.Foster 38*); AUSTRALIANS 561 for 6 dec (J.L.Langer 87, M.L.Hayden 150, S.M.Katich 72, B.J.Hodge 166, B.J.Haddin 59). *MATCH DRAWN.*

Among current conjectures, the Australians were expected to call up Shane Watson, recently a double-centurion for Hampshire and bowling briskly. Mike Hussey was another seen as a possible replacement for, perhaps, Hayden; but the prolific Hussey was now on his way to play for Australia A in Pakistan. Instead, the tall 29-year-old fast bowler Stuart Clark was enlisted as cover for Glenn McGrath, with whom he once opened the bowling for Sutherland in Sydney grade cricket. Clark had been playing for Middlesex and bowling steadily: no more than that. It looked as if the Old Guard, for all their recent failings and insecurities, would be trusted to fight this last-ditch stand for the Ashes.

Meanwhile, on the omens-superstitions front, news came through on this opening day that the Australian author Donald Horne had died at the age of 83. His most famous book was *The Lucky Country*. How lucky might Ponting's men be now, when it mattered more than ever?

FIRST DAY. Thursday, September 8, 2005

England's captain in the Bodyline series of 1932-33, D.R.Jardine, was more liverish than usual when the Harbour Bridge, Sydney's new pride and joy, was shown to him. As some RAAF aircraft flew above it, he sneered, "I wish they were Japs and I wish they'd bomb that bridge into their harbour." Had such an outrage occurred, the resulting structural profile remaining above water level would not have been dissimilar to the new £25-million construction at the Vauxhall end at The Oval which stretches from near the famous gas-holders almost across to Stoddart House. Despite the development, the ground still accommodates no more than 23,000. There we sat in the new media centre, the lucky ones such as myself in the fresh air, brushed by the crowd's noise throughout, while less fortunate media brethren sat cramped in the stuffy room behind us. This is the fifth Press box I've known here since the mid-1960s, and none of them has been much good. Surrey County Cricket Club's priorities have long been a puzzle.

But one should not complain, for this was the most compelling Test match for an age. And it started with Vaughan winning the very important toss and taking first use of an immaculate pitch. The superstitious tried hard to ignore the fact that it was pitch number 13 on this historic square.

Collingwood was in England's XI, so the prospect faded of an unaltered team for all five Tests – the first since 1884-85 (when Arthur Shrewsbury's side on the long tour of Australia consisted of only 13 players). The weather remained an urgent topic of discussion, but for now the sun burned all in its compass as the rousingly-sung *Jerusalem* rose from the loudspeakers. For anybody to whom cricket is a form of religion, it was like being in church.

McGrath bounced the new ball extravagantly and Lee was again hot stuff, though Trescothick and Strauss were on alert for anything loose. England's policy of search and destroy, for all its risks, was clearly still in force. In the 14 overs before the first drinks break 70 runs were chalked up from skilful strokeplay interwoven with determined defence, and home expectation was high. But the second hour changed that. Warne, carrying almost all of Australia's hopes on his brawny shoulders, took the ball for the 14th over and soon lured Trescothick (43) into jabbing at one coming in. Hayden took a sharp two-handed catch at slip. Vaughan (11), serene as ever, pulled Warne and played a lyrical cover-drive, but with the hundred up, right heel flung high behind him, he squirted a catch to midwicket. The picture altered further when Bell, without a run, fell to Warne's straight ball a few minutes later: a shaky 104 for three just before lunch.

Pietersen is incurable. Lunch pending? So what? Tait came on and KP laced him through the covers, was beaten, glanced for another four, cover-drove a two, and walked off satisfied: 115 for three, Strauss a watchful 42, Pietersen 10.

It was obvious that Warne was going to bowl heaps of overs in supposedly his final Test on English soil, with support coming mainly from McGrath and Lee bringing bounce and sparks from time to time. A rasping lifter had Strauss risking whiplash as he jerked his head away from danger. A back-cut four gave him a 79-ball fifty, but a fierce cut was wonderfully intercepted by Hayden. Australian pressure stemmed from desperation. Let England recover the Ashes from some wretched future generation of Australian cricketers, not us. And now, to advance this desperate cause, they rid themselves of the dangerous Pietersen. Warne's 13th ball to him whipped through a gaping hole to bowl him: 131 for four.

Flintoff misjudged his first ball but survived and Warne was patted on the back by half the team at the end of the over. In him their desperate hopes rested. The concerted effort to finish Flintoff off quickly continued with bouncers from Lee, all little short of 100 mph: one nearly hit his throat, another clanged his helmet and went for four leg-byes.

When Warne held a long conference with his captain, from the terraces came catcalls and whistles, to which he responded in mime. Warne is a performer in every sense of the word, and he craves control of any situation. Flintoff does too, and he hit Lee through cover off the back foot and played him to third man. The ball was coming to him at lightning speed but without much deviation. Unusually wicketless, McGrath returned at the pavilion end, and Strauss played him through midwicket: 161 for four at the drinks break.

The consolidation continued until tea: 213 for four. There had been a raucous appeal (in truth, the only kind of appeal heard all summer) when Flintoff floundered against Warne. All the fielders went berserk, but umpire Bowden kept his crooked finger by his side. A steer through the covers off Warne which Clarke just failed to flick back on the rope took Strauss to 75, and the left-hander actually had the lion's share of the fifty stand with Flintoff. The tension subsided when Warne took a short rest and Tait and Katich were tried, and there was a sizzling straight-drive by Flintoff off the fast man. The 200 came in the 52nd over, a healthy rate, as it should have been on this splendid surface.

Strauss flashed twice at Tait, but his big partner played a model cover-drive, and after the interval Warne returned, to be smashed through the open midwicket area by Flintoff, and, in the spinner's next over, to concede three successive fours – two swept, one banged down the ground on the full – as the Lancastrian heavyweight reached his fifty and raised the century stand. He closed the over with an immaculate forward defensive, cheered just as enthusiastically.

Now the spotlight returned to Strauss, who was about to become the only batsman to register two hundreds in this historic series. He pushed Lee wide of mid-on for four off the 150th ball he had faced, taking England to 239 for four, and recovery.

Flintoff's bat had sounded bad and he now changed it. With the sun shining gloriously he proved the solidity of the new weapon with cuts and drives, while Strauss also got every run he could. Lee lifted one at his face, which was saved only by the bat-handle, and the bowler was very agitated when umpire Koertzen refused a shout for caught behind later that over.

The first six of the match came from Flintoff off Warne, into the Barmy Army's ranks at long-on, and soon the batsman was cooling off at the drinks break with a large ice-pack on his head that conjured visions of William "Braveheart" Wallace. Like the Scottish warrior, he was not to survive long. McGrath found the edge and Warne held a good low catch at slip. Flintoff (72) and Strauss had reshaped the match with a stand of 143, and England supporters were reassured by the entry of Collingwood at No.7. The Durham man had been a run machine for his county this summer.

Andrew Strauss continued to run with great purpose for a man who had begun batting mid-morning. This did seem, though, to be a bowler's graveyard – unless you happened to spin the ball like a top. Shane Warne wants always to command the show. An lbw shout against Strauss was followed by a long freeze by the side of the pitch with horrified expression, and then a lengthy parliamentary session with the umpire. Much of the fire of the celebrated "Tiger" O'Reilly burns within him. As he toiled away, the occasional googly restored to his repertoire, it seemed an outside possibility that he might even come close to O'Reilly's 85 overs here in 1938, when England made 903 for seven and Len Hutton 364.

Collingwood (7) was unlucky. Tait struck him just outside the line as he played at the ball, and umpire Koertzen granted the appeal, reigniting the worst fear of all: that this supremely important Test match might hang at the last on a dubious umpiring decision. Three overs later Australia clawed back more territory when they got rid of Strauss after his admirable performance. His 129 extended over almost six hours before he pad-batted to short leg off Warne, who thus claimed his fifth wicket, and for the first time in his 128 Tests had dismissed the first four in the batting order (a further mark, surely, of Australia's reduced new-ball power). Strauss said later that this was the best of his seven centuries (all scored in a mere 19 Tests and 16 months), though he hadn't really enjoyed it, so intense was the situation. "Lord Brocket", as the only public-school-educated member of the side is known to his chums, will never play a more important innings than this.

Geraint Jones acquired some handsome fours and survived a narrow run-out call, and as the shadows lengthened Warne's

Andrew Strauss was caught at short leg off Warne in both innings, but the century he had made in the first set England up after a wobbly start.

marathon of 34 overs ended for the day, full effort going into that shoulder, wrist and finger right to the end. Ponting claimed the new ball 10 minutes from the close, but England finished with a reasonably satisfying 319 for seven.

SECOND DAY. Friday, September 9, 2005
The day broke mistily, the haze restricting visibility to 100 metres at dawn. Soon, though, the sun was burning through it and it was hot in the centre when Jones and Giles resumed. Australia quickly broke through. The wicketkeeper forced his first ball, from Lee, to the cover boundary and was bowled by the next: 325 for eight.

This brought together the heroes of the crisis at Trent Bridge, and Hoggard immediately became the coconut at the fairground as McGrath sprayed him with bouncers. Giles hooked him for four, but his partner, still scoreless, survived a low left-hand catch to

Ponting before finally notching his first run from the 30th ball he faced. Then a ball from McGrath finished in Gilchrist's gloves, to roared appeals, only for umpire Koertzen to shake his head. A run came every two minutes until Warne stepped into the attack again after 50 minutes.

But it was McGrath who broke this irritating stand when Hoggard (2) lobbed tamely to cover. Rudi Koertzen was unmoved again when the Australians went up for caught-behind with Giles on 24, and after Harmison had heaved and top-edged four fours in his merry 20, Giles was given out lbw to Warne, a poor decision by Billy Bowden in a session where the umpires earned far more attention than was normal.

England 373, respectable but far from formidable. This Ashes decider was still wide open as Langer and Hayden sought to find some form when it mattered more than ever before in this series. Harmison bowled fast bouncers at them and Hoggard swung the ball late, and when Collingwood hurled his lithe body to intercept at square cover, the crowd thought it was a miracle catch, and their roars died in their throats. Hoggard then beat Hayden both on the hook and on the defensive.

Nineteen without loss at lunch, the Australians resumed under a sky across which clouds were gathering. Soon the ground began to lose its glare and the Barmy Army chorus was at its most tedious, willing the fall of an Australia wicket which simply refused to materialise. Hayden was playing the quiet role. The highest of his previous eight innings was 36 and his career was on the line. It was the 18th over before he tiptoed into double figures.

For the 19th over, from the pavilion end, Ashley Giles was called up. There was a big surprise in store. Justin Langer whacked his second ball into the nearby Bedser Stand and took another six, slightly wider, from the fourth. A two to long-on brought him 50 from 63 balls, out of 66, a fine piece of targeting – Langer had twice fallen to Giles via short-leg catches – that persuaded Vaughan to switch his spinner to the other end. There he gamely looped the first ball to Langer and nearly did him.

It was thought that Collingwood would be no real replacement for Simon Jones, with his 18 cheap wickets in the four preceding Tests; but he now beat Langer and then found the edge. The catch went high to Trescothick's right. He failed to hold it. Langer survived to go on quietly murdering Giles.

With 12 added, Langer, now 65, might have been stumped had Jones reacted a flash faster, and when he swept at Giles there was an appeal from over 20,000 throats – justified, as it transpired, though umpire Bowden thought not. Giles himself had been robbed of his wicket this very morning. Whoever expects justice from the game of cricket is a fool.

Soon these prolific left-handers posted their 14th century opening stand together, Langer 75, Hayden 25, the circus strong man playing second fiddle to the little fella. Their rich association had begun on this ground four years ago, when Langer was brought in to replace the disorientated Michael Slater (who was now up in the TV commentary box). Langer's career was rekindled with a century in that 2001 Oval Test, an innings ended when Andy Caddick knocked him to the canvas, bells ringing in his head so soon after he had reached three figures. Four days later Australia sealed their fourth substantial victory of the series: all part of the repetitive humiliation which England were currently fighting so hard to overturn.

It therefore came as an enormous surprise when Australia, bursting for a victory which would save the Ashes, accepted the umpires' offer to leave the field before resumption after tea because of poor light. They (captain, batsmen and senior players) had reasoned that if a wicket were to fall a new batsman could struggle against Harmison and Flintoff in such conditions, and three or four wickets could easily topple before the light deteriorated enough for the umpires to make a further offer. The reasoning was supported by the knowledge that with time to be made up the net loss would not be so great, and most Tests now seem to be over in only four days. The lighting on both scoreboards gleamed eerily and raindrops began to fall. Notwithstanding, a few Australians, journalists included, were furious at what seemed such a weak withdrawal.

THIRD DAY. Saturday, September 10, 2005

The start was delayed for half-an-hour while surface moisture was cleared and the light lifted a little, though it remained murky. But Australia needed to press on. Hoggard's first ball should have earned him Langer's wicket, leg-before, but he was reprieved. His bat more like the railway sleeper of old, former world record-holder Hayden played a booming cover-drive, and English anxiety intensified.

A further half-hour was lost to rain, but the batsmen settled in again, and a ball after Flintoff had hit him in the guts Hayden raced off for a single to post his first fifty of the series. It had taken him 191 minutes, and with the sun poking through, Australia were looking good at 141 without loss.

Flintoff again seemed to be far and away England's best bowler, reverse-swinging and varying his length. But he had to be rested, and Harmison came on opposite the faithful Hoggard. Lunch was taken at 157 for none off 47 overs, Langer 91, Hayden 60.

The afternoon brought more sub-standard light, so much so that boundary fieldsmen often failed to pick up the ball and moved either in the wrong direction or not at all. It was no fun facing Harmison in these conditions, especially for Langer, whose score had climbed to 97. Twice bouncers went so far over his helmet that they were called as wides. Then he got one in the slot, back-cut it, and had his fourth century against England, 22nd in all (this four also took him past Bradman's aggregate of 6996). A flick over the slips for four straight afterwards brought up his 7000th Test run.

In a flurry of records, the opening pair next overtook an old first-wicket partnership best for Australia at The Oval, the 180 made by Warren Bardsley and Syd Gregory in 1909, and drew level with England's even more venerable Ashes first-wicket best on this ground, the 185 by F.S. Jackson and Tom Hayward in 1899.

Here England's frustration suddenly ended. Langer (105) played a lifting ball from Harmison down onto his thigh and thence the off stump. Ponting was halfway down the steps when light rain drove the players from the field. Nor did the poor light and specks of rain soon let up. It was 3.30 pm, almost two hours later, before play resumed. Needless to say the crowd were content with the hold-up. Every minute was a minute closer to that euphoric moment when England reclaimed the Ashes. Every time the umpires, having checked conditions with their light-meters, returned to their room they were cheered as if they had taken another couple of wickets.

Harmison loped in to bowl to Ponting, the crowd's lungs like factory hooters. Australia's skipper was made to hop about. On 83, Hayden edged Giles just wide of Jones, and in the same over Ponting, on 13, inside-edged to silly point off his pad, a dismissal clearly detected by television for the benefit of countless millions watching television but not for the umpire. Roll on the day when commonsense prevails.

Rain, we were told, was falling on Lord's and Chelmsford and other places, and was the predominant consideration for both sides. Matthew Hayden, though, ground on, reaching his 1000 runs against England (25th innings), and then his fourth century, driving Flintoff to the pavilion, then for a single, then for another four to the pavilion. He received not only a big hug from his captain but a friendly half-hug from the bowler. It was Hayden's 21st Test century, his first for 31 innings in just over a year, and he had also reached 6000 Test runs. It took him 289 minutes and was seemingly a career-saver.

There were lustier cheers shortly afterwards when rain fell again, and this time just over an hour was lost. Australia, 243 for one, with Ponting an agitated and lucky 20, were 130 behind England.

At least the interruptions kept England's reduced squad of bowlers fresh. When the players re-entered the arena it was still gloomy and there was distant thunder. Harmison and Flintoff would be menacing in these conditions. Vaughan set an in-and-out field, aimed at curbing singles and boundaries. Huge pressure was building up for Australia, who simply had to win. If the truth be known, both sides were a little scared of each other in this situation. Giles's accuracy against Hayden built that pressure further. With Harmison once again strangely failing to live up to expectation, Flintoff took over. It worked. His second ball jumped at Ponting

Matthew Hayden, his dismal series rounded off with a painstaking century at The Oval, is congratulated by Steve Harmison as he leaves the field.

(35), who could only fend it to gully, where Strauss took a very good plunging catch. Martyn's second ball was not dissimilar, but he played it for four through point. But in Flintoff's next over he almost removed Martyn's head, beat him twice more as he tried to persuade the ball to third man. And a touch to the wicketkeeper was unrecognised by the umpire.

At 6.23 pm the umpires had yet another little chat and the field was emptied of players for the last time this day, Australia 277 for two,

96 in arrears, Hayden 110, Martyn 9, three days now gone. Soon the selected players came into the interview room. Justin Langer wanted to talk about Hayden – "my big mate". He reckoned he had started to look loose and free in that high-scoring Essex match. Asked whether Langer himself hoped to return for the 2009 Ashes series, he said self-mockingly, "Maybe, but we're a very old team!"

Matt Hayden smiled from under his prize eyebrows as he admitted that he was practically "relearning how to bat in Test cricket", concentrating on trying to play fairly straight. He thought the pitch slow and the game now had to be taken to England.

Freddie Flintoff would have known that full well, and his mission statement was clear enough over the "massive" two days remaining: "Every ounce we've got left we're going to leave out there."

FOURTH DAY. Sunday, September 11, 2005

It was again overcast, but the spots of rain were few, and a prompt 10.30 am start was made. And in the third over, Martyn was gone. A fast one from Flintoff came through at an awkward height, catching the batsman halfway through his leg-side shot. The ball spooned to square leg: 281 for three.

The new ball was taken and Hoggard bowled a skilful over of outswingers to Clarke, who soon touched one, only for Flintoff surprisingly to miss the high catch at second slip. Hayden got the strike and launched two hefty drives to the boundary, leaving Vaughan sprawling. Then he nearly played on.

A whippy throw by Collingwood, England's ace fieldsman, was worth a try, but gave Hayden a five. England contained Australia to 42 in the first hour before drinks were taken, and straight afterwards Hayden's seven-hour effort was terminated for 138. Flintoff brought the ball back at him and hit the pad as he played forward: 323 for four.

Katich played and missed, and with the disappointing Harmison giving way to Hoggard again Clarke hit square on the off side, the ball falling just short of Bell in the deep. With the match poised we were in for some very absorbing cricket.

Australia's collapse was hastened now by Katich's timid downfall, walking across his wicket, as he usually does, and trapped lbw by Flintoff. Hoggard beat Gilchrist first ball, but this match-turning left-hander played him to the square-leg boundary and pulled another four, with the square-leg fieldsman raising his hands helplessly, unable to see the ball, so dim was the light. Next, Flintoff was through Gilchrist – only for the next ball, a half-volley, to be sent skimming to the rope. Gilchrist's luck seemed to be in this time as he edged Hoggard for four, and only a brilliant save by Collingwood cut off another. There was mass hand-clapping, accelerating as Hoggard ran in to bowl, followed by a resounding "Ooooooh!" as the ball flew through to the keeper. None thought of constraining their emotions.

Michael Clarke, in his 17th Test, reached 1000 runs (average still just above 40), and with Gilchrist he seemed capable of building fast to an Australian lead that would make life uncomfortable for England in the remaining time. There would be no appeal against the light today – not by the batsmen at any rate.

There now came what seemed a conclusive slide of fortunes. The remaining five wickets were soaked up fast. Just after Gilchrist seemed to have edged Flintoff to Jones (appeal refused by Koertzen) he was lbw to Hoggard. Lunch was taken there and then. But upon resumption, Clarke (25) was also lbw to Hoggard, having just been put down high to his right by wicketkeeper Jones. That was the fourth leg-before in a row. And the extraordinary thing about it was that they were all perfect verdicts.

Flintoff's fifth wicket of the innings came when Warne went for a duck, trying to pull a 90-mph ball over mid-on. "Super Fred!" screamed the fans after Vaughan, not the greatest fielder in the side, secured the catch after a little bobble. McGrath (0) now edged Hoggard to second slip, and with six fieldsmen patrolling the boundary Lee hit Hoggard to wide deep midwicket, where Giles held a running catch and held the ball aloft as if betokening victory.

Well, there were still risks ahead, but to widespread surprise Australia had been dispatched for 367 to give England the unexpected bonus of a six-run lead on first innings. The last seven wickets had crashed for 44 runs in 90 balls.

But there were still many overs to come in this match, and the figure of Shane Warne loomed like the sinister ghost of Australian Triumphs Past. Anybody who said he might not be capable of destroying England's second innings, letting Australia snatch the Ashes at the last gasp, knew nothing of cricket.

And that sinister ghost, because of the threat posed by continuing poor light, came on for the fourth over of England's second innings, and struck instantly. Strauss played tamely to short leg and England were 2 for one wicket. As the comedians on the terraces struck up *Singin' in the Rain* and tried to con the umpires by raising their umbrellas, every forward defensive was cheered as if it were a six out of the ground. Warne showed off with a leg-break which turned almost square. One kept low. Another beat the edge. Such tension: and we still had tomorrow to endure.

At 2.23 pm the umpires offered the light to Trescothick (who had just become the first batsman in the series to reach 400 runs) and Vaughan, who accepted it almost before the words had been uttered. Shortly, umpire Koertzen was explaining – perhaps not quite capturing the precise adjective – that the Australians had been "happy" at the decision.

The covers were wheeled on. The scoreboard lights gleamed merrily. Raindrops fell here and there. Young Australians in the crowd tried to demonstrate what a beautiful day it was by stripping to the waist. And we serious chaps began working out just how long England had to survive to feel safe. It seemed they would need to bat for most of the final day tomorrow, when the weather was expected to be good.

There was just over half an hour's further play on this truncated day and England's tall, serious pair negotiated it safely. Warne and McGrath were the defenders of Australia's faith, but Vaughan is never willing to miss a scoring opportunity, whatever the match situation. Cuts either side of point showed McGrath that there was no fear. When Warne spun one past Vaughan's outside edge, however, the umpires concerned themselves again as to whether the light enabled a fair contest and decided that it didn't. Warne took it upon himself to engage one of the umpires in conversation, but their minds were made up. England 34 for one, Trescothick 14, Vaughan 19. It was still only 3.43 pm but there was to be no further play today.

The most important artefact in the world of cricket – every bit as significant as the Ashes urn itself – was now the light-meter. The men in white shirts came out periodically to check the reading and each time there was no improvement. The two top teams in the world were poised a day away from a conclusion of supreme significance. Alfred Hitchcock never came near to staging such a sustained thriller as this series or even this day.

The cricket lost over the first four days amounted to 134 overs. The Australians' frustration may easily be imagined.

FIFTH DAY. Monday, September 12, 2005

Ninety-eight overs were scheduled to be bowled on this fateful day. While English confidence and brewing excitement were at high levels, there was still a long way to go. I thought of the premature mock obituary published around Manchester in 1902, 20 years after the *Sporting Times* joke announcement which led to the creation of the Ashes urn after the 1882 upset at The Oval. On the penultimate evening of the 1902 Old Trafford Test, Australia were 122 ahead with two wickets in hand. A Mr Griffiths of Ardwick thought this a strong enough position to guarantee England victory. Beneath a sketch of a horse-drawn funeral carriage he printed the following on his cards:

> *The Australia men, their players feel*
> *The blighting, withering blast,*
> *For full of hope, they thought to steal*
> *The verdict at last:*
> *Twas not to be, so let them lie*
> *Deep in the silent grave,*
> *And shed a tear, o'er their bier,*
> *And the match they tried to save.*

Mr Griffiths was forced to withdraw the cards from sale when Australia were bowled to victory by Trumble and Saunders by three runs.

Forty ahead, nine wickets in hand, up to 98 overs to play. Would England prevail or might Ponting's men roll them over quickly and knock off the runs? The pre-lunch session pointed resoundingly towards the latter course and completely ruined the digestion of millions of England supporters.

For a time it went smoothly. Superstitions were put firmly in their place. While the Aussies must have been praying that Warne would not fall down the stairs and break his right wrist, I merely gave my customary nod towards the grave of Lewis Carroll in the church-yard on the way to the railway station early on this autumnal morning, urging the creator of *Alice* not to spring anything too illogical or bizarre upon the realm of cricket this day.

Again, had there been floodlights at The Oval they might have been switched on at the start. But the sky was clearing gradually as England went about their business. Warne and McGrath, 1132 Test wickets between them to date, began their desperate mission. England's two seniors played them calmly. Vaughan even drove the second ball of the day, from Warne, to the long-on boundary. Lee took over from Warne, but Vaughan took a four backward of point and edged McGrath for another. The fifty came up. Trescothick reached 1000 runs against Australia. It was all too serene.

Then McGrath made a double strike. He found Vaughan's edge and Gilchrist completed a magnificent diving catch low down. A man and a woman clad in scanty swimwear ran uncaringly across the field (until apprehended) between this dismissal and Ian Bell's first ball, which also proved fatal. He edged to Warne at slip, and sloped off, victim of a "pair".

Kevin Pietersen came in on the hat-trick. McGrath slipped him a vicious lifter. He rocked back like a boxer pole-axed and the ball flew high to second slip. The appeals were frenzied, insistent, un-receptive to refusal. But in what was probably the most important decision he'll ever make, umpire Bowden said "Not out!" The ball had struck Pietersen's shoulder and nothing else. So he got down the other end and nicked Warne. The ball touched Gilchrist's glove and eluded Hayden's desperate grasp. It could be said that KP would be lucky to make nought.

More jumping and hollering from Warne as a gyrating ball hit Trescothick's pads, but Pietersen hooked McGrath for four and at drinks England had calmed down somewhat at 79 for three.

The sky was clearing and 85 overs remained, so if anything Australia were in control and might have had strong expectations of yet saving the series. Warne had the usual intimidating box of four close fieldsmen, and when a throw from Clarke tried for a run-out and plucked a stump out of the ground, nerves jangled.

On 15, Pietersen edged Lee to Warne collarbone-high at first slip. He couldn't hold it. And with that, though it was some time before it became obvious, the Ashes were lost. It was the cruellest stroke of fate against the most powerful bowling agent of the series.

The key moment: Kevin Pietersen has touched a ball from Brett Lee to slip fieldsman Shane Warne, who fails to cling to the catch.

It seemed to matter little when Trescothick (33) was lbw to a sharply-spinning ball from Warne, reducing England to 109 for four. This took Shane Warne to 168 wickets against England, passing Dennis Lillee's record, a matter to be savoured later, for battle now was raging full bore. Flintoff's early dismissal, caught for 8 from a return catch to Warne, saw the Australians absolutely exultant. England 126 for five, a mere 132 ahead with all the top-order men bar Pietersen accounted for, and bags of time remaining.

Just before Trescothick's dismissal, Pietersen had belted two sixes off a Warne over, one over midwicket, the other swept over square, with a crude swipe in between. Now the Hampshire batsman took one in the ribs from Lee and sought attention. He later claimed he was being a bit of a "drama queen", but it must have hurt. When Lee bounced him again, with half a Bodyline field in position, there was booing. Maybe some knew about Larwood's blow to Woodfull's chest at Adelaide in '33, and of how, when he was recovered, he was bounced again, this time to a fully-manned Bodyline field.

By the grace of God, Pietersen made it to lunch (127 for five) with his head still attached to his neck. He was 35, Collingwood was still with him, having scored no runs, and much of the nationwide cocksuredness had been deflated.

England's aggressive approach was ingrained by now, and upon resumption Pietersen hooked Lee for six, way over the waiting fieldsman. Seventy-one overs were left and England led by 147. Not only were Collingwood's forward defensives being noisily applauded; so were the leaves. Pietersen reached his half-century from 71 balls, but soon Lee was after him again with rockets of close to 100 mph. He hooked him and the ball seemed to be threatening the gas-holder. The next was hooked too, but Tait just failed to make a catch of it in the deep. KP then *hit* a glance for four: not merely letting the ball run off the blade of the bat.

Brett Lee was bowling his heart out and at blistering pace. It was Tom Richardson at Old Trafford all over again, when England tried to stop Australia getting 125 in the 1896 Test match, and he sent down 42.3 consecutive five-ball overs. A vital catch was dropped by England wicketkeeper Lilley (yes, they did it in those days too) and Australia got home by three wickets. The dazed Richardson was led from the field, wrote the fantasist Cardus, "like some fine animal baffled at the uselessness of great strength and effort in this world" (whereas another account states that Tom had sunk a couple of pints before the players had got their boots off). This was the kind of distraction needed to pacify the nerves on this electrifying afternoon at The Oval in 2005. Like Richardson of old, Lee "did bowl and bowl and bowl, and his fury diminished not a jot".

What might Cardus have made of Kevin Pietersen though? Another four under the body of the diving Clarke, another slammed through mid-on, and when the fifty stand came, Collingwood's staunch contribution was a mere four runs. We were seeing fresh folklore under construction.

Katich went off for a while after being struck by a Collingwood pull. While England would have had a super-athletic substitute on in his place, Kasprowicz came on for Australia.

God Save Your Queen rose from the Barmy Army ranks now. They were getting their confidence back after the shocks. "Five-nil! Five-nil!" they taunted Glenn McGrath when he fielded in front of them. Four leg-side byes off Warne were cheered gratefully. Then the next breakthrough: Collingwood (10) fell to Warne, Ponting launching into a dive at short leg: 186 for six.

Geraint Jones gave his impression of the infamously dogged Trevor Bailey forward defensive as clouds seemed to be gathering again, and the strains of *Jerusalem* once more sent shivers down the spine. The climax was upon us. England led by 195 with 56 overs remaining. Australia, in their desperate position, would surely be capable of lashing anything up to 10 or even 12 runs an over when the time came?

Pietersen slashed Tait for two fours when he bowled for the first time in the 57th over. But the young quickie beat Jones (1) with sheer pace, the ball not rising quite as expected either: 199 for seven. Again an interloper had inspired a wicket, for a large man in a ballerina's tutu had just run across the ground before being carted away by a handful of the hundreds of zealous security men in attendance, with Johnny Dennis on the PA pleading desperately for people not to run on.

Ashley Giles took a calm single to bring up 200, and Pietersen showed he could play copybook as well as kindergarten shots by placing Tait off his toes for four. He was now in the nineties, and Warne teased him with wide balls, one of which was called. Then, just on tea, Pietersen cover-drove Tait for four to raise his first Test century (124 balls, 10 fours, four sixes), an ecstatic moment for him and millions of others. It is hard to see how any hundred he may make in the years ahead could carry such weight of significance.

At tea England were 221 for seven, and close now, surely, to safety?

And so to the final session of the greatest series in 128 years of Test cricket. Giles was the target of bouncers, which he rode well. One from Lee was timed at 96.7 mph. He swayed clear. When Lee

Pietersen, whose fiery 158 led England's final surge to Ashes success at The Oval, deals combatively with another of Lee's thunderbolts.

bounced Pietersen, however, he smote it into the Peter May Enclosure, and in the next over he pounded his sixth six, straight off
Warne. That equalled Ian Botham's overall record for an Ashes
innings, and it wasn't long before he had the record all to himself,
lofting an on-drive off his pal Warne for a seventh six. The audacity
and the exuberance of it all took the breath away.

McGrath replaced the exhausted Lee, and Giles looked at ease.
Warne was beginning to look slightly slumped. His match effort
would be 75 overs, his tally 12 wickets, giving him 40 for the series,
a record for Australia against England in a five-Test rubber. He had
seen the tantalising hopes of the morning slowly give way to blank
despair: the Ashes were lost. And he'd put Pietersen down at 15;
here he was 152 not out.

Transfer of the Ashes was not official yet, of course. The new ball
was taken at 298 for seven, after 80 overs, and a quick single to
cover by Giles raised the hundred stand (143 balls), resistance that
made certain of the outcome. The partnership had reached 109 – a
new eighth-wicket record for England against Australia at The
Oval, passing the 90 by Walter Read and Johnny Briggs in 1886 –
when Pietersen's amazing effort came to an end. McGrath knocked
his off stump out when he was 158, coincidentally the score made by
another South Africa-born England batsman, Basil D'Oliveira, on
this ground in 1968, a century that had major political repercus-
sions. It's a team game, but if anybody above all others could be said
to have secured the Ashes it was 25-year-old Kevin Peter Pietersen,
whose brave assault had saved England's hopes from melting in the
white-hot crucible.

Even the stuffiest onlooker forgave him his hair-style and his
diamond ear-stud as he saluted the crowd on his way from the
arena (using his third bat after breaking two). And to reconfirm
the lovely spirit in which this series was played, Warne ran a long
way after him to congratulate him. I fancied, too, that the ghosts of
F.S.Jackson and his players of 1905 might have been applauding
from the balconies – though they might have been difficult to spot
midst all the gaudy commercial tack attached to that grand old

pavilion. And it so happened that Pietersen's going practically coincided with Richie Benaud's departure from the Channel 4 commentary seat for the last time.

Pietersen's innings was orthodox and original, defiant, daring, cautious where unavoidable. "There's a little bit of a genius in him," Vaughan summed up later, while KP stressed that "Australia have been playing this kind of cricket for a decade." He let loose more "fantastics" that evening than he had hit sixes, and he revealed that his mother had been watching. He would not be seeing her again for some time.

McGrath now plucked Giles's off stump out too, though only jokingly. The batsman had pulled away, unsighted, and the bowler didn't fancy rupturing himself by slamming on the brakes. Giles punched him through the covers then pulled him through mid-on to reach his fifty off 87 balls, an indescribably precious supporting job. And when drinks were summoned by the umpires some spectators mistook it for the end of the match and became very excited.

Shortly after smacking Warne through cover, Giles (59) was bowled by him, having achieved his highest score in Tests in this his 50th appearance. Harmison's swift dismissal gave Warne his dozen for the match and a final haul of 40, a record for Australia in a five-Test series against England, only Terry Alderman (twice) and Rodney Hogg having taken more in a six-Test rubber. But there was little elation about the greatest spin bowler of all time, and the adrenalin had long been replaced by molten concrete in the stomachs of his team-mates.

Eighteen overs now remained and Australia needed an unreachable 342 as England took the field all wearing their navy caps with coronet and three lions. A few bouncers from Harmison, one of which reared well over Jones's upstretched glove, convinced the umpires that there was no future in this light, so off they all trooped. The crowd, unsure as to whether this was it, booed. But the stumps remained in place and it was not until some time later, at 6.15 pm, that the anti-climax gave way to a realisation, with the uprooting of the stumps, that the match was over.

After 5886 days, eight series, and 44 Tests against Australia under seven captains, all unwanted records, England had the Ashes back. Delirium swept across The Oval, across England, across British outposts around the world.

It was regrettable that spectators were forbidden from running across the grass to the players' area, as they had done in 1926 and 1953. Instead, the players came to them, doing a slow lap of honour while *Jerusalem* was played, and *Rule Britannia* and *Land of Hope and Glory*. For the multitude, the author included, it was emotionally overwhelming.

The England winners' extended celebrations were highlighted by a triumphal bus ride through London into Trafalgar Square: Giles, Jones (S.), Strauss, captain Vaughan (with replica Ashes urn), Pietersen, Trescothick (with large crystal Ashes reproduction), Jones (G.), and Flintoff.

FIFTH TEST MATCH
The Oval, September 8, 9, 10, 11, 12, 2005

ENGLAND		mins	ball	4s			mins	balls	4s
M.E.Trescothick	c Hayden b Warne	43	77	65	8	lbw b Warne	33	150	84	1
A.J.Strauss	c Katich b Warne	129	351	210	17	c Katich b Warne	1	16	7	–
*M.P.Vaughan	c Clarke b Warne	11	26	25	2	c Gilchrist b McGrath	45	80	65	6
I.R.Bell	lbw b Warne	0	9	7	–	c Warne b McGrath	0	2	1	–
K.P.Pietersen	b Warne	14	30	25	2	b McGrath	158	285	187	15#
A.Flintoff	c Warne b McGrath	72	162	115	12+	c & b Warne	8	20	13	1
P.D.Collingwood	lbw b Tait	7	26	26	1	c Ponting b Warne	10	72	51	1
#G.O.Jones	b Lee	25	60	41	5	b Tait	1	24	12	–
A.F.Giles	lbw b Warne	32	120	70	1	b Warne	59	159	97	7
M.J.Hoggard	c Martyn b McGrath	2	47	36	–	not out	4	45	35	–
S.J.Harmison	not out	20	25	20	4	c Hayden b Warne	0	2	2	–
Extras	b 4, lb 6, w 1, nb 7	18				b 4, w 7, nb 5	16		
Total	(105.3 overs, 471 mins)	373				(91.3 overs, 432 mins)	335		

+ plus 1 six   # plus 7 sixes

Fall: 1/82 2/102 3/104 4/131 5/274   1/2 2/67 3/67 4/109 5/126
    6/289 7/297 8/325 9/345   6/186 7/199 8/306 9/335

BOWLING: McGrath 27-5-72-2 (1w), Lee 23-3-94-1 (3nb), Tait 15-1-61-1 (3nb), Warne 37.3-5-122-6, Katich 3-0-14-0
SECOND INNINGS: McGrath 26-3-85-3 (1nb), Lee 20-4-88-0 (4nb, 1w), Warne 38.3-3-124-6 (1w), Clarke 2-0-6-0, Tait 5-0-28-1 (1w)

AUSTRALIA		mins	balls	4s			mins	balls	4s
J.L.Langer	b Harmison	105	233	146	11#	not out	0	3	4	–
M.L.Hayden	lbw b Flintoff	138	416	303	18	not out	0	3	0	–
*R.T.Ponting	c Strauss b Flintoff	35	81	56	3				
D.R.Martyn	c Collingwood b Flintoff	10	36	29	1				
M.J.Clarke	lbw b Hoggard	25	119	59	2				
S.M.Katich	lbw b Flintoff	1	12	11	–				
#A.C.Gilchrist	lbw b Hoggard	23	32	20	4				
S.K.Warne	c Vaughan b Flintoff	0	18	10	–				
B.Lee	c Giles b Hoggard	6	22	10	–				
G.D.McGrath	c Strauss b Hoggard	0	6	6	–				
S.W.Tait	not out	1	7	2	–				
Extras	b 4, lb 8, w 2, nb 9	23				lb 4	4		
Total	(107.1 overs, 494 mins)	367				(0.4 overs, 3 mins)	0 wkt	4	

plus 2 sixes

Fall: 1/185 2/264 3/281 4/323 5/329 6/356 7/359 8/363 9/363

BOWLING: Harmison 22-2-87-1 (2nb, 2w), Hoggard 24.1-2-97-4 (1nb), Flintoff 34-10-78-5 (6nb), Giles 23-1-76-0, Collingwood 4-0-17-0
SECOND INNINGS: Harmison 0.4-0-0-0

Toss won by England	Umpires: B.F.Bowden (NZ) & R.E.Koertzen (SAf)
Test debut: none	Replay umpire: J.W.Lloyds (Eng)
Match award: K.P.Pietersen	Match referee: R.S.Madugalle (SL)
Series awards: A.Flintoff (Eng) & S.K.Warne (Aus)	

MATCH DRAWN

Reflections

So, did England benefit from the luck so necessary to carry them to victory with the sides so evenly matched? In recalling Glenn McGrath's shock injury, the spoiling weather in the decisive Test at The Oval, the favour of the last three tosses of the coin to England, and a few umpiring quirks, the answer seems to be "Yes". And yet even I, in my assertion to my unsuspecting friends in Sydney eight months earlier, did not fully anticipate the *strength of purpose* instilled into this England team. To lose the opening encounter at Lord's and yet come back so strongly in the second Test, to overcome so readily the crushing disappointment of not quite finishing off Australia at Old Trafford in the third Test, this was the mark of astonishing resiliency and determination.

It seems, too, that the in-depth pre-series study of Australia's make-up, player by player, raised strategic planning to new levels. To pick out a couple of examples: two of the world's most destructive batsmen, Gilchrist and Hayden, found themselves having to deal with pace channelled into a constricting zone, with a sometimes unorthodox field waiting for the faulty stroke. All the planning in the world would have been in vain if the bowlers had not pursued the planned course. And the surprise packet was Simon Jones with his ability to swerve the ball either way, against the shine, at top speed. Reverse swing became the topic of the day.

The result rocked the world. And yet it was almost foiled on the very last afternoon when Australia's situation was laid bare for all to see. They had the most formidable bowler in the world pressing hard, as he had done in the petrifying final stages at Trent Bridge. But even Shane Warne cannot bowl at both ends.

Was cricket ever so cruel as when he put down the catch that mattered? Australia missed 16 chances in the series, against 24 errors by England. But while Pietersen's gaffe at Lord's (one of his six in the series) gave Michael Clarke 70 extra runs, Warne's at The Oval was to gift Pietersen 143. The second-costliest miss was Gilchrist's at Old Trafford, where the wicketkeeper had a nightmare match with the gloves. Vaughan, then 41, went on to 166. The damage, put into stark figures, was 388 runs to Australian batsmen after they had been reprieved by English fieldsmen and wicket-keeper, against 547 runs handed to England.

How noticeably the images of the key figures changed between the start and finish of the campaign. Ricky Ponting, sometimes accused of captaining by committee, shrewdly projected an air of amusement when things went wrong in the one-day matches. He played one of the most outstanding captain's innings in the Old Trafford Test. He lost his cool in the following Test over England's dubious utilisation of Olympic substitute fieldsmen (did he not know that England have been at it since Syd Copley, the ground-staff sub, caught Stan McCabe and swung the Trent Bridge Test of 1930?). And he handled the obituaristic farewell Press conference with admirable aplomb. Australia's coach, John Buchanan, who had had such a triumphant ride throughout his term of employment, for most of the tour would have scanned the papers in vain for complimentary remarks about himself.

Michael Vaughan, in contrast, had a bit of the Jardine about him. He would have made an excellent superintendent of police, or even a High Court judge. Not that he didn't know how to smile and relax. Even the stern, composed Jardine did a funny little jig when Bradman got out first ball, and Vaughan had much to rejoice about this summer. His sturdy No.2, Marcus Trescothick, would have fitted in well at Rorke's Drift – with apologies for the war correlation – so unflappable was he whether dismissed for modest scores (he only once in 10 innings failed to make double figures) or raising his bat for a fifty (still he awaits his first hundred against Australia). Would Andrew Strauss, for all his runs in his maiden Test year, make it against McGrath and Co? He did. Nobody else scored two centuries. "Merlyn" the spin machine was the secret weapon.

Nor should Matthew Hoggard's efforts be overlooked. As in Australia last time, he can look ordinary, but he then produces the outswinger that counts. Oddly enough his part in the 2005 series may well be portrayed in that cover-drive in the acute crisis of Trent Bridge. Ashley Giles? Another lower-order batsman who gained immortality in that match, though his steadiness under fire as a bowler will not be forgotten.

Principally though, credit goes to the master architect, Duncan Fletcher, one of whose rewards was belated British citizenship, to be followed, so they say, by a knighthood come New Year, while the rest of the lads get MBEs or somesuch. Fletcher first defeated Australia as skipper of Zimbabwe in the 1983 World Cup. It was a fortuitous day for English cricket when he chose to live in the United Kingdom.

Fletcher said at the end that it was his team's aggression during the early one-day matches that he liked: "We got into their faces and into their space. It was so well done. Then the win at Bristol followed and we realised we could do something this summer." That first morning at Lord's stunned everyone with its intensity. The Englishmen simply pounded the Australians, drawing blood, then standing off indifferently. It was an amazing statement of intent. None of it lasted. Steve Harmison did not go on to get 30 wickets. He took only 17. Nor did England, having made their point, stay nasty. They treated the cricket thereafter as hard but sporting contests.

The 2005 Ashes series was without question the most enthralling and exciting of all the many Test series ever played. There can be no question about it. There were not only an unprecedented *three* nerve-shredding thrillers in a row, but the match to end it all, do or die for both sides, concluded with a fifth day every bit as exciting, lasting for several white-knuckle hours. The battle that had raged for several weeks, with the welcome life-saving recovery periods between Tests, was sustained well into the final scheduled passage of play. Speaking on behalf of the wives and girlfriends, Rachael Flintoff said, "We've been crying at the end of every match. It's been getting a bit ridiculous." Millions and millions all around the world thought likewise. It will be tough watching the average fare which inevitably follows. Not that there is any guarantee that the 2006–07 Ashes series will be as gripping. There will be no forecasts from this man this time.

A glance backwards does no harm. Sid Barnes's observation when the 1953 Australians landed in England – that "our lads were going to meet some determined opposition this time" – has turned out to be a valid simile for 2005. It was five years before the ageing Australian side beaten by Len Hutton's combination was succeeded by a vibrant new Test XI. Today, Australia contemplates an over-mature group of players, some of whom will have retired or been pensioned off when England next tour. As for 2009, the Ashes series could easily be as lopsided as those in England's dark period between 1989 and 2002–03.

You need a thick skin if you're the butt of opposition jokes, even more so if you have attachments to both sides. Probably the cruellest jibe directed at England's Australian-raised wicketkeeper was: "What does he have in common with Michael Jackson? Answer: Both wear gloves without apparent reason." Well, Geraint Jones now has the Ashes to his credit. But if you should get to handle the precious original little urn, be careful Jonesy!

They seem a level-headed lot, these England players. Kevin Pietersen's considered view on the past and the present is that "what happened 10 seconds ago in a cricket match is the same as what happened 100 years ago: it's history." Who could argue with that? Warne's fatal missed catch at The Oval will be talked about 100 years from now – as will KP's six dropped catches in the series. When he eventually holds one how the stadium will rock.

Atop the stack of congratulatory messages for England was a precious one from the Queen which said *inter alia*: "Both sides can take credit for giving us all such a wonderfully exciting and entertaining summer of cricket at its best." One can only assume that Her Majesty's attention was elsewhere when the 40 chances were spilt! And we may never know whether she heard one of the Barmy Army's more provocative anti-Australian ditties in her name. If she did, she would surely have giggled at the cheek of it all.

If one image stood out from the summer it was of Freddie Flintoff in England's moment of glory at Edgbaston sparing a thought for the shattered Brett Lee. It was an iconic picture, a champion sportsman understanding the despair felt by his opponent and extending a comforting arm. This was the true, if elusive, spirit of Anglo-Australian athletic combat.

Flintoff would have won the inaugural Compton/Miller medal anyway. Although Pietersen stole the thunder at the climax of this ultimate series, the burly Lancashire lad's stride through the campaign was ever-dominant, and his name would have come almost automatically to the minds of the respective chairmen of selectors, David Graveney and Trevor Hohns, who were asked to adjudicate. Freddie has much in common with Denis Compton and Keith Miller, for he has an almost permanent smile on his face, radiates optimism, and has no time for anything petty. He also happens to have their kind of talent. Apart from Ian Botham he is the only player to take 20 wickets and score 300 runs for England in an Ashes series. In fact he finished with 402 runs (40.20) and 24 wickets (27.29): this against the world's No.1 side. Flintoff and Pietersen were also mainly responsible for the 36 sixes hit by England in the series, another record. Remember that text message so long ago concerning their intention to "do some damage together"? It was decent of Ricky Ponting to say at the end, "It would be nice if we could find an Andrew Flintoff somewhere."

At the closing Press conference I asked both captains who they thought was now the top team in the world. Obediently observing the terms of the ICC World Championship table, both said it was still Australia. Some of us prefer the logic of the boxing ring. When the champion is beaten his conqueror is the new champion. Yes, there is usually a return match. In Ashes cricket this will occur in Australia in 14 months' time. Michael Clarke will surely be there, wiser and full of sparkling runs. So will Justin Langer, the archetypal battler, almost certainly with "my big mate" Hayden. Damien Martyn, Simon Katich, Michael Kasprowicz, Jason Gillespie? Time will tell. While his hot pace lasts Brett Lee will probably lead the attack, even if there is still some juice left in McGrath's tank, while Shaun Tait has been blooded and will surely progress from here.

❊ ❊ ❊

London went wild when Vaughan and his lads were driven through the streets in an open-top red double-decker to the celebrations in Trafalgar Square. This fulfilment of an omen was not quite envisaged when reference was made early in this book to the 200th anniversary of Nelson's triumph off Cape Trafalgar against the Spanish fleet. But it will serve.

So too will all the other omens, principally the 100-years-on phenomenon. Archie MacLaren probably lived again through Kevin Pietersen. As Archie Mac said of Cotter, KP might have shouted, "Lee? I'll bloody well Lee him!" Might there have been supernatural intervention at the moment when Langer and Hayden equalled F.S.Jackson and Hayward's record 185 first-wicket stand at The Oval? Don't forget that Justin Langer was born on the exact centenary of Jackson's birth. Let's recall, too, how C.B.Fry recorded that "we all liked and admired the Australians . . . but, by Jove! We did like beating them." Some things will never change. Remember, equally, how the great rarity of three thrilling finishes in a row also occurred on the 1905 Australians' tour of England: nine down with Jessop still in, Gloucestershire blocked out for a draw; Darling's Australians scrambled a leg-bye in W.G.Grace's direction to win by one wicket at Bournemouth; and Essex hung on for a draw with their last pair at the crease and no television on hand to examine the five late lbw appeals turned down. They probably said there would never ever be three nail-biters in succession again. Well, 100 years later we've just experienced three more.

It may be recalled that Joe Darling, leaning on the ship's railing on the voyage back to Australia, was asked if he was searching for the Ashes. Like Ricky Ponting, he could only reply, "No, unfortunately we left them behind us." While Darling never played for Australia again, it is inconceivable that Ponting will be absent from the next few Ashes series. He will have his chance for revenge. We'll see. Doubtless Warne is still glaring over his shoulder and snarling, "I'll be back!" Meanwhile, there will be some Englishmen who will now puff out their chests, radiating the aura of a superior race – having suppressed already the memories of 16 years of enslavement imposed by Messrs Border, Taylor and Waugh.

The outcome of the 2005 Ashes series came as a great relief to one who was probably regarded as being on the fringe of senile dementia after his prediction that evening in Sydney, months before the series got under way. Now we are all in need of proper recovery from this most exhausting of Ashes encounters, players, writers, spectators, viewers and listeners. And I've waited long enough. The little bottle of celebratory champagne kindly provided by England's Test match sponsors npower needs to be uncorked now. Here's to the Ashes – not forgetting the power of superstition.

Averages

ENGLAND

	M	Ins	NO	Runs	HS	Av	100s	50s	Catches
K.P.Pietersen	5	10	1	473	158	52.56	1	3	0
M.E.Trescothick	5	10	0	431	90	43.10	0	3	3
A.Flintoff	5	10	0	402	102	40.20	1	3	3
A.J.Strauss	5	10	0	393	129	39.30	2	0	6
S.P.Jones	4	6	4	66	20*	33.00	0	0	1
M.P.Vaughan	5	10	0	326	166	32.60	1	1	2
G.O.Jones	5	10	1	229	85	25.44	0	1	15/1 st
A.F.Giles	5	10	2	155	59	19.38	0	1	5
I.R.Bell	5	10	0	171	65	17.10	0	2	8
S.J.Harmison	5	8	2	60	20*	10.00	0	0	1
P.D.Collingwood	1	2	0	17	10	8.50	0	0	1
M.J.Hoggard	5	9	2	45	16	6.43	0	0	0

J.C.Hildreth held 1 catch as substitute

	O	M	R	W	Av	5w/i	10w/m	Best
S.P.Jones	102	17	378	18	21.00	2	0	6-53
A.Flintoff	194	32	655	24	27.29	1	0	5-78
M.J.Hoggard	122.1	15	473	16	29.56	0	0	4-97
S.J.Harmison	161.1	22	549	17	32.29	1	0	5-43
A.F.Giles	160	18	578	10	57.80	0	0	3-78
P.D.Collingwood	4	0	17	0	–	0	0	
I.R.Bell	7	2	20	0	–	0	0	
M.P.Vaughan	5	0	21	0	–	0	0	

AUSTRALIA

	M	Ins	NO	Runs	HS	Av	100s	50s	Catches
J.L.Langer	5	10	1	394	105	43.78	1	2	2
R.T.Ponting	5	9	0	359	156	39.89	1	1	4
M.J.Clarke	5	9	0	335	91	37.22	0	2	2
G.D.McGrath	3	5	4	36	20*	36.00	0	0	1
M.L.Hayden	5	10	1	318	138	35.33	1	0	10
S.K.Warne	5	9	0	249	90	27.67	0	1	5
S.M.Katich	5	9	0	248	67	27.56	0	2	4
B.Lee	5	9	3	158	47	26.33	0	0	2
A.C.Gilchrist	5	9	1	181	49*	22.63	0	0	18/1 st
D.R.Martyn	5	9	0	178	65	19.78	0	1	4
M.S.Kasprowicz	2	4	0	44	20	11.00	0	0	3
S.W.Tait	2	3	2	8	4	8.00	0	0	0
J.N.Gillespie	3	6	0	47	26	7.83	0	0	1

B.J.Hodge held 2 catches as substitute

	O	M	R	W	Av	5w/i	10w/m	Best
R.T.Ponting	6	2	9	1	9.00	0	0	1-9
S.K.Warne	252.5	37	797	40	19.93	3	2	6-46
G.D.McGrath	134	22	440	19	23.16	2	0	5-53
B.Lee	191.1	25	822	20	41.10	0	0	4-82
S.W.Tait	48	5	210	5	42.00	0	0	3-97
S.M.Katich	12	1	50	1	50.00	0	0	1-36
M.S.Kasprowicz	52	6	250	4	62.50	0	0	3-80
J.N.Gillespie	67	6	300	3	100.00	0	0	2-91
M.J.Clarke	2	0	6	0	–	0	0	